D1501490

FREE DVD FREE FREE DVD

Essential Test Tips DVD from Trivium Test Prep

Dear Customer,

Thank you for purchasing from Cirrus Test Prep! Whether you're looking to join the military, get into college, or advance your career, we're honored to be a part of your journey.

To show our appreciation (and to help you relieve a little of that test-prep stress), we're offering a **FREE** *Praxis Essential Test Tips DVD* by Cirrus Test Prep. Our DVD includes 35 test preparation strategies that will help keep you calm and collected before and during your big exam. All we ask is that you email us your feedback and describe your experience with our product. Amazing, awful, or just so-so: we want to hear what you have to say!

To receive your **FREE** *Praxis Essential Test Tips DVD*, please email us at 5star@cirrustestprep.com. Include "Free 5 Star" in the subject line and the following information in your email:

1. The title of the product you purchased.

2. Your rating from 1 – 5 (with 5 being the best).

3. Your feedback about the product, including how our materials helped you meet your goals and ways in which we can improve our products.

4. Your full name and shipping address so we can send your **FREE** *Praxis Essential Test Tips DVD*.

If you have any questions or concerns please feel free to contact us directly at 5star@cirrustestprep.com.

Thank you, and good luck with your studies!

Praxis Core Academic Skills for Educators (5712, 5722, 5732) Study Guide

Test Prep and Practice Test Questions for the Praxis Core Reading, Math and Writing Exams

Table of Contents

PART III: MATHEMATICS 93

PART IV: PRACTICE 201

Introduction

Congratulations on choosing to take the Praxis Core Academic Skills for Educators Tests (5712, 5722, and 5732)! By purchasing this book, you've taken the first step toward becoming a teacher, an enriching and satisfying career.

This guide will provide you with a detailed overview of the Praxis Core Academic Skills for Educators Tests, also known as the Praxis Core Tests or Praxis Series, so you know exactly what to expect on test day. It will prepare you for all three of the Core Academic Skills for Educators tests: Reading (5712), Writing (5722), and Mathematics (5732). We'll take you through all the concepts covered on these tests and give you the opportunity to test your knowledge with practice questions. Even if it's been a while since you last took a major test, don't worry; we'll make sure you're more than ready!

WHAT IS THE PRAXIS CORE ACADEMIC SKILLS FOR EDUCATORS?

The Praxis Core Tests are used by teacher preparation programs in many states to measure applicants' aptitude in mathematics, reading, and writing. They are generally all required and may be referred to as the Praxis Series. You may take the tests individually on separate dates, or you may take them all on the same date by registering for the Praxis Core Academic Skills for Educators: Combined Test. In addition to its use as a determinant for entry into teaching programs, the Praxis Series is also used by many states to determine whether individuals receive teaching licenses. While there are other Praxis tests for specific academic subjects you may also be required to take, these core subjects are essential for anyone entering the teaching profession. Some states, however, require their own, independently created exam in lieu of the Praxis Series. It is important to check the specific requirements of *your* state to ensure you take the right exams.

What's on the Praxis Core Academic Skills for Educators?

The Praxis Core Tests gauge college-level skills in mathematics, reading, and writing in accordance with the Common Core State Standards. Each test—Reading, Writing, and Mathematics—is broken down into different categories based on the skills needed to succeed in a teacher preparation program.

On the Reading Test (5712) you will read and answer questions about fiction and non-fiction passages, which will be of varying length. Some will be paired. They may be taken from any reading material an educated adult is likely to encounter, including novels, newspapers, magazines, articles on current events, and visual representations.

The Writing Test (5722) tests your ability to analyze purpose, production, and types of text and your language and research skills. You will write two essays and answer multiple-choice questions.

The Mathematics Test (5732) focuses on numbers, algebra and functions, geometry, and statistics and probability. There may be more than one answer choice on some multiple-choice questions (these are designated with boxes rather than ovals or circles). A calculator will appear on screen when you are permitted to use one.

What's on the Praxis Core Academic Skills for Educators: Combined Test?			
Section	**Concepts**	**Number of Questions**	**Time**
Reading (5712)	Main idea and supporting details, text structure, and integration of ideas	56 multiple-choice questions following paired, long, and short passages and brief statements	85 minutes
Writing (5722)	Text types, purposes and production; language; research skills for writing	40 multiple-choice questions and 2 essays	40 minutes + 30 minutes each for each essay (a total of 100 minutes)
Mathematics (5732)	Number and quantity; algebra and functions; geometry, probability and statistics	56 multiple-choice and numeric entry questions	85 minutes

Section	Concepts	Number of Questions	Time
Total		152 (and 2 essays)	**5 hours is allotted in total for the combined test; 2 hours in total for each individual test if they are taken separately. Allotted time provides for tutorials and review of background information.**

How Is the Praxis Core Academic Skills for Educators Scored?

Your scores become available 2 – 3 weeks after the exam on your online account; you will be notified via email when they are released. In most cases, your Praxis scores will automatically be sent to the credentialing agency of the state in which you test. In addition, when you register you may choose four recipient institutions for your scores; they will be sent directly for free. (If you complete or plan to complete a teacher preparation program in Guam, Maine, New Mexico, Texas, the US Virgin Islands, or Wisconsin, you *must* list your educational institution as a score recipient). After your scores become available, you may send them to other institutions for an additional charge. Check http://www.ets.org to determine how this applies to your specific situation.

Each multiple-choice question is worth one raw point. The total number of questions you answer correctly is added up to obtain your raw score. Essay responses are scored on a holistic scale of 1 – 6 by two separate graders who are unaware of each other's evaluations of your work. Their scores are added together for a total of 2 – 12; if they differ substantially, to ensure fairness a third scorer determines your final essay score. This number is added to your raw score, which is then scaled to result in your final score.

Upon completion of the test, you will immediately receive an unofficial score report. Before receiving the report, however, you have the option to cancel your scores. You will receive your official score report 10 – 16 days after taking the exam.

Keep in mind that a small number of multiple-choice questions are experimental and will not count toward your overall score. ETS uses these to test out new questions for future exams. However, as those questions are not indicated on the test, you must respond to every question.

There is no penalty for guessing on the test, so be sure to eliminate answer choices and answer every question. If you still do not know the answer, guess; you may get it right!

How Is the Praxis Core Academic Skills for Educators Administered?

The Praxis is a computer-based test offered continuously at a range of universities and testing centers. It may be taken in its individual parts or all at once. Check https://www.ets.org/praxis/register/centers_dates/ for more information. You will need to print your registration ticket from your online account and bring it, along with your identification, to the testing site on test day. No pens, pencils, erasers, or calculators are allowed; on the Mathematics portion of the exam, a calculator will automatically appear on the computer screen for certain questions. You may take the test once every 21 days.

About Cirrus Test Prep

Cirrus Test Prep study guides are designed by current and former educators and are tailored to meet your needs as an incoming educator. Our guides offer all of the resources necessary to help you pass teacher certification tests across the nation.

Cirrus clouds are graceful, wispy clouds characterized by their high altitude. Just like cirrus clouds, Cirrus Test Prep's goal is to help educators "aim high" when it comes to obtaining their teacher certification and entering the classroom.

About This Guide

This guide will help you master the most important test topics and also develop critical test-taking skills. We have built features into our books to prepare you for your tests and increase your score. Along with a detailed summary of the test's format, content, and scoring, we offer an in-depth overview of the content knowledge required to pass the test. Our sidebars provide interesting information, highlight key concepts, and review content so that you can solidify your understanding of the exam's concepts. Test your knowledge with sample questions and detailed answer explanations in the text that help you think through the problems on the exam and two full-length practice tests that reflect the content and format of the Praxis. We're pleased you've chosen Cirrus to be a part of your professional journey!

ONLINE MATERIALS INCLUDED WITH YOUR PURCHASE

To help you fully prepare for your Praxis Core Academic Skills exam, Cirrus includes online resources with the purchase of this study guide.

PRACTICE TEST

In addition to the practice test included in this book, we also offer an online exam. Since many exams today are computer-based, getting to practice your test-taking skills on the computer is a great way to prepare.

FLASHCARDS

A convenient supplement to this study guide, Cirrus's e-flashcards enable you to review important terms easily on your computer or smartphone.

CHEAT SHEETS

Review the core skills you need to master with easy-to-read Cheat Sheets. Topics covered include Numbers and Operations, Algebra, Geometry, Statistics and Probability, and Grammar.

FROM STRESS TO SUCCESS

Watch *From Stress to Success*, a brief but insightful YouTube video that offers the tips, tricks, and secrets experts use to score higher on the exam.

REVIEWS

Leave a review, send us helpful feedback, or sign up for Cirrus's promotions—including free books!

To access these materials, please enter the following URL into your browser: **http://www.cirrustestprep.com/praxis-core-academic-skills-for-educators-online-resources**.

Part I: Reading

Reading Skills

INTRODUCTION

The Reading test assesses overall proficiency in several key reading skills, including building inferences, understanding themes, and describing the organization and craft of writing.

The Reading test contains 56 multiple-choice questions, presented following brief passages of text or other types of media, such as graphs. The number of questions following each passage depends on the length of the passage: four to seven questions follow a 200-word passage or a pair of passages may be followed by four to seven questions; three questions follow a 100-word passage; and single questions follow statements and briefer passages. Question stems may be presented as fill-in-the-blank sentences, straightforward questions, or *LEAST/NEVER/EXCEPT* questions, which ask the test taker to choose the answer that does not fit.

The Praxis Reading test consists of three main question categories based on the Common Core State Standards. In the sections that follow, several strategies and terms will be briefly discussed, and they will be fully addressed throughout this book.

KEY IDEAS AND DETAILS

Questions in this category focus on the text as a whole; they ask for explanations of the main ideas and how those ideas lead to specific inferences and conclusions. Answers should reflect connections between various sections of the text, discuss the consistency and overall meaning of the author's argument, and identify the piece's theme, summarizing it accurately. To accomplish this, the test taker should incorporate details that support the author's argument and are considered the most important.

Strategies for approaching this type of question include previewing the questions and outlining. Reading through the questions before reading the passage is a way to find a focus. The questions describe what to look for, and wrong answer choices can be eliminated quickly by identifying the main ideas and supporting details. Building an outline of the text assists in accurately identifying these things: jotting down words or phrases that describe the main idea of each paragraph and underlining important details that uphold that idea.

CRAFT, STRUCTURE, AND LANGUAGE SKILLS

This category tests understanding of the craft of writing, including the use of language, point of view, and organization. Questions may require relating the details of a passage to the overall organization and meaning of that passage. Such questions ask for evaluations of specific areas of the text as they relate to the author's purpose and argument, and descriptions of how the author uses specific words, figurative language, or transitions.

For these craft-related questions, the best strategy entails returning to the passage after reading each question and looking for the specific context and location of each question in order to be as accurate as possible. Marking out incorrect answers plus circling the important aspects of the question stem and answer are also helpful strategies.

INTEGRATING KNOWLEDGE AND SKILLS

This final category blends the strategies used with the other two categories. The synthesis of skills employed with previous questions extends in these questions into evaluation and judgment.

Questions may require an assessment of a text, a comparison of multiple texts, or an examination of other kinds of texts, such as visual media. In order to compare two texts, for example, the test taker must understand the purpose and main idea of each text as well as specific details. Determining what to pay attention to is accomplished by reviewing each question before reading its relative passage and returning to the passage as needed. A passage that employs diverse media, such as visuals, requires the same skills used while reading text. Carefully considering each question resolves which skills and knowledge should be integrated to answer it, and deconstructing the question stem best determines what sort of question it is.

The rest of this book will focus on describing in detail the skills, terms, and general content familiarity needed to approach the Praxis Reading test. Each section contains examples of the sorts of questions the test may ask about each of these topics. These examples are meant to exercise the skills needed for each type of question.

THE MAIN IDEA

The **main idea** of a text describes the author's main topic and general concept; it also generalizes the author's point of view about a subject. It is contained within and throughout the text. The reader can easily find the main idea by considering how the main topic is addressed throughout a passage. In the reading test, the expectation is not only to identify the main idea but also to differentiate it from a text's theme and to summarize the main idea clearly and concisely.

The main idea is closely connected to topic sentences and how they are supported in a text. Questions may deal with finding topic sentences, summarizing a text's ideas, or locating supporting details. The sections and practice examples that follow detail the distinctions between these aspects of text.

IDENTIFYING THE MAIN IDEA

To identify the main idea, first identify the **topic**. The difference between these two things is simple: the **topic** is the overall subject matter of a passage; the **main idea** is what the author wants to say about that topic. The main idea covers the author's direct perspective about a topic, as distinct from the **theme**, which is a generally true idea that the reader might derive from a text. Most of the time, fiction has a theme, whereas nonfiction has a main idea. This is the case because in a nonfiction text, the author speaks more directly to the audience about a topic—his or her perspective is more visible. For example, the following passage conveys the topic as well as what the author wants to communicate about that topic.

> **HELPFUL HINT**
>
> The author's perspective on the subject of the text and how he or she has framed the argument or story hints at the main idea. For example, if the author framed the story with a description, image, or short anecdote, this suggests a particular idea or point of view.

The "shark mania" of recent years can be largely pinned on the sensationalistic media surrounding the animals: from the release of *Jaws* in 1975 to the week of ultra-hyped shark feeding frenzies and "worst shark attacks" countdowns known as Shark Week, popular culture both demonizes and fetishizes sharks until the public cannot get enough. Swimmers and beachgoers may look nervously for the telltale fin skimming the surface, but the reality is that shark bites are extremely rare and they are almost never unprovoked. Sharks attack people at very predictable times and for very predictable reasons. Rough surf, poor visibility, or a swimmer sending visual and physical signals that mimic a shark's normal prey are just a few examples.

Of course, some places are just more dangerous to swim. Shark attack "hot spots," such as the coasts of Florida, South Africa, and New Zealand, try a variety of solutions to protect tourists and surfers. Some beaches employ "shark nets," meant to keep sharks away from the beach, though these are controversial because they frequently trap other forms of marine life as well. Other beaches use spotters in helicopters and boats to alert beach officials when there are sharks in the area. In addition, there is an array of products that claim to offer personal protection from sharks, ranging from wetsuits in different colors to devices that broadcast electrical signals in an attempt to confuse the sharks' sensory organs. At the end of the day, though, beaches like these remain dangerous, and swimmers must assume the risk every time they paddle out from shore.

The author of this passage has a clear topic: sharks and the relationship between humans and sharks. In order to identify the main idea of the passage, the reader must ask what the author wants to say about this topic, what the reader is meant to think or understand. The author makes sure to provide information about several different aspects of the relationship between sharks and humans, and points out that humans must respect sharks as dangerous marine animals, without sensationalizing the risk of attack. This conclusion results from looking at the various pieces of information the author includes as well as the similarities between them. The passage describes sensationalistic media, then talks about how officials and governments try to protect beaches, and ends with the observation that people must take personal responsibility. These details clarify what the author's main idea is. Summarizing that main idea by focusing on the connection between the different details helps the reader draw a conclusion.

HELPFUL HINT

Readers should identify the topic of a text and pay attention to how the details about it relate to one another. A passage may discuss, for example, topic similarities, characteristics, causes, and/or effects.

SAMPLE QUESTIONS

The art of the twentieth and twenty-first centuries demonstrates several aspects of modern societal advancement. A primary example is the advent and ascendancy of technology: New technologies have developed new avenues for art making, and the globalization brought about by the Internet has both diversified the art world and brought it together simultaneously. Even as artists are able to engage in a global conversation about the categories and characteristics of art, creating a more uniform understanding, they can now express themselves in a diversity of ways for a diversity of audiences. The result has been a rapid change in how art is made and consumed.

1) **This passage is primarily concerned with**

   A.   the importance of art in the twenty-first century.

   B.   the use of art to communicate overarching ideals to diverse communities.

   C.   the importance of technology to art criticism.

   D.   the change in understanding and creation of art in the modern period.

   E.   artists' desires to diversify the media with which art is created.

   Answers:

   A.   Incorrect. The focus of the passage is what the art of the twentieth and twenty-first centuries demonstrates.

   B.   Incorrect. Although the passage mentions a diversity of audiences, it discusses the artists expressing themselves, not attempting to communicate overarching ideals.

   C.   Incorrect. The passage discusses how new technologies have "developed new avenues for art making," but nothing about criticism.

   D.   Correct. The art of the modern period reflects the new technologies and globalization possible through the Internet.

   E.   Incorrect. The passage mentions the diversity of ways artists express themselves, not the media specifically.

2) **Which of the following best describes the main idea of the passage?**

   A.   Modern advances in technology have diversified art making and connected artists to distant places and ideas.

   B.   Diversity in modern art is making it harder for art viewers to understand and talk about that art.

   C.   The use of technology to discuss art allows us to create standards for what art should be.

   D.   Art making before the invention of technology such as the Internet was disorganized and poorly understood.

   E.   Art making in the twenty-first century is dependent on the use of technology in order to meet current standards.

   Answers:

   A.   Correct. According to the text, technology and the Internet have "diversified the art world and brought it together simultaneously."

   B.   Incorrect. The passage explains that the global conversation about art has created a more uniform understanding.

   C.   Incorrect. The passage indicates that artists now engage in a global conversation about art, but this is one detail in the passage. The main idea of the passage concerns the advances in art in the twentieth and twenty-first centuries.

D.   Incorrect. The invention of technology and the Internet have diversified art; however, that does not mean it was disorganized previously.

E.   Incorrect. Technology is a means to an end; art is not dependent on it.

TOPIC AND SUMMARY SENTENCES

Identifying the main idea requires understanding the structure of a piece of writing. In a short passage of one or two paragraphs, the topic and summary sentences quickly relate what the paragraphs are about and what conclusions the author wants the reader to draw. These sentences function as bookends to a paragraph or passage, telling readers what to think and keeping the passage tied tightly together.

Generally, the **topic sentence** is the first, or very near the first, sentence in a paragraph. It is a general statement that introduces the topic, clearly and specifically directing the reader to access any previous experience with that topic.

QUICK REVIEW

A **summary** is a very brief restatement of the most important parts of an argument or text. Building a summary begins with the most important idea in a text. A longer summary also includes supporting details. The text of a summary should be much shorter than the original.

The **summary sentence**, on the other hand, frequently—but not always!—comes at the end of a paragraph or passage, because it wraps up all the ideas presented. This sentence provides an understanding of what the author wants to say about the topic and what conclusions to draw about it. While a topic sentence acts as an introduction to a topic, allowing the reader to activate his or her own ideas and experiences, the summary statement asks the reader to accept the author's ideas about that topic. Because of this, a summary sentence helps the reader quickly identify a piece's main idea.

SAMPLE QUESTIONS

Altogether, Egypt is a land of tranquil monotony. The eye commonly travels either over a waste of waters, or over a green plain unbroken by elevations. The hills which inclose (*sic*) the Nile valley have level tops, and sides that are bare of trees, or shrubs, or flowers, or even mosses. The sky is generally cloudless. No fog or mist enwraps the distance in mystery; no rainstorm sweeps across the scene; no rainbow spans the empyrean; no shadows chase each other over the landscape. There is an entire absence of picturesque scenery. A single broad river, unbroken within the limits of Egypt even by a rapid, two flat strips of green plain at its side, two low lines of straight-topped hills beyond them, and a boundless open space where the river divides itself into half a dozen sluggish branches before reaching the sea, constitute Egypt, which is by nature a southern Holland—"weary, stale, flat and unprofitable."

—from *Ancient Egypt* by George Rawlinson

3) **Which of the following best explains the general idea and focus indicated by the topic sentence?**

   A.   Egypt is a boring place without much to do.

   B.   The land of Egypt is undisturbed; the reader will read on to find out what makes it so dull.

   C.   Egypt is a peaceful place; its people live with a sense of predictability.

   D.   The land of Egypt is quiet; the reader wants to know what is missing.

   E.   The reader is curious about how people survive in an area of worn-out uniformity.

   Answers:

   A.   Incorrect. The word *monotony* does suggest the idea of being bored; however, the focus is the land of Egypt, not what people have to do. In addition, tranquility is part of the general idea.

   B.   Correct. This option indicates both the main idea and what the reader will focus on while reading.

   C.   Incorrect. This option leaves out what the focus will be.

   D.   Incorrect. This option leaves out the general idea of monotony.

   E.   Incorrect. This option is inaccurate; the topic sentence does not suggest anything about survival.

4) **Which of the following best states what the author wants the reader to understand after reading the summary sentence?**

   A.   There is not much to get excited about while visiting Egypt.

   B.   Egypt is a poverty-stricken wasteland.

   C.   The land of Egypt is worn out from overuse.

   D.   The land of Egypt lacks anything fresh or inspiring.

   E.   The land of Egypt lacks anything fresh or inspiring.

   Answers:

   A.   Incorrect. The summary describes the place, not a visit to the place.

   B.   Incorrect. The word *unprofitable* suggests that the land of Egypt is unrewarding, not poverty stricken.

   C.   Incorrect. The reason the land is stale and weary may not be due to overuse. This summary describes; it does not explain the reasons the land is worn.

   D.   Incorrect. The first part of the sentence is correct, but the summary sentence does not indicate that Egypt is not worth visiting.

   E.   Correct. The words *weary*, *stale*, and *unprofitable* suggest a lack of freshness or anything that stimulates enthusiasm.

SUPPORTING DETAILS

Between a topic sentence and a summary sentence, the rest of a paragraph is built with **supporting details**. Supporting details come in many forms; the purpose of the passage dictates the type of details that will support the main idea. A persuasive passage may use facts and data or detail specific reasons for the author's opinion. An informative passage will primarily use facts about the topic to support the main idea. Even a narrative passage will have supporting details—specific things the author says to develop the story and characters.

The most important aspect of supporting details is exactly what the term states: They support the main idea. Examining the various supporting details and how they work with one another will solidify how the author views a topic and what the main idea of the passage is. Supporting details are key to understanding a passage.

IDENTIFYING SUPPORTING DETAILS

How can the reader identify the most important pieces of information in a passage? Supporting details build an argument and contain the concepts upon which the main idea rests. While supporting details will help the reader determine the main idea, it is actually easier to find the most important supporting details by first understanding the main idea; the pieces that make up the main argument then become clear.

Signal words—transitions and conjunctions—explain to the reader how one sentence or idea is connected to another. These words and phrases can be anywhere in a sentence, and it is important to understand what each signal word means. Signal words can add information, provide counterarguments, create organization in a passage, or draw conclusions. Some common signal words include *in particular*, *in addition*, *besides*, *contrastingly*, *therefore*, and *because*.

SAMPLE QUESTIONS

The war is inevitable—and let it come! I repeat it, sir, let it come! It is in vain, sir, to extenuate the matter. Gentlemen may cry, "Peace! Peace!"—but there is no peace. The war is actually begun! The next gale that sweeps from the north will bring to our ears the clash of resounding arms! Our brethren are already in the field! Why stand we here idle? What is it that gentlemen wish? What would they have? Is life so dear, or peace so sweet, as to be purchased at the price of chains and slavery? Forbid it, Almighty God! I know not what course others may take; but as for me, give me liberty or give me death!

—from "Give Me Liberty or Give Me Death" speech
by Patrick Henry

5)   In the fourth sentence of the text, the word *but* signals

A.   an example.

B.   a consequence.

C.   an exception.

D.   a counterargument.

E.   a reason.

Answers:

A.   Incorrect. The author includes an example that the war has begun when he says "Our brethren are already in the field!" The word *but* does not signal this example.

B.   Incorrect. The phrase "but there is no peace" is a fact, not a consequence.

C.   Incorrect. In order to be an exception, the word *but* would have to be preceded by a general point or observation. In this case, *but* is preceded by a demand for peace.

D.   Correct. The argument or claim that the country should be at peace precedes the word *but*. *But* counters the demand for peace with the argument that there is no peace; the war has begun.

E.   Incorrect. *But* does not introduce a reason in this text; it introduces a contradictory point.

6)   **What argument does the author use to support his main point?**

A.   Life in slavery is not the goal of the country.

B.   To die bravely is worthwhile.

C.   Life without freedom is intolerable.

D.   The cost of going to war is too great.

E.   People cannot live in peace without going to war.

Answers:

A.   Incorrect. The main point is that the country has to go to war with England to be free. The author does not support his point with a discussion of the goals of the country.

B.   Incorrect. This does not relate to the main point of going to war.

C.   Correct. The author indicates that life is not so dear, or peace so sweet, "as to be purchased at the price of chains and slavery."

D.   Incorrect. This is inaccurate. The author insists that the cost of not fighting for freedom is too great.

E.   Incorrect. Those who opposed going to war believed that Americans could find a way to live peacefully, without a war; the author's main point is the opposite.

EVALUATING SUPPORTING DETAILS

Besides using supporting details to help understand a main idea, the reader must evaluate them for relevance and onsistency. An author selects details to help organize a passage and support its main idea. Sometimes, the author's bias results in details left out that don't directly support the main idea or that support an opposite idea. The reader has to be able to notice not only what the author says but also what the author leaves out.

To understand how a supporting detail relates to the main idea, the purpose of the passage should be discerned: what the author is trying to communicate and what the author wants from the reader. Every passage has a specific goal, and each paragraph in a passage is meant to support that goal. For each supporting detail, the position in the text, the signal words, and the specific content work together to alert the reader to the relationship between the supporting ideas and the main idea.

Close reading involves noticing the striking features of a text. For example, does a point made in the text appeal to the reader's sense of justice? Does a description seem rather exaggerated or overstated? Do certain words—such as *agonizing*—seem emotive? Are rhetorical questions being used to lead the reader to a certain conclusion?

Though the author generally includes details that support the text's main idea, the reader must decide how those details relate to one another as well as find any gaps in the support of the author's argument. This is particularly important in a persuasive piece of writing, when an author may allow bias to show through. Discovering the author's bias and how the supporting details reveal that bias is also key to understanding a text.

SAMPLE QUESTIONS

In England in the 'fifties came the Crimean War, with the deep stirring of national feeling which accompanied it, and the passion of gratitude and admiration which was poured forth on Miss Florence Nightingale for her work on behalf of our wounded soldiers. It was universally felt that there was work for women, even in war—the work of cleansing, setting in order, breaking down red tape, and soothing the vast sum of human suffering which every war is bound to cause. Miss Nightingale's work in war was work that never had been done until women came forward to do it, and her message to her countrywomen was educate yourselves, prepare, make ready; never imagine that your task can be done by instinct, without training and preparation. Painstaking study, she insisted, was just as necessary as a preparation for women's work as for men's work; and she bestowed the whole of the monetary gift offered her by the gratitude of the nation to form training-schools for nurses at St. Thomas's and King's College Hospitals.

—from *Women's Suffrage: A Short History of a Great Movement*
by Millicent Garrett Fawcett

7) **Which of the following best states the bias of the passage?**

   A. Society underestimates the capacity of women.

   B. Generally, women are not prepared to make substantial contributions to society.

   C. If women want power, they need to prove themselves.

   D. One strong woman cannot represent all women.

   E. The strength of women is their ability to take care of others.

   Answers:

   A. Correct. The author is suggesting that the work Florence Nightingale did had not been done before women came forward. Up till that point, what a woman could do had not been recognized.

   B. Incorrect. This fact may have been true at the time this text was written, but only because educational opportunities were not available to women, and women were not encouraged to develop their abilities. Including this fact reveals the bias that women should be granted opportunities to train and to contribute.

   C. Incorrect. This option does not apply; Florence Nightingale did more than prove herself.

   D. Incorrect. The fact that Florence Nightingale donated the money awarded her to the training of women indicates that other women were preparing themselves to contribute.

   E. Incorrect. This may or may not be true. It does not matter what kind of strength women have; the bias is that the strength of women wasn't really known.

8) **Which of the following best summarizes what the author left out of the passage?**

   A. Women can fight in wars.

   B. Other women should be recognized.

   C. Women need to stop wasting time giving speeches at conventions and start proving themselves.

   D. Without the contributions of women, society suffers.

   E. Women are the ones who get the important work done.

   Answers:

   A. Incorrect. "It was universally felt that there was work for women, even in war" suggests that women had much to offer and didn't need to be sheltered; however, "there was work" does not mean the author thought women should engage in combat.

   B. Incorrect. Since the passage is specifically about Florence Nightingale, nothing in it suggests the author included information about what other women did.

C.   Incorrect. Information about women's suffrage conventions is unrelated to the topic of the paragraph.

D.   Correct. The author emphasizes that "Miss Nightingale's work in war was work that never had been done until women came forward to do it."

E.   Incorrect. The author shows the importance of Miss Nightingale's work, but that does not suggest it was the only important work being done.

Facts and Opinions

Authors use both facts and opinions as supporting details. While it is usually a simple task to identify the two, authors may mix facts with opinions or state an opinion as if it were a fact. The difference between the two is simple: A **fact** is a piece of information that can be verified as true or false, and it retains the quality of truthfulness or falsity no matter who verifies it. An **opinion** reflects a belief held by the author and may or may not be something each reader agrees with.

HELPFUL HINT

To distinguish between fact and opinion, the reader should rely on what can be proven. Subjectivity is determined by asking if an observation varies according to the situation or the person observing.

SAMPLE QUESTIONS

I remember thinking how comfortable it was, this division of labor which made it unnecessary for me to study fogs, winds, tides, and navigation, in order to visit my friend who lived across an arm of the sea. It was good that men should be specialists, I mused. The peculiar knowledge of the pilot and captain sufficed for many thousands of people who knew no more of the sea and navigation than I knew. On the other hand, instead of having to devote my energy to the learning of a multitude of things, I concentrated it upon a few particular things, such as, for instance, the analysis of Poe's place in American literature—an essay of mine, by the way, in the current *Atlantic*. Coming aboard, as I passed through the cabin, I had noticed with greedy eyes a stout gentleman reading the *Atlantic*, which was open at my very essay. And there it was again, the division of labor, the special knowledge of the pilot and captain which permitted the stout gentleman to read my special knowledge on Poe while they carried him safely from Sausalito to San Francisco.

—from *The Sea-Wolf* by Jack London

9) **Which of the following best summarizes an opinion stated by the narrator?**

   A.   Poe has a place in American literature.

   B.   People have the time to read magazines like the *Atlantic* because there are other people to take care of other tasks.

   C.   The narrator has no knowledge of the sea and navigation.

   D.   Having specialized knowledge sets people apart and makes them superior.

   E.   Division of labor is a beneficial practice.

   Answers:

   A.   Incorrect. This is a fact. The *significance* of Poe's place in American literature is an opinion.

   B.   Incorrect. This is a fact. The reader is expected to agree with the point that if someone else had not been managing the boat, the people who wanted to get across the water would have had to do the work of getting themselves across.

   C.   Incorrect. This is a fact. The narrator admits to "this division of labor which made it unnecessary for me to study fogs, winds, tides, and navigation."

   D.   Incorrect. Although the narrator acknowledges that specialized knowledge exists, he does not indicate that he believes it creates superiority.

   E.   **Correct.** The narrator provides several facts proving that he and the other passengers benefit from the specialized knowledge and labor of others.

10) **Which of the following is an opinion expressed by the narrator that is not supported by facts within the passage?**

   A.   People should live life focusing on and learning about only a few things.

   B.   Having general knowledge is good.

   C.   He has time to focus on writing about literature.

   D.   People depend on other people.

   E.   People can experience more freedom by depending on others.

   Answers:

   A.   **Correct.** When the narrator says "instead of having to devote my energy to the learning of a multitude of things, I concentrated it upon a few particular things," he conveys his view that he does not have to learn much. There are no facts to support the view that he has to learn only a few particular things in life.

B.   Incorrect. The narrator does not express this opinion. He is speaking about specialized knowledge.

C.   Incorrect. This is a fact that the narrator shares about his life.

D.   Incorrect. The passage does offer facts to support this; both the narrator and the passenger reading depend on the pilot to navigate the boat safely.

E.   Incorrect. This opinion is supported by the fact that the passenger has the freedom to sit back and read, and the narrator has the freedom to watch him read, while they both depend on the pilot.

TEXT STRUCTURE

The structure of a text determines how the reader understands the argument and how the various details interact to form the argument. There are many ways to arrange text, and various types of arrangements have distinct characteristics.

The organizing structure of a passage is defined by the order in which the author presents information and the transitions used to connect those pieces. Problem-and-solution and cause-and-effect structures use transitions that show causal relationships: *because, as a result, consequently, therefore*. These two types of structures may also use transitions that show contradiction. A problem-and-solution structure may provide alternative solutions; a cause-and-effect structure may explain alternative causes: *however, alternatively, although*.

> **HELPFUL HINT**
>
> Authors often use repetition to reinforce an idea, including repeated words, phrases, or images.

Specific text structures include not only problem and solution and cause and effect, but also compare and contrast, descriptive, order of importance, and chronological. When analyzing a text, the reader should consider how text structure influences the author's meaning. Most important, the reader needs to be aware of how an author emphasizes an idea by the way he or she presents information. For instance, including a contrasting idea makes a central idea stand out, and including a series of concrete examples creates a force of facts to support an argument.

SAMPLE QUESTIONS

It was the green heart of the canyon, where the walls swerved back from the rigid plan and relieved their harshness of line by making a little sheltered nook and filling it to the brim with sweetness and roundness and softness. Here all things rested. Even the narrow stream ceased its turbulent down-rush long enough to form a quiet pool....On one side, beginning at the very lip of the pool, was a tiny meadow, a cool, resilient surface of green that extended to the base of the frowning wall. Beyond the pool a gentle slope of earth ran up and up to meet the opposing wall. Fine grass covered the slope—grass that was spangled with flowers, with here and there patches of color, orange and purple and golden. Below, the canyon was shut in. There was no view. The walls leaned together abruptly and the canyon ended in a chaos of rocks, moss-covered and hidden by a green screen of vines and creepers and boughs of trees. Up the canyon rose far hills and peaks, the big foothills, pine-covered and remote. And far beyond, like clouds upon the border of the slay, towered minarets of white, where the Sierra's eternal snows flashed austerely the blazes of the sun.

—from "All Gold Canyon" by Jack London

11) **The organizational structure of the passage is**

    A.   order of importance.

    B.   cause and effect.

    C.   problem and solution.

    D.   descriptive.

    E.   chronological.

Answers:

    A.   Incorrect. A series of reasons is not presented from most to least or least to most important. The passage describes a restful nook in the canyon.

    B.   Incorrect. The passage does not explain the origin of this nook or its effect on anything, although the reader understands from the details what makes the nook so restful.

    C.   Incorrect. The description of the nook presents no problem, although time in the nook could be seen as a solution for many problems.

    D.   **Correct.** The description of the nook begins with a general impression, moves from one side, to the area beyond the pool, to below the heart of the canyon, and finally to what is above the canyon.

    E.   Incorrect. The description does not include a sequence of events in time.

12) **How does the text structure emphasize the central idea of the passage?**

    A.   The logical reasons for needing to rest while hiking make the author's argument compelling.

    B.   By explaining the activities within the canyon, the author convinces the reader that the canyon is safe.

    C.   By describing the areas to the side, below, and above the canyon, the author is able to emphasize the softness at the heart of the canyon.

    D.   The concrete examples included in the passage demonstrate the author's view that beauty is found in nature.

    E.   The sensory details of the description make it easy for the reader to visualize and enjoy.

Answers:

A. Incorrect. The passage does not indicate anything about a hike, although the valley is described as a restful place.

B. Incorrect. The heart of the canyon is still, without activity; even the water stops rushing and forms a pool.

C. Correct. The little restful nook is surrounded by the wall of the mountain, a "chaos of rocks," "boughs of trees," "far hills and peaks."

D. Incorrect. The central idea of the passage is not finding beauty in nature but simply the restfulness of this nook.

E. Incorrect. The passage does include sensory detail that's easy to visualize; however, this option does not indicate how the detail relates to the central idea.

DRAWING CONCLUSIONS

Reading text begins with making sense of the explicit meanings of information or a narrative. Understanding occurs as the reader draws conclusions and makes logical inferences. To draw a conclusion, the reader considers the details or facts. He or she then comes to a conclusion—the next logical point in the thought sequence. For example, in a Hemingway story, an old man sits alone in a café. A young waiter says that the café is closing, but the old man continues to drink. The waiter starts closing up, and the old man signals for a refill. Based on these details, the reader might conclude that the old man has not understood the young waiter's desire for him to leave.

An inference is distinguished from a conclusion drawn. An **inference** is an assumption the reader makes based on details in the text as well as his or her own knowledge. It is more of an educated guess that extends the literal meaning. Inferences begin with the given details; however, the reader uses the facts to determine additional facts. What the reader already knows informs what is being suggested by the details of decisions or situations in the text. Returning to the example of the Hemingway story, the reader might infer that the old man is lonely, enjoys being in the café, and is reluctant to leave.

> **DID YOU KNOW?**
>
> When considering a character's motivations, the reader should ask what the character wants to achieve, what the character will get by accomplishing this, and what the character seems to value the most.

When reading fictional text, inferring character motivations is essential. The actions of the characters move the plot forward; a series of events is understood by making sense of why the characters did what they did. Hemingway includes contrasting details as the young waiter and an older waiter discuss the old man.

The older waiter sympathizes with the old man; both men have no one at home and experience a sense of emptiness in life, which motivates them to seek the café.

Another aspect of understanding text is connecting it to other texts. Readers may connect the Hemingway story about the old man in the café to other Hemingway stories about individuals struggling to deal with loss and loneliness in a dignified way. They can extend their initial connections to people they know or their personal experiences. When readers read a persuasive text, they often connect the arguments made to counterarguments and opposing evidence of which they are aware. They use these connections to infer meaning.

HELPFUL HINT

Conclusions are drawn by thinking about how the author wants the reader to feel. A group of carefully selected facts can cause the reader to feel a certain way.

SAMPLE QUESTIONS

I believe it is difficult for those who publish their own memoirs to escape the imputation of vanity; nor is this the only disadvantage under which they labor: it is also their misfortune, that what is uncommon is rarely, if ever, believed, and what is obvious we are apt to turn from with disgust, and to charge the writer with impertinence. People generally think those memoirs only worthy to be read or remembered which abound in great or striking events, those, in short, which in a high degree excite either admiration or pity: all others they consign to contempt and oblivion. It is therefore, I confess, not a little hazardous in a private and obscure individual, and a stranger too, thus to solicit the indulgent attention of the public; especially when I own I offer here the history of neither a saint, a hero, nor a tyrant. I believe there are few events in my life, which have not happened to many: it is true the incidents of it are numerous; and, did I consider myself an European, I might say my sufferings were great: but when I compare my lot with that of most of my countrymen, I regard myself as a *particular favorite of Heaven*, and acknowledge the mercies of Providence in every occurrence of my life. If then the following narrative does not appear sufficiently interesting to engage general attention, let my motive be some excuse for its publication. I am not so foolishly vain as to expect from it either immortality or literary reputation. If it affords any satisfaction to my numerous friends, at whose request it has been written, or in the smallest degree promotes the interests of humanity, the ends for which it was undertaken will be fully attained, and every wish of my heart gratified. Let it therefore be remembered, that, in wishing to avoid censure, I do not aspire to praise.

—from *The Interesting Narrative of the Life of Olaudah Equiano, or Gustavus Vassa, The African* by Olaudah Equiano

Go on →

13) **Which of the following best explains the primary motivation of the narrator?**

   A.   He wants his audience to know that he is not telling his story out of vanity.

   B.   He is hoping people will praise his courage.

   C.   He wants to give credit to God for protecting him.

   D.   He is honoring the wishes of his friends.

   E.   He is not seeking personal notoriety; he is hoping people will be influenced by his story and the human condition will improve.

   Answers:

   A.   Incorrect. That motive is how the passage begins, but it is not his primary motive.

   B.   Incorrect. He says he does not aspire to praise, and he does not suggest that he was courageous.

   C.   Incorrect. He does state that the "mercies of Providence" were always with him; however, that acknowledgement is not his primary motive.

   D.   Incorrect. Although he says that he wrote it at the request of friends, the story is meant to improve humanity.

   E.   **Correct.** In the passage "If it…in the smallest degree promotes the interests of humanity, the ends for which it was undertaken will be fully attained, and every wish of my heart gratified," the narrator's use of the word *humanity* could mean he wants to improve the human condition or he wants to increase human benevolence, or brotherly love.

14) **Given the details of what the narrator says he is *not*, as well as what he claims his story is *not*, it can be inferred that his experience was**

   A.   a story that could lead to his success.

   B.   an amazing story of survival and struggle that will be unfamiliar to many readers.

   C.   an adventure that will thrill the audience.

   D.   a narrow escape from suffering.

   E.   an interesting story that is worthy of publication.

   Answers:

   A.   Incorrect. The narrator says that what is obvious in his story is what people "are apt to turn from with disgust, and to charge the writer with impertinence." The narrator is telling a story that his audience couldn't disagree with and might consider rude.

   B.   **Correct.** By saying "what is uncommon is rarely, if ever, believed, and what is obvious we are apt to turn from with disgust," the narrator suggests that his experience wasn't common or ordinary and could cause disgust.

C. Incorrect. The reader can infer that the experience was horrific; it will inspire disgust, not excitement.

D. Incorrect. The narrator admits he suffered; he indicates that he narrowly escaped death. This is not an inference.

E. Incorrect. By saying "If then the following narrative does not appear sufficiently interesting to engage general attention, let my motive be some excuse for its publication," the narrator makes clear that he does not think his narrative is interesting, but he believes his motive to help humanity makes it worthy of publication.

UNDERSTANDING THE AUTHOR

Many questions on the Praxis Reading test will ask for an interpretation of an author's intentions and ideas. This requires an examination of the author's perspective and purpose as well as the way the author uses language to communicate these things.

In every passage, an author chooses words, structures, and content with specific purpose and intent. With this in mind, the reader can begin to comprehend why an author opts for particular words and structures and how these ultimately relate to the content.

THE AUTHOR'S PURPOSE

The author of a passage sets out with a specific goal in mind: to communicate a particular idea to an audience. The **author's purpose** is determined by asking why the author wants the reader to understand the passage's main idea. There are four basic purposes to which an author can write: narrative, expository, technical, and persuasive. Within each of these general purposes, the author may direct the audience to take a clear action or respond in a certain way.

The purpose for which an author writes a passage is also connected to the structure of that text. In a **narrative**, the author seeks to tell a story, often to illustrate a theme or idea the reader needs to consider. In a narrative, the author uses characteristics of storytelling, such as chronological order, characters, and a defined setting, and these characteristics communicate the author's theme or main idea.

In an **expository** passage, on the other hand, the author simply seeks to explain an idea or topic to the reader. The main idea will probably be a factual statement or a direct assertion of a broadly held opinion. Expository writing can come in many forms, but one essential feature is a fair and balanced representation of a topic. The author may explore one detailed aspect or a broad range of characteristics, but he or she mainly seeks to prompt a decision from the reader.

Similarly, in **technical** writing, the author's purpose is to explain specific processes, techniques, or equipment in order for the reader to use that process or equipment to obtain a desired result. Writing like this employs chronological or spatial structures, specialized vocabulary, and imperative or directive language.

In **persuasive** writing, though the reader is free to make decisions about the message and content, the author actively seeks to convince him or her to accept an opinion or belief. Much like expository writing, persuasive writing is presented in many organizational forms, but the author will use specific techniques, or **rhetorical strategies**, to build an argument. Readers can identify these strategies in order to clearly understand what an author wants them to believe, how the author's perspective and purpose may lead to bias, and whether the passage includes any logical fallacies.

Common rhetorical strategies include the appeals to ethos, logos, and pathos. An author uses these to build trust with the reader, explain the logical points of his or her argument, and convince the reader that his or her opinion is the best option.

An **ethos—ethical—appeal** uses balanced, fair language and seeks to build a trusting relationship between the author and the reader. An author might explain his or her credentials, include the reader in an argument, or offer concessions to an opposing argument.

A **logos—logical—appeal** builds on that trust by providing facts and support for the author's opinion, explaining the argument with clear connections and reasoning.

At this point, the reader should beware of logical fallacies that connect unconnected ideas and build arguments on incorrect premises. With a logical appeal, an author strives to convince the reader to accept an opinion or belief by demonstrating that not only is it the most logical option but it also satisfies his or her emotional reaction to a topic.

A **pathos—emotional—appeal** does not depend on reasonable connections between ideas; rather, it seeks to remind the reader, through imagery, strong language, and personal connections, that the author's argument aligns with his or her best interests.

Many persuasive passages seek to use all three rhetorical strategies to best appeal to the reader.

Clues will help the reader determine many things about a passage, from the author's purpose to the passage's main idea, but understanding an author's purpose is essential to fully understanding the text.

SAMPLE QUESTIONS

Evident truth. Made so plain by our good Father in Heaven, that all *feel* and *understand* it, even down to brutes and creeping insects. The ant, who has toiled and dragged a crumb to his nest, will furiously defend the fruit of his labor, against whatever robber assails him. So plain, that the most dumb and stupid slave that ever toiled for a master, does constantly *know* that he is wronged. So plain that no one, high or low, ever does mistake it, except in a plainly *selfish* way; for although volume upon volume is written to prove slavery a very good thing, we never hear of the man who wishes to take the good of it, *by being a slave himself.*

Most governments have been based, practically, on the denial of the equal rights of men, as I have, in part, stated them; *ours* began, by *affirming* those rights. *They* said, some men are too *ignorant*, and *vicious*, to share in government. Possibly so, said we; and, by your system, you would always keep them ignorant and vicious. We proposed to give *all* a chance; and we expected the weak to grow stronger, the ignorant, wiser; and all better, and happier together.

We made the experiment; and the fruit is before us. Look at it. Think of it. Look at it, in its aggregate grandeur, of extent of country, and numbers of population, of ship, and steamboat.

—from Abraham Lincoln's speech fragment on slavery

15) **The author's purpose is to**

    A.   explain ideas.

    B.   narrate a story.

    C.   describe a situation.

    D.   persuade to accept an idea.

    E.   define a problem.

Answers:

    A.   Incorrect. The injustice of slavery in America is made clear, but only to convince the audience that slavery cannot exist in America.

    B.   Incorrect. The author briefly mentions the narrative of America in terms of affirming the equal rights of all people, but he does not tell a story or relate the events that led to slavery.

    C.   Incorrect. The author does not describe the conditions of slaves or the many ways their human rights are denied.

    D.   **Correct.** The author provides logical reasons and evidence that slavery is wrong, that it violates the American belief in equal rights.

    E.   Incorrect. Although the author begins with a short definition of evident truth, he is simply laying the foundation for his persuasive argument that slavery violates the evident truth Americans believe.

Go on

16) To achieve his purpose, the author primarily uses

   A.   concrete analogies.

   B.   logical reasoning.

   C.   emotional appeals.

   D.   images.

   E.   figurative language.

Answers:

   A.   Incorrect. The author mentions the ant's willingness to defend what is his but does not make an explicit and corresponding conclusion about the slave; instead, he says, "So plain, that the most dumb and stupid slave that ever toiled for a master, does constantly *know* that he is wronged." The implied parallel is between the ant's conviction about being wronged and the slave knowing he is wronged.

   B.   Correct. The author uses logic when he points out that people who claim slavery is good never wish "to take the good of it, *by being a slave.*" The author also points out that the principle of our country is to give everyone, including the "ignorant," opportunity; then he challenges his listeners to look at the fruit of this principle, saying, "Look at it, in its aggregate grandeur, of extent of country, and numbers of population, of ship, and steamboat."

   C.   Incorrect. The author relies on logic and evidence, and makes no emotional appeals about the suffering of slaves.

   D.   Incorrect. The author does offer evidence of his point with an image of the grandeur of America, but his primary appeal is logic.

   E.   Incorrect. Initially, the author uses hyperbole when he says, "Evident truth. Made so plain by our good Father in Heaven, that all *feel* and *understand it*, even down to brutes and creeping insects." However, the author's primary appeal is logos.

THE AUDIENCE

The structure, purpose, main idea, and language of a text all converge on one target: the intended audience. An author makes decisions about every aspect of a piece of writing based on that audience, and readers can evaluate the writing through the lens of that audience. By considering the probable reactions of an intended audience, readers can determine many things: whether or not they are part of that intended audience; the author's purpose for using specific techniques or devices; the biases of the author and how they appear in the writing; and how the author uses rhetorical strategies. While readers evaluate each

TEACHING TIP
When reading a persuasive text, students should maintain awareness of what the author believes about the topic.

of these things separately, identifying and considering the intended audience adds depth to the understanding of a text and helps highlight details with more clarity.

Several aspects identify the text's intended audience. First, when the main idea of the passage is known, the reader considers who most likely cares about that idea, benefits from it, or needs to know about it. Many authors begin with the main idea and then determine the audience in part based on these concerns.

Then the reader considers language. The author tailors language to appeal to the intended audience, so the reader can narrow down a broad understanding of that audience. The figurative language John Steinbeck uses in his novel *The Grapes of Wrath* reveals the suffering of the migrant Americans who traveled to California to find work during the Great Depression of the 1930s. Steinbeck spoke concretely to the Americans who were discriminating against the migrants. Instead of finding work in the "land of milk and honey," migrants faced unbearable poverty and injustice. The metaphor that gives the novel its title is "and in the eyes of the people there is the failure; and in the eyes of the hungry there is a growing wrath. In the souls of the people the grapes of wrath are filling and growing heavy, growing heavy for the vintage." Steinbeck, used the image of ripening grapes, familiar to those surrounded by vineyards, to condemn this harsh treatment, provide an education of the human heart, and inspire compassion in his audience. Readers who weren't directly involved in the exodus of people from Oklahoma to the West, could have little difficulty grasping the meaning of Steinbeck's language in the description: "66 is the path of a people in flight, refugees from dust and shrinking land, from the thunder of tractors and invasion, from the twisting winds that howl up out of Texas, from floods that bring no richness to the land and steal what little richness is there."

> **QUICK REVIEW**
>
> A logical argument includes a claim, a reason that supports the claim, and an assumption that the reader makes based on accepted beliefs. All parts of the argument need to make sense to the reader, so authors often consider the beliefs of their audience as they construct their arguments.

SAMPLE QUESTIONS

In the following text, consideration should be made for how an English political leader of 1729 might have reacted.

It is a melancholy object to those, who walk through this great town, or travel in the country, when they see the streets, the roads and cabin-doors crowded with beggars of the female sex, followed by three, four, or six children, all in rags, and importuning every passenger for an alms. These mothers instead of being able to work for their honest livelihood, are forced to employ all their time in strolling to beg sustenance for their helpless infants who, as they grow up, either turn thieves for want of work, or leave their dear native country, to fight for the Pretender in Spain, or sell themselves to the Barbados.

I shall now therefore humbly propose my own thoughts, which I hope will not be liable to the least objection.

I have been assured by a very knowing American of my acquaintance in London, that a young healthy child well nursed, is, at a year old, a most delicious nourishing and wholesome food, whether stewed, roasted, baked, or boiled; and I make no doubt that it will equally serve in a fricassee.

I do therefore humbly offer it to public consideration, that of the hundred and twenty thousand children, already computed, twenty thousand may be reserved for breed, whereof only one fourth part to be males; which is more than we allow to sheep, black cattle, or swine, and my reason is, that these children are seldom the fruits of marriage, a circumstance not much regarded by our savages, therefore, one male will be sufficient to serve four females. That the remaining hundred thousand may, at a year old, be offered in sale to the persons of quality and fortune, through the kingdom, always advising the mother to let them suck plentifully in the last month, so as to render them plump, and fat for a good table. A child will make two dishes at an entertainment for friends, and when the family dines alone, the fore or hind quarter will make a reasonable dish, and seasoned with a little pepper or salt, will be very good boiled on the fourth day, especially in winter.

—from *A Modest Proposal for Preventing the Children of Poor People in Ireland From Being a Burden on Their Parents or Country, and for Making Them Beneficial to the Public* by Jonathan Swift

17) **Which of the following best states the central idea of the passage?**

A. Irish mothers are not able to support their children.

B. The Irish people lived like savages.

C. The people of England are quality people of fortune.

D. The poverty of the Irish forces their children to become criminals.

E. The kingdom of England has exploited the weaker country of Ireland to the point that the Irish people cannot support their families.

Answers:

A. Incorrect. This is a fact alluded to in the passage, not a central idea.

B. Incorrect. Although the author does refer to the Irish as savages, the reader recognizes that the author is being outrageously satirical.

C. Incorrect. The author does say "That the remaining hundred thousand may, at a year old, be offered in sale to the persons of quality and fortune, through the kingdom," referring to the English. However, this is not the central idea; the opposite is, given that this is satire.

D. Incorrect. The author does mention children growing up to be thieves, but this is not the central idea.

E. **Correct.** The author is hoping to use satire to shame England.

18) The author's use of phrases like "humbly propose," "liable to the least objection," "wholesome food" suggests which of the following purposes?

- A. to inform people about the attitudes of the English
- B. to use satire to reveal the inhumane treatment of the Irish by the English
- C. to persuade people to survive by any means
- D. to express his admiration of the Irish people
- E. to narrate the struggles of the English people

Answers:

- A. Incorrect. The author's subject is the poverty of the Irish, and his audience is the English who are responsible for the suffering of the Irish.
- **B. Correct.** The intended meaning of a satire sharply contradicts the literal meaning. Swift's proposal is not humble; it is meant to humble the arrogant. He expects the audience to be horrified. The children would make the worst imaginable food.
- C. Incorrect. The author is not serious. His intent is to shock his English audience.
- D. Incorrect. The author is expressing sympathy for the Irish.
- E. Incorrect. It is the Irish people who are struggling.

TONE AND MOOD

Two important aspects of the communication between author and audience occur subtly. The **tone** of a passage describes the author's attitude toward the topic, distinct from the **mood**, which is the pervasive feeling or atmosphere in a passage that provokes specific emotions in the reader. The distinction between these two aspects lies once again in the audience: the mood influences the reader's emotional state in response to the piece, while the tone establishes a relationship between the audience and the author. Does the author intend to instruct the audience? Is the author more experienced than the audience, or does he or she wish to convey a friendly or equal relationship? In each of these cases, the author uses a different tone to reflect the desired level of communication.

> **TEACHING TIP**
>
> To determine the author's tone, students should examine what overall feeling they are experiencing.

Primarily **diction**, or word choice, determines mood and tone in a passage. Many readers make the mistake of thinking about the ideas an author puts forth and using those alone to determine particularly tone; a much better practice is to separate specific words from the text and look for patterns in connotation and emotion. By considering categories of words used by the author, the reader can discover both the overall emotional atmosphere of a text and the attitude of the author toward the subject.

HELPFUL HINT

To decide the connotation of a word, the reader examines whether the word conveys a positive or negative association in the mind. Adjectives are often used to influence the feelings of the reader, such as in the phrase "an ambitious attempt to achieve."

Every word has not only a literal meaning but also a **connotative meaning**, relying on the common emotions, associations, and experiences an audience might associate with that word. The following words are all synonyms: *dog, puppy, cur, mutt, canine, pet*. Two of these words—*dog* and *canine*—are neutral words, without strong associations or emotions. Two others—*pet* and *puppy*—have positive associations. The last two—*cur* and *mutt*—have negative associations. A passage that uses one pair of these words versus another pair activates the positive or negative reactions of the audience.

SAMPLE QUESTIONS

Day had broken cold and grey, exceedingly cold and grey, when the man turned aside from the main Yukon trail and climbed the high earth-bank, where a dim and little-travelled trail led eastward through the fat spruce timberland. It was a steep bank, and he paused for breath at the top, excusing the act to himself by looking at his watch. It was nine o'clock. There was no sun nor hint of sun, though there was not a cloud in the sky. It was a clear day, and yet there seemed an intangible *pall* over the face of things, a subtle gloom that made the day dark, and that was due to the absence of sun. This fact did not worry the man. He was used to the lack of sun. It had been days since he had seen the sun, and he knew that a few more days must pass before that cheerful orb, due south, would just peep above the sky-line and dip immediately from view.

—from "To Build a Fire" by Jack London

19) **Which of the following best describes the mood of the passage?**

    A.   exciting and adventurous

    B.   fierce and determined

    C.   bleak and forbidding

    D.   grim yet hopeful

    E.   intense yet filled with fear

Answers:

    A.   Incorrect. The man is on some adventure as he turns off the main trail, but the context is one of gloom and darkness, not excitement.

    B.   Incorrect. The cold, dark day is fierce, and the man may be determined; however, the overall mood of the entire passage is one of grim danger.

    C.   **Correct.** The man is oblivious to the gloom and darkness of the day, which was "exceedingly cold and grey."

    D.   Incorrect. The atmosphere is grim, and there is no indication the man is hopeful about anything. He is aware only of his breath and steps forward.

    E.   Incorrect. The cold, grey scene of a lone man walking off the trail is intense, but "this fact did not worry the man."

20) **The connotation of the words *intangible pall* is**

    A.   a death-like covering.

    B.   a vague sense of familiarity.

    C.   an intimation of communal strength.

    D.   an understanding of the struggle ahead.

    E.   a refreshing sense of possibility.

Answers:

    A.   **Correct.** Within the context of the sentence "It was a clear day, and yet there seemed an intangible *pall* over the face of things, a subtle gloom that made the day dark," the words *gloom* and *dark* are suggestive of death; the words *over the face* suggest a covering.

    B.   Incorrect. The word *intangible* can mean a vague sense, but there is nothing especially familiar about a clear day that is dark, with no sunlight.

    C.   Incorrect. The word *intangible* suggests intimation; however, from the beginning, the author shows the man alone, and reports, "the man turned aside from the main Yukon trail."

    D.   Incorrect. A struggle may be indicated by the darkness and gloom, but the man has no understanding of this possibility. The text refers to the darkness, saying, "This fact did not worry the man. He was used to the lack of sun."

    E.   Incorrect. The man is hiking this trail for some possibility, but he is not refreshed; he is pausing to catch his "breath at the top, excusing the act to himself by looking at his watch."

MEANING OF WORDS AND PHRASES

CONTEXT CLUES

Vocabulary in context questions ask about the meaning of specific words in the passage. The questions will ask which answer choice is most similar in meaning to the specified word, or which answer choice could be substituted for that word in the passage.

When confronted with unfamiliar words, the passage itself can help clarify their meaning. Often, identifying the tone or main idea of the passage can help eliminate answer choices. For example, if the tone of the passage is generally positive, try eliminating the answer choices with a negative connotation. Or, if the passage is about a particular occupation, rule out words unrelated to that topic.

Passages may also provide specific **context clues** that can help determine the meaning of a word.

One type of context clue is a **definition**, or **description**, **clue**. Sometimes, authors use a difficult word, then include *that is* or *which is* to signal that they are providing a definition. An author also may provide a synonym or restate the idea in more familiar words:

> *Teachers often prefer teaching students with intrinsic motivation; these students have an internal desire to learn.*

The meaning of *intrinsic* is restated as an *internal desire*.

Similarly, authors may include an **example clue**, providing an example phrase that clarifies the meaning of the word:

> *Teachers may view extrinsic rewards as efficacious; however, an individual student may not be interested in what the teacher offers. For example, a student who is diabetic may not feel any incentive to work when offered a sweet treat.*

Efficacious is explained with an example that demonstrates how an extrinsic reward may not be effective.

Another commonly used context clue is the **contrast**, or **antonym**, **clue**. In this case, authors indicate that the unfamiliar word is the opposite of a familiar word:

> *In contrast to intrinsic motivation, extrinsic motivation is contingent on teachers offering rewards that are appealing.*

The phrase "in contrast" tells the reader that *extrinsic* is the opposite of *intrinsic*.

SAMPLE QUESTIONS

21) One challenge of teaching is finding ways to incentivize, or to motivate, learning.

Which of the following is the meaning of *incentivize* as used in the sentence?

A. encourage

B. determine

C. challenge

D. improve

E. dissuade

Answers:

A. **Correct.** The word *incentivize* is defined immediately with the synonym *motivate*, or *encourage*.

B. Incorrect. *Determine* is not a synonym for *motivate*. In addition, the phrase "to determine learning" does not make sense in the sentence.

C. Incorrect. *Challenge* is not a synonym for motivate.

D. Incorrect. *Improve* is closely related to motivation, but it is not the best synonym provided.

E. Incorrect. *Dissuade* is an antonym for motivate.

22) **If an extrinsic reward is extremely desirable, a student may become so apprehensive he or she cannot focus. The student may experience such intense pressure to perform that the reward undermines its intent.**

Which of the following is the meaning of *apprehensive* as used in the sentence?

A. uncertain

B. distracted

C. anxious

D. forgetful

E. resentful

Answers:

A. Incorrect. Nothing in the sentence suggests the student is uncertain.

B. Incorrect. *Distracted* is related to the clue "focus" but does not address the clue "pressure to perform."

C. **Correct.** The reader can infer that the pressure to perform is making the student anxious.

D. Incorrect. Nothing in the sentence suggests the student is forgetful.

E. Incorrect. The clues describe the student as feeling pressured but does not suggest the student is resentful.

WORD STRUCTURE

In addition to the context of a sentence or passage, an unfamiliar word itself can give the reader clues about its meaning. Each word consists of discrete pieces that determine meaning; the most familiar of these pieces are word roots, prefixes, and suffixes.

Word roots are the bases from which many words take their form and meaning. The most common word roots are Greek and Latin, and a broad knowledge of these roots can greatly improve a reader's ability to determine the meaning of words in context. The root of a word does not always point to the word's exact meaning, but combined with an understanding of the word's place in a sentence and the context of a passage, it will often be enough to answer a question about meaning or relationships.

Table 1.1. Common Word Roots

Root	Meaning	Examples
alter	other	alternate, alter ego
ambi	both	ambidextrous
ami, amic	love	amiable
amphi	both ends, all sides	amphibian
anthrop	man, human, humanity	misanthrope, anthropologist
apert	open	aperture
aqua	water	aqueduct, aquarium
aud	to hear	audience
auto	self	autobiography
bell	war	belligerent, bellicose
bene	good	benevolent
bio	life	biology
ced	yield, go	secede, intercede
cent	one hundred	century
chron	time	chronological
circum	around	circumference
contra, counter	against	contradict
crac, crat	rule, ruler	autocrat, bureaucrat
crypt	hidden	cryptogram, cryptic
curr, curs, cours	to run	precursory
dict	to say	dictator, dictation
dyna	power	dynamic
dys	bad, hard, unlucky	dysfunctional
equ	equal, even	equanimity
fac	to make, to do	factory
form	shape	reform, conform
fort	strength	fortitude
fract	to break	fracture
grad, gress	step	progression
gram	thing written	epigram
graph	writing	graphic
hetero	different	heterogeneous
homo	same	homogenous
hypo	below, beneath	hypothermia
iso	identical	isolate
ject	throw	projection

Root	Meaning	Examples
logy	study of	biology
luc	light	elucidate
mal	bad	malevolent
meta, met	behind, between	metacognition (behind the thinking)
meter, metr	measure	thermometer
micro	small	microbe
mis, miso	hate	misanthrope
mit	to send	transmit
mono	one	monologue
morph	form, shape	morphology
mort	death	mortal
multi	many	multiple
phil	love	philanthropist
port	carry	transportation
pseudo	false	pseudonym
psycho	soul, spirit	psychic
rupt	to break	disruption
scope	viewing instrument	microscope
scrib, scribe	to write	inscription
sect, sec	to cut	section
sequ, secu	follow	consecutive
soph	wisdom, knowledge	philosophy
spect	to look	spectator
struct	to build	restructure
tele	far off	telephone
terr	earth	terrestrial
therm	heat	thermal
vent, vene	to come	convene
vert	turn	vertigo
voc	voice, call	vocalize, evocative

In addition to understanding the base of a word, it is vital to recognize common affixes that change the meaning of words and demonstrate their relationships to other words. **Prefixes** are added to the beginning of words and frequently change their meaning, sometimes to an opposite meaning.

Go on

Table 1.2. Common Prefixes

Prefix	Meaning	Examples
a, an	without, not	anachronism, anhydrous
ab, abs, a	apart, away from	abscission, abnormal
ad	toward	adhere
agere	act	agent
amphi, ambi	round, both sides	ambivalent
ante	before	antedate, anterior
anti	against	antipathy
archos	leader, first, chief	oligarchy
bene	well, favorable	benevolent, beneficent
bi	two	binary, bivalve
caco	bad	cacophony
circum	around	circumnavigate
corpus	body	corporeal
credo	belief	credible
demos	people	demographic
di	two, double	dimorphism, diatomic
dia	across, through	dialectic
dis	not, apart	disenfranchise
dynasthai	be able	dynamo, dynasty
ego	I, self	egomaniac, egocentric
epi	upon, over	epigram, epiphyte
ex	out	extraneous, extemporaneous
geo	earth	geocentric, geomancy
ideo	idea	ideology, ideation
in	in	induction, indigenous
in, im	not	ignoble, immoral
inter	between	interstellar
lexis	word	lexicography
liber	free, book	liberal
locus	place	locality
macro	large	macrophage
micro	small	micron
mono	one, single	monocle, monovalent
mortis	death	moribund
olig	few	oligarchy
peri	around	peripatetic, perineum
poly	many	polygamy
pre	before	prescient

Prefix	Meaning	Examples
solus	alone	solitary
subter	under, secret	subterfuge
un	not	unsafe
utilis	useful	utilitarian

Suffixes, on the other hand, are added to the end of words, and they generally point out a word's relationship to other words in a sentence. Suffixes might change a part of speech or indicate if a word is plural or related to a plural.

Table 1.3. Common Suffixes

Suffix	Meaning	Examples
able, ible	able, capable	visible
age	act of, state of, result of	wreckage
al	relating to	gradual
algia	pain	myalgia
an, ian	native of, relating to	riparian
ance, ancy	action, process, state	defiance
ary, ery, ory	relating to, quality, place	aviary
cian	processing a specific skill or art	physician
cule, ling	very small	sapling, animalcule
cy	action, function	normalcy
dom	quality, realm	wisdom
ee	one who receives the action	nominee
en	made of, to make	silken
ence, ency	action, state of, quality	urgency
er, or	one who, that which	professor
escent	in the process of	adolescent, senescence
esis, osis	action, process, condition	genesis, neurosis
et, ette	small one, group	baronet, lorgnette
fic	making, causing	specific
ful	full of	frightful
hood	order, condition, quality	adulthood
ice	condition, state, quality	malice
id, ide	connected with, belonging to	bromide
ile	relating to, suited for, capable of	puerile, juvenile
ine	nature of	feminine
ion, sion, tion	act, result, state of	contagion
ish	origin, nature, resembling	impish
ism	system, manner, condition, characteristic	capitalism

Table 1.3. Common Suffixes (continued)

Suffix	Meaning	Examples
ist	one who, that which	artist, flautist
ite	nature of, quality of, mineral product	graphite
ity, ty	state of, quality	captivity
ive	causing, making	exhaustive
ize, ise	make	idolize, bowdlerize
ment	act of, state or, result	containment
nomy	law	autonomy, taxonomy
oid	resembling	asteroid, anthropoid
some	like, apt, tending to	gruesome
strat	cover	strata
tude	state of, condition of	aptitude
um	forms single nouns	spectrum
ure	state of, act, process, rank	rupture, rapture
ward	in the direction of	backward
y	inclined to, tend to	faulty

SAMPLE QUESTIONS

Width and intensity are leading characteristics of his writings—width both of subject-matter and of comprehension, intensity of self-absorption into what the poet contemplates and expresses. He scans and presents an enormous panorama, unrolled before him as from a mountain-top; and yet, whatever most large or most minute or casual thing his eye glances upon, that he enters into with a depth of affection which identifies him with it for a time, be the object what it may. There is a singular interchange also of actuality and of ideal substratum and suggestion. While he sees men, with even abnormal exactness and sympathy, as men, he sees them also "as trees walking," and admits us to perceive that the whole show is in a measure spectral and unsubstantial, and the mask of a larger and profounder reality beneath it, of which it is giving perpetual intimations and auguries.

—from "Prefatory Notice," in the first edition of Walt Whitman's *Leaves of Grass*, by W. M. Rossetti

23) **Which of the following is the best definition of the word *substratum*?**

   A.   meaningful crest

   B.   distracting idea

   C.   reduction

   D.   establishment

   E.   underlying foundation

Answers:

A.   Incorrect. Within the context of the sentence "There is a singular interchange also of actuality and of ideal substratum and suggestion," to say an "ideal meaningful crest" would be inaccurate because the *sub* prefix suggests *under*, a foundation.

B.   Incorrect. Within the context, an "ideal distracting idea" sounds contradictory.

C.   Incorrect. The word *reduction* suggests less than, not under.

D.   Incorrect. This possibility is close because something established could be foundational; however, the meaning of an "ideal establishment and suggestion" is unclear.

E.   Correct. Combining the prefix *sub* (*under*) and the root *strata* (*cover*) with the singular suffix *um*, the word *substratum* means underlying layer or substance. An "ideal underlying foundation" makes sense.

24)   **The prefix *un* in a word like *unsubstantial* indicates the meaning of the word is**

A.   not whatever the root word is.

B.   suggestive of an undercurrent of whatever the root word is.

C.   a lower value of the root word.

D.   in opposition to whatever the root word is.

E.   within or part of the root word.

Answers:

A.   **Correct.** The prefix *un* means not, and the root word *substantial* means real. *Unsubstantial* means not of physical reality.

B.   Incorrect. The prefix *un* does not suggest under.

C.   Incorrect. The prefix *un* does not suggest less than; it is the opposite of the root word.

D.   Incorrect. "In opposition to" suggests working against something, not being the opposite of.

E.   Incorrect. The prefix *un* suggests not being anything like or in any way part of the root word.

FIGURATIVE LANGUAGE

A figure of speech is an expression that is understood to have a nonliteral meaning. Instead of meaning what is actually said, figurative language suggests meaning by pointing to something else. When Shakespeare says "All the world's a stage, / And all men and women merely players," he is speaking of the world as if it were a stage. Since the world is not literally a stage, the reader has to ask how the world is a stage and what Shakespeare is implying about the world.

Figurative language extends the meaning of words by giving readers a new way to view a subject. Thinking of the world as a stage on which people are performing is a new way of thinking about life. After reading Shakespeare's metaphor, people may reflect on how often they play a role, act a part. Their minds may go in many directions; they may wonder when their behavior is genuine, whether they're too worried about others evaluating their performance, and so on. Figurative language—such as metaphors and similes—generates thought after thought; with just a few words, it engages the reader's imagination and adds emphasis to different aspects of the text's subject.

A **metaphor** describes a *topic* that may be unfamiliar to the reader as though it were something else—a *vehicle*—that is probably familiar to the reader. The familiar vehicle is used to help the reader understand a new or unfamiliar topic. As the reader reflects on the similarities between the topic and the vehicle, he or she forms a new idea about the topic. For example, if a person refers to an issue as "the elephant in the room," the topic is the issue, and "the elephant in the room" is a vehicle communicating how overwhelming the issue is or that the issue is undeniable.

Similarly, in **personification** an object is anthropomorphized in some way or receives a human attribute. In the sentence "The earth swallowed him whole," *earth* is personified because it is described as carrying out a human action. Personification may also represent an abstract quality. For instance, a timid individual may be the "personification of cowardice."

A **simile** directly points to similarities between two things. The author uses a familiar vehicle to express an idea about the topic. For example, in his poem "The Rime of the Ancient Mariner," Samuel Taylor Coleridge describes his ship as "Idle as a painted ship upon a painted ocean." Readers have most likely seen a painting of a ship; Coleridge has used this knowledge to convey that the ship was completely motionless. Like a simile, an **analogy** is a correspondence between two things; it shows a partial similarity.

HELPFUL HINT

Aristotle claimed that "the greatest thing by far is to have a command of metaphor. This alone cannot be imparted by another; it is the mark of genius, for to make good metaphors implies an eye for resemblances." The resemblance between two unlike things enables understanding of the ideas suggested by metaphoric language.

SAMPLE QUESTIONS

In shape Egypt is like a lily with a crooked stem. A broad blossom terminates it at its upper end; a button of a bud projects from the stalk a little below the blossom, on the left-hand side. The broad blossom is the Delta, extending from Aboosir to Tineh, a direct distance of a hundred and eighty miles, which the projection of the coast—the graceful swell of the petals—enlarges to two hundred and thirty. The bud is the Fayoum, a natural depression in the hills that shut in the Nile valley on the west, which has been rendered cultivable for many thousands of years....

The long stalk of the lily is the Nile valley itself, which is a ravine scooped in the rocky soil for seven hundred miles from the First Cataract to the apex of the Delta, sometimes not more than a mile broad, never more than eight or ten miles. No other country in the world is so strangely shaped, so long compared to its width, so straggling, so hard to govern from a single center.

—from *Ancient Egypt* by George Rawlinson

25) **What kind of figurative language does the author of *Ancient Egypt* use?**

A.   a metaphor

B.   a simile

C.   a comparison

D.   an analogy

E.   personification

Answers:

A.   Incorrect. A metaphor involves speaking of one thing as if it is something else, not just like something else.

B.   Correct. To describe Egypt, the author uses a simile. "Egypt is like a lily with a crooked stem." The blossom is the Delta region of Egypt, the bud is the hills on the west, and the long stalk is the Nile valley.

C.   Incorrect. Similes show only how one thing is similar to another. A comparison usually shows both similarities and differences.

D.   Incorrect. An analogy is a correspondence between two things; it shows a partial similarity.

E.   Incorrect. With personification, an object is given a human attribute or represents an abstract quality. Personification indicates that the object somehow suggests the quality. An example is *whispering pines*.

26) **What does the figurative language used in *Ancient Egypt* help the reader understand?**

A.   how outsiders perceive Egypt

B.   the dominance of the Nile River

C.   how difficult it is to live in Egypt

D.   how strange the shape of the country is

E.   the expansiveness of the Delta of Egypt

Answers:

A.   Incorrect. The problem with this option is the word *outsiders*. Anyone looking at a map can see the similarity between the shape of Egypt and a lily.

B.   Incorrect. The Nile River does run through Egypt, but this does not account for the hills or Delta region.

C.   Incorrect. Egypt being shaped like a lily does not suggest difficulty in living there. Something like a lack of rainfall could create difficulty.

D.   Correct. By showing the similarities between a lily and the shape of the country, the author puts a memorable image in the mind of the reader and provides a clear understanding of his point: that there is no center from which to govern the country.

E.   Incorrect. The Delta is the blossom of the lily, not the stem or the bud.

COMPARING PASSAGES

Some of the questions in the Praxis Reading exam require test takers to compare texts that have similar themes or topics. Questions involve identifying the similarities and differences in main ideas, styles, supporting details, and text structures. Test takers will find it helpful to preview the questions and to note pertinent similarities and differences in texts while reading.

The following example passages discuss Walt Whitman's text *Leaves of Grass*. The first is from the preface of *Leaves of Grass* and is written by Whitman himself. The second is from a critical essay by Ed Folsom and Kenneth M. Price about *Leaves of Grass*.

Readers should keep in mind the following questions:

▸   What central idea about Whitman's response to slavery is being expressed in the passages?

▸   How does Folsom and Price's explanation of Whitman's response to the issue of slavery in America differ from Whitman's own statement of his intention?

SAMPLE QUESTIONS

One

No great literature, nor any like style of behavior or oratory or social intercourse or household arrangements or public institutions, can long elude the jealous and passionate instinct of American standards. Whether or not the sign appears from the mouths of the people, it throbs a live interrogation in every freeman's and freewoman's heart after that which passes by.

Are its disposals without ignominious distinctions? Is it for the ever-growing communes of brothers and lovers, large, well united, proud beyond the old models, generous beyond all models?

I know that what answers for me, an American, must answer for any individual or nation that serves for a part of my materials. Does this answer? Or is it without reference to universal needs?

Does this acknowledge liberty with audible and absolute acknowledgment, and set slavery at naught, for life and death? Will it help breed one good-shaped man, and a woman to be his perfect and independent mate?

—from preface to *Leaves of Grass* by Walt Whitman

Two

A pivotal and empowering change came over Whitman at this time of poetic transformation. His politics—and especially his racial attitudes—underwent a profound alteration. As we have noted, Whitman the journalist spoke to the interests of the day and from a particular class perspective when he advanced the interests of white workingmen while seeming, at times, unconcerned about the plight of blacks. Perhaps the New Orleans experience had prompted a change in attitude, a change that was intensified by an increasing number of friendships with radical thinkers and writers who led Whitman to rethink his attitudes toward the issue of race. Whatever the cause, in Whitman's future-oriented poetry blacks become central to his new literary project and central to his understanding of democracy....His first notebook lines in the manner of *Leaves of Grass* focus directly on the fundamental issue dividing the United States. His notebook breaks into free verse for the first time in lines that seek to bind opposed categories, to link black and white, to join master and slave:

> *I am the poet of the body*
> *And I am the poet of the soul*
> *I go with the slaves of the earth equally with the masters*
> *And I will stand between the masters and the slaves,*
> *Entering into both so that both shall understand me alike.*

The audacity of that final line remains striking. While most people were lining up on one side or another, Whitman placed himself in that space—...*between* master and slave. His extreme political despair led him to replace what he now named the "scum" of corrupt American politics in the 1850s with his own persona—a shaman, a culture-healer, an all-encompassing "I."

—from "Walt Whitman: Racial Politics and the Origins of *Leaves of Grass*" by Ed Folsom and Kenneth M. Price, http://www.whitmanarchive.org/biography/walt_whitman/index.html#racial

27) **What main idea do both sources make about Walt Whitman's perspective?**

    A.   Slavery is anti-American.

    B.   Democracy is a force of brotherhood.

    C.   Walt Whitman is the voice of American individuality.

    D.   American politics is corrupt.

    E.   Issues divide Americans.

Answers:

    A.   **Correct.** The main idea of both passages reveals that Whitman's perspective about the issue of slavery is that slavery is anti-American because it is undemocratic. Whitman saw the liberty of America as a unifying force, a force of brotherhood that could not permit slavery to continue.

    B.   Incorrect. Whitman does view democracy this way; however, he is speaking specifically about slavery being undemocratic.

C.   Incorrect. This option is true but far too broad an interpretation of the passages. A main idea is more specific statement.

D.   Incorrect. This option is mentioned in only one passage.

E.   Incorrect. This option is vague, not a focused main point made by both passages.

28)   **What is the main difference between the passages?**

A.   In the first passage, the writer is concerned about slavery, but in the second passage the writers reveal the American confusion about slavery.

B.   The first passage is a biography of Whitman; the second passage discusses Whitman's poetry.

C.   The second passage reveals Whitman's consistent opposition to slavery; the first passage details Whitman's pain in relation to slavery.

D.   In the first passage, Whitman states his perspective on slavery, but the second passage is about Whitman's change of perspective on slavery.

E.   The first passage is about practical problems connected to holding people in slavery; the second passage is an idealistic description of slavery.

Answers:

A.   Incorrect. In the first passage, Whitman explains his viewpoint. In the second passage, the authors critique Whitman's changing views on slavery. Initially, as a journalist, Whitman was sympathetic to the white working class, not the blacks. The authors go on to explain that, in time, Whitman's poetic response to the issue of slavery in America displayed his sympathy for the slave that originated in his soul and his ability to form a union with what he observed. He could see the spiritual significance of different aspects of life and nature, including slavery.

B.   Incorrect. The first passage is written by Whitman; he is expressing his own perspective.

C.   Incorrect. The second passage clearly states that Whitman's view of slavery changed. The first passage is not about pain.

D.   Correct. Whitman's perspective is abstract. The second passage helps to make Whitman's thinking clear.

E.   Incorrect. The first passage is abstract and idealistic; it is not practical. The second passage is not practical or idealistic; it is a straightforward explanation of Whitman's thinking over time.

Part II: Writing

Language and Research Skills

PARTS OF SPEECH

The **parts of speech** are the building blocks of sentences, paragraphs, and entire texts. Grammarians have typically defined eight parts of speech—nouns, pronouns, verbs, adverbs, adjectives, conjunctions, prepositions, and interjections—all of which play unique roles in the context of a sentence. Thus, a fundamental understanding of the parts of speech is necessary in order to form an understanding of basic sentence construction.

> **DID YOU KNOW?**
>
> Although some words fall easily into one category or another, many words can function as different parts of speech based on their usage within a sentence.

NOUNS AND PRONOUNS

Nouns are the words used to give names to people, places, things, and ideas. Most often, nouns fill the position of subject or object within a sentence. The category of nouns has several subcategories: common nouns (*chair, car, house*), proper nouns (*Julie, David*), abstract nouns (*love, intelligence, sadness*), concrete nouns (*window, bread, person*), compound nouns (*brother-in-law, rollercoaster*), non-countable nouns (*money, water*), countable nouns (*dollars, cubes*), and verbal nouns (*writing, diving*). There is much crossover between these subcategories (for example, *chair* is common, concrete, and countable).

Sometimes, a word that is typically used as a noun will be used to modify another noun. The word then would be labeled as an adjective because of its usage within the sentence. In the following example, *cabin* is a noun in the first sentence and an adjective in the second:

> The family visited the <u>cabin</u> by the lake.

> Our <u>cabin</u> stove overheated during vacation.

Pronouns replace nouns in a sentence or paragraph, allowing a writer to achieve a smooth flow throughout a text by avoiding unnecessary repetition. The unique aspect of the pronoun as a part of speech is that the list of pronouns is finite: while there are innumerable nouns in the English language, the list of pronouns is rather limited in contrast. The noun that a pronoun replaces is called its **antecedent**.

Pronouns fall into several distinct categories. **Personal pronouns** act as subjects or objects in a sentence:

> <u>She</u> received a letter; I gave the letter to <u>her</u>.

Possessive pronouns indicate possession:

> <u>My</u> coat is red; <u>our</u> car is blue.

Reflexive (intensive) **pronouns** intensify a noun or reflect back upon a noun:

> I <u>myself</u> made the dessert. I made the dessert <u>myself</u>.

Personal, possessive, and reflexive pronouns must all agree with the noun that they replace both in gender (male, female, or neutral), number (singular or plural), and person. **Person** refers to the point of view of the sentence. First person is the point of view of the speaker (I, me), second person is the person being addressed (you), and third person refers to a person outside the sentence (he, she, they).

HELPFUL HINT

The subject performs the action of a sentence, while the object has the action performed on it.

Table 2.1. Personal, Possessive, and Reflexive Pronouns

Case	First Person		Second Person		Third Person	
	singular	**plural**	**singular**	**plural**	**singular**	**plural**
Subject	I	we	you	you (all)	he, she, it	they
Object	me	us	you	you (all)	him, her, it	them
Possessive	my	our	your	your	his, her, its	their
Reflexive	myself	ourselves	yourself	yourselves	himself, herself, itself	themselves

Relative pronouns begin dependent clauses. Like other pronouns, they may appear in subject or object case, depending on the clause. Take, for example, the sentence below:

> Charlie, <u>who</u> made the clocks, works in the basement.

LANGUAGE AND RESEARCH SKILLS

Here, the relative pronoun *who* is substituting for Charlie; that word indicates that Charlie makes the clocks, and so *who* is in the subject case because it is performing the action (*makes the clocks*).

In cases where a person is the object of a relative clause, the writer would use the relative pronoun *whom*. For example, read the sentence below:

My father, <u>whom</u> I care for, is sick.

Even though *my father* is the subject of the sentence, in the relative clause the relative pronoun *whom* is the object of the preposition *for*. Therefore that pronoun appears in the object case.

When a relative clause refers to a non-human, *that* or *which* is used. (*I live in Texas, which is a large state.*) The relative pronoun *whose* indicates possession. (*I don't know whose car that is.*)

Table 2.2. Relative Pronouns

Pronoun Type	Subject	Object
Person	who	whom
Thing	which, that	
Possessive	whose	

Interrogative pronouns begin questions (*Who worked last evening?*). They request information about people, places, things, ideas, location, time, means, and purposes.

Table 2.3. Interrogative Pronouns

Interrogative Pronoun	Asks About	Example
who	person	<u>Who</u> lives there?
whom	person	To <u>whom</u> shall I send the letter?
what	thing	<u>What</u> is your favorite color?
where	place	<u>Where</u> do you go to school?
when	time	<u>When</u> will we meet for dinner?
which	selection	<u>Which</u> movie would you like to see?
why	reason	<u>Why</u> are you going to be late?
how	manner	<u>How</u> did the ancient Egyptians build the pyramids?

Demonstrative pronouns point out or draw attention to something or someone. They can also indicate proximity or distance.

⟶
Go on

Table 2.4. Demonstrative Pronouns

Number	Subject/ Proximity	Example	Object/ Distance	Example
Singular	this (subject)	This is my apartment—please come in!	that (object)	I gave that to him yesterday.
	this (proximity)	This is the computer you will use right here, not the one in the other office.	that (distance)	That is the Statue of Liberty across the harbor.
Plural	these (subject)	These are flawless diamonds.	those (object)	Give those to me later.
	these (proximity)	These right here are the books we want, not the ones over there.	those (distance)	Those mountains across the plains are called the Rockies.

Indefinite pronouns simply replace nouns to avoid unnecessary repetition:

Several came to the party to see both.

Indefinite pronouns can be either singular or plural (and some can act as both depending on the context). If the indefinite pronoun is the subject of the sentence, it is important to know whether that pronoun is singular or plural so that the verb can agree with the pronoun in number.

Table 2.5. Common Indefinite Pronouns

Sigular		Plural	Singular or Plural
each	everybody	both	some
either	nobody	few	any
neither	somebody	several	none
one	anybody	many	all
everyone	everything		most
no one	nothing		more
someone	something		*These pronouns take their singularity or plurality from the object of the prepositions that follow: Some of the pies were eaten. Some of the pie was eaten.*
anyone	anything		
	another		

VERBS

Verbs express action (*run, jump, play*) or state of being (*is, seems*). The former are called action verbs, and the latter are linking verbs. Linking verbs join the subject of the sentence to the subject complement, which follows the verb and provides more information about the subject. See the sentence below:

> The dog is cute.

The dog is the subject, *is* is the linking verb, and *cute* is the subject complement.

Verbs can stand alone or they can be accompanied by **helping verbs**, which are used to indicate tense. Verb tense indicates the time of the action. The action may have occurred in the past, present, or future. The action may also have been simple (occurring once) or continuous (ongoing). The perfect and perfect continuous tenses describe when actions occur in relation to other actions.

Table 2.6. Verb Tenses

Tense	Past	Present	Future
Simple	I <u>answered</u> the question.	I <u>answer</u> your questions in class.	I <u>will answer</u> your question.
Continuous	I <u>was answering</u> your question when you interrupted me.	I <u>am answering</u> your question; please listen.	I <u>will be answering</u> your question after the lecture.
Perfect	I <u>had answered</u> all questions before class ended.	I <u>have answered</u> the questions already.	I <u>will have answered</u> every question before the class is over.
Perfect Continuous	I <u>had been answering</u> questions when the students started leaving.	I <u>have been answering</u> questions for 30 minutes and am getting tired.	I <u>will have been answering</u> students' questions for 20 years by the time I retire.

Helping Verbs: is/am/are/was/were, be/being/been, has/had/have, do/does/did, should, would, could, will

Changing the spelling of the verb and/or adding helping verbs is known as **conjugation**. In addition to being conjugated for tense, verbs are conjugated to indicate *person* (first, second, and third person) and *number* (whether they are singular or plural). The conjugation of the verb must agree with the subject of the sentence. A verb that has not be conjugated is called an infinitive and begins with *to* (*to swim, to be*).

> **HELPFUL HINT**
>
> A noun that receives the direct object is the indirect object.
>
> The pitcher will throw <u>Antoine</u> the ball.

→ Go on

Table 2.7. Verb Conjugation (Present Tense)

Person	Singular	Plural
First Person	I answer	we answer
Second Person	you answer	you (all) answer
Third Person	he/she/it answers	they answer

Verbs may be regular, meaning they follow normal conjugation patterns, or irregular, meaning they do not follow a regular pattern.

Table 2.8. Regular and Irregular Verbs

	Simple Present	Present Participle	Simple Past	Past Participle
Regular	help	helping	helped	(have) helped
	jump	jumping	jumped	(have) jumped
Irregular	am	been	was	(have) been
	swim	swimming	swam	(have) swum
	sit	sitting	sat	(have) sat
	set	setting	set	(have) set
	lie	lying	lay	(have) lain
	lay	laying	laid	(have) laid
	rise	rising	rose	(have) risen
	raise	raising	raised	(have) raised

Verbs can be written in the active or passive voice. In the **active voice**, the subject of the sentence performs the main action of the sentence. In the sentence below, Alexis is performing the action:

Alexis played tennis.

In the passive voice, the subject of the sentence is receiving the action of the main verb. In the sentence below, the subject is *tennis*, which receives the action *played*:

Tennis was played.

Note that, in the passive voice, there is no indication of who performed the action. For this reason, passive voice is used when the subject is unknown or unimportant. For example, in science, it is common to use the passive voice:

The experiment was performed three times.

At most other times, it is considered more appropriate to use the active voice because it is more dynamic and gives more information.

Finally, verbs can be classified by whether they take a **direct object**, which is a noun that receives the action of the verb. Transitive verbs require a direct object. In the sentence below, the transitive verb *throw* has a direct object (ball):

The pitcher will throw <u>the ball</u>.

Intransitive verbs do not require a direct object. Verbs like *run*, *jump*, and *go* make sense without any object:

He will run.

She jumped.

Many sets of similar verbs include one transitive and one intransitive verb, which can cause confusion. These troublesome verbs include combinations such as *lie* or *lay*, *rise* or *raise*, and *sit* or *set*.

Table 2.9. Intransitive and Transitive Verbs

Intransitive Verbs	Transitive Verbs	
lie – to recline	lay – to put	lay <u>something</u>
rise – to go or get up	raise – to lift	raise <u>something</u>
sit – to be seated	set – to put	set <u>something</u>
Hint: These intransitive verbs have *i* as the second letter. *Intransitive* begins with *i*.	Hint: The word *transitive* begins with a *t*, and it *TAKES* an object.	

ADJECTIVES AND ADVERBS

Adjectives modify or describe nouns and pronouns. In English, adjectives are usually placed before the word being modified, although they can also appear after a linking verb such as *is* or *smells*.

<u>The</u> <u>beautiful</u> <u>blue</u> <u>jade</u> necklace will go perfectly with my dress.

I think that lasagna smells <u>delicious</u>.

When multiple adjectives are used, they should be listed in the following order:

1. Determiners: articles (*a*, *an*, and *the*), possessive adjectives (e.g., *my*, *her*), and descriptors of quantity (e.g., *three*, *several*)
2. Opinions: modifiers that imply a value (e.g., *beautiful*, *perfect*, *ugly*)
3. Size: descriptions of size (e.g., *small*, *massive*)
4. Age: descriptions of age (e.g., *young*, *five-year-old*)
5. Shape: descriptions of appearance or character (e.g., *smooth*, *loud*)

HELPFUL HINT

Adverbs typically answer the questions Where? When? Why? How? How often? To what extent? Under what conditions?

6. Color: descriptions of color (e.g., *blue*, *dark*)
7. Origin: modifiers that describe where something came from (e.g., *American*, *homemade*)
8. Material: modifiers that describe what something is made from (e.g., *cotton*, *metallic*)
9. Purpose: adjectives that function as part of the noun to describe its purpose (e.g., *sewing machine*, *rocking chair*)

Adverbs, which are often formed by adding the suffix *–ly*, modify any word or set of words that isn't a noun or pronoun. They can modify verbs, adjectives, other adverbs, phrases, or clauses.

> He <u>quickly</u> ran to the house next door. (*Quickly* modifies the verb *ran*.)
>
> Her <u>very</u> effective speech earned her a promotion. (*Very* modifies the adjective *effective*.)
>
> <u>Finally</u>, the table was set and dinner was ready. (*Finally* modifies the clause *the table was set and dinner was ready*.)

CONJUNCTIONS

Conjunctions join words into phrases, clauses, and sentences by use of three mechanisms. There are three main types of conjunctions. **Coordinating conjunctions** join together two independent clauses (i.e., two complete thoughts). These include *and, but, or, for, nor, yet, so* (FANBOYS). Note that some of these can also be used to join items in a series.

> I'll order lunch, <u>but</u> you need to go pick it up.
>
> Make sure to get sandwiches, chips, <u>and</u> sodas.

Correlative conjunctions (whether/or, either/or, neither/nor, both/and, not only/but also) work together to join items:

> <u>Both</u> the teacher <u>and</u> the students needed a break after the lecture.

Subordinating conjunctions join dependent clauses (thoughts that cannot stand alone as sentences) to the related independent clause. They usually describe some sort of relationship between the two parts of the sentence, such as cause/effect or order. They can appear at the beginning or in the middle of a sentence:

> We treat ourselves during football season to several orders <u>because</u> we love pizza.
>
> <u>Because</u> we love pizza, we treat ourselves during football season to several orders.

Table 2.10 Subordinating Conjunctions

Subordinating Conjunctions	
Time	after, as, as long as, as soon as, before, since, until, when, whenever, while
Manner	as, as if, as though
Cause	because
Condition	although, as long as, even if, even though, if, provided that, though, unless, while
Purpose	in order that, so that, that
Comparison	as, than

When using correlative conjunctions, be sure that the structure of the word, phrase, or clause that follows the first part of the conjunction mirrors the structure of the word, phrase, or clause that follows the second part.

> I will neither mow the grass nor pull the weeds today. (correct)
>
> I will neither mow the grass nor undertake the pulling of the weeds today. (incorrect)

PREPOSITIONS

Prepositions set up relationships in time (*after the party*) or space (*under the cushions*) within a sentence. A preposition will always function as part of a prepositional phrase, which includes the preposition along with the object of the preposition. If a word that usually acts as a preposition is standing alone in a sentence, the word is likely functioning as an adverb:

> She hid underneath.

Table 2.11 Common Prepositions

Prepositions	**Compound Prepositions**
along, among, around, at, before, behind, below, beneath, beside, besides, between, beyond, by, despite, down, during, except, for, from, in, into, near, of, off, on, onto, out, outside, over, past, since, through, till, to, toward, under, underneath, until, up, upon, with, within, without	according to, as of, as well as, aside from, because of, by means of, in addition to, in front of, in place of, in respect to, in spite of, instead of, on account of, out of, prior to, with regard to

INTERJECTIONS

Interjections have no grammatical attachment to the sentence itself other than to add expressions of emotion. These parts of speech may be punctuated with commas or exclamation points and may fall anywhere within the sentence itself:

> <u>Ouch</u>! He stepped on my toe.
>
> She shopped at the stores after Christmas and, <u>hooray</u>, found many items on sale.
>
> I have seen his love for his father in many expressions of concern—<u>Wow</u>!

SAMPLE QUESTIONS

1) List all of the adjectives used in the following sentence:

   Her camera fell into the turbulent water, so her frantic friend quickly grabbed the damp item.

   A. turbulent, frantic, damp
   B. turbulent, frantic, quickly, damp
   C. her, turbulent, frantic, damp
   D. the, turbulant, frantic, damp
   E. her, the, turbulent, frantic, damp

   Answers:

   A. Incorrect. This list is incomplete; it does not include the articles or possessive adjectives.
   B. Incorrect. This list is incomplete and inaccurate; *quickly* is an adverb.
   C. Incorrect. This list is incomplete; it does not include the articles.
   D. Incorrect. This list is incomplete; it does not include the possessive adjectives.
   E. Correct. *Turbulent, frantic,* and *damp* are adjectives; *her* is modifying first *camera* and then *friend*; and *the* is always a limiting adjective—the definite article.

2) List all of the pronouns used in the following sentence:

   Several of the administrators who had spoken clearly on the budget increase gave both of the opposing committee members a list of their ideas.

   A. several, of, their
   B. several, who, both
   C. several, who, both, their
   D. several, both
   E. several, who, their

Answers:

A.   Incorrect. The word *of* is a preposition; the word *their* is being used as a possessive adjective.

B.   Correct. *Several* is an indefinite plural pronoun; *who* is a relative pronoun introducing the adjectival clause *who had spoken clearly on the budget increase*; *both* is an indefinite plural pronoun.

C.   Incorrect. The word *their* is being used as a possessive adjective.

D.   Incorrect. The list is missing the word *who* which is a relative pronoun introducing the adjectival clause *who had spoken clearly on the budget increase*.

E.   Incorrect. This list is missing *both*, which is an indefinite plural pronoun.

3)   **Which of the following words is functioning as a coordinating conjunction in the sentence below?**

The political parties do not know if the most popular candidates will survive until the election, but neither the voters nor the candidates will give up their push for popularity.

A.   if

B.   until

C   but

D.   neither

E.   nor

Answers:

A.   Incorrect. *If* is a subordinating conjunction.

B.   Incorrect. *Until* is a preposition.

C.   Correct. *But* is a coordinating conjunction joining two clauses.

D.   Incorrect. *Neither* is half of the correlative conjunction pair *neither/nor*.

E.   Incorrect. *Nor* is half of the correlative conjunction pair *neither/nor*.

CONSTRUCTING SENTENCES

Syntax is the study of how words are combined to create sentences. In English, words are used to build phrases and clauses, which, in turn, are combined to create sentences. By varying the order and length of phrases and clauses, writers can create sentences that are diverse and interesting.

Phrases and clauses are made up of either a subject, a predicate, or both. The **subject** is what the sentence is about. It will be a noun that is usually performing the main action of the sentence, and it may be accompanied by modifiers. The **predicate** describes what the subject is doing or being. It contains the verb(s) and any modifiers or objects that accompany it.

PHRASES

A **phrase** is a group of words that communicates a partial idea and lacks either a subject or a predicate. Several phrases may be strung together, one after another, to add detail and interest to a sentence.

> The animals crossed <u>the large bridge to eat the fish on the wharf</u>.

Phrases are categorized based on the main word in the phrase. A **prepositional phrase** begins with a preposition and ends with an object of the preposition; a **verb phrase** is composed of the main verb along with its helping verbs; and a **noun phrase** consists of a noun and its modifiers.

> prepositional phrase: The dog is hiding <u>under the porch</u>.
>
> verb phrase: The chef <u>would have created</u> another soufflé, but the staff protested.
>
> noun phrase: The big, red barn rests beside <u>the vacant chicken house</u>.

An **appositive phrase** is a particular type of noun phrase that renames the word or group of words that precedes it. Appositive phrases usually follow the noun they describe and are set apart by commas.

> My dad, <u>a clock maker</u>, loved antiques.

Verbal phrases begin with a word that would normally act as a verb but is instead filling another role within the sentence. These phrases can act as nouns, adjectives, or adverbs. **Gerund phrases** begin with gerunds, which are verbs that end in –*ing* and act as nouns. The word *gerund* has an *n* in it, a helpful reminder that the gerund acts as a noun. Therefore, the gerund phrase might act as the subject, the direct object, or the object of the preposition just as another noun would.

> gerund phrase: <u>Writing numerous Christmas cards</u> occupies her aunt's time each year.

A **participial phrase** is a verbal phrase that acts as an adjective. These phrases start with either present participles (which end in –*ing*) or past participles (which usually end in –*ed*). Participial phrases can be extracted from the sentence, and the sentence will still make sense because the participial phrase is playing only a modifying role:

> <u>Enjoying the stars that filled the sky</u>, Dave lingered outside for quite a while.

Finally, an **infinitive phrase** is a verbal phrase that may act as a noun, an adjective, or an adverb. Infinitive phrases begin with the word *to*, followed by a simple form of a verb (to eat, to jump, to skip, to laugh, to sing).

> <u>To visit Europe</u> had always been her dream.

CLAUSES

Clauses contain both a subject and a predicate. They can be either independent or dependent. An **independent** (or main) **clause** can stand alone as its own sentence:

> The dog ate her homework.

Dependent (or subordinate) **clauses** cannot stand alone as their own sentences. They start with a subordinating conjunction, relative pronoun, or relative adjective, which will make them sound incomplete:

> <u>Because</u> the dog ate her homework

Table 2.12. Words That Begin Dependent Clauses

Subordinating Conjunctions	Relative Pronouns and Adjectives
after, before, once, since, until, when, whenever, while, as, because, in order that, so, so that, that, if, even if, provided that, unless, although, even though, though, whereas, where, wherever, than, whether	who, whoever, whom, whomever, whose, which, that, when, where, why, how

TYPES OF SENTENCES

Sentences can be classified based on the number and type of clauses they contain. A **simple sentence** will have only one independent clause and no dependent clauses. The sentence may contain phrases, complements, and modifiers, but it will comprise only one independent clause, one complete idea.

> The cat under the back porch jumped against the glass yesterday.

A **compound sentence** has two or more independent clauses and no dependent clauses:

> The cat under the back porch jumped against the glass yesterday, and he scared my grandma.

A **complex sentence** has only one independent clause and one or more dependent clauses:

> The cat under the back porch, who loves tuna, jumped against the glass yesterday.

A **compound-complex sentence** has two or more independent clauses and one or more dependent clause:

> The cat under the back porch, who loves tuna, jumped against the glass yesterday; he left a mark on the window.

Go on →

Table 2.13. Sentence Structure and Clauses

Sentence Structure	Independent Clauses	Dependent Clauses
Simple	1	0
Compound	2 +	0
Complex	1	1 +
Compound-complex	2 +	1 +

Writers can diversify their use of phrases and clauses in order to introduce variety into their writing. Variety in **sentence structure** not only makes writing more interesting but also allows writers to emphasize that which deserves emphasis. In a paragraph of complex sentences, a short, simple sentence can be a powerful way to draw attention to a major point.

SAMPLE QUESTIONS

4) Identify the prepositional phrase in the following sentence:

Wrapping packages for the soldiers, the kind woman tightly rolled the t-shirts to see how much space remained for the homemade cookies.

    A.   Wrapping packages for the soldiers

    B.   the kind woman

    C.   rolled the t-shirts

    D.   to see how much space

    E.   for the homemade cookies

Answers:

    A.   Incorrect. This is a participial phrase that begins with the participle *wrapping*.

    B.   Incorrect. This is a noun phrase that contains the noun *woman* and modifiers.

    C.   Incorrect. This is a verb phrase that contains the verb and its object.

    D.   Incorrect. This is an infinitive phrase that begins with the infinitive *to see*.

    E.   **Correct.** This phrase begins with the preposition *for*.

5) Which of the following sentences is complex?

    A.   The grandchildren and their cousins enjoyed their day at the beach.

    B.   Most of the grass has lost its deep color despite the fall lasting into December.

    C.   The committee members cheered when the amendment passed.

    D.   The recipes calls for many ingredients that are hard to find or too expensive.

    E.   The orchestra, which included six cellos, two pianos, and a drum set, would not fit on the small stage.

Answers:

A. Incorrect. This sentence is simple with only one independent clause.

B. Incorrect. This sentence is simple with one independent clause but several phrases.

C. Correct. This sentence is complex. It has an indpendent clause (The committee members cheered) and a dependent clause (when the amendment passed).

D. Incorrect. This sentence is simple with only one independent clause.

E. Incorrect. This sentence is simple with only one independent clause.

PUNCTUATION

Many of the choices writers must make relate to **punctuation**. While creative writers have the liberty to play with punctuation to achieve their desired ends, academic and technical writers must adhere to stricter conventions. The main punctuation marks are periods, question marks, exclamation marks, colons, semicolons, commas, quotation marks, and apostrophes.

> **DID YOU KNOW?**
>
> Many people are taught that a comma represents a pause for breath. While this trick is useful for helping young readers, it is not a helpful guide for comma usage when writing.

There are three terminal punctuation marks that can be used to end sentences. The **period** is the most common and is used to end declarative (statement) and imperative (command) sentences. The **question mark** is used to end interrogative sentences, and exclamation marks are used to indicate that the writer or speaker is exhibiting intense emotion or energy.

> Sarah and I are attending a concert.
>
> How many people are attending the concert?
>
> What a great show that was!

The **colon** and the **semicolon**, though often confused, have a unique set of rules surrounding their respective uses. While both punctuation marks are used to join clauses, the construction of the clauses and the relationship between them varies.

The **semicolon** is used to show a general relationship between two independent clauses (IC; IC):

> The disgruntled customer tapped angrily on the counter; she had to wait nearly ten minutes to speak to the manager.

Coordinating conjunctions (FANBOYS) cannot be used with semi-colons. However, conjunctive adverbs can be used following a semi-colon:

> She may not have to take the course this <u>year; however,</u> she will eventually have to sign up for that specific course.

The **colon**, somewhat less limited than the semicolon in its usage, is used to introduce a list, definition, or clarification. While the clause preceding the colon must be an independent clause, the clause that follows does not have to be one:

> The buffet offers three choices that include: ham, turkey, or roast. (incorrect)
>
> The buffet offers three choices: ham, turkey, or roast. (correct)
>
> The buffet offers three choices that include the following: ham, turkey, or roast. (correct)

Note that neither the semicolon nor the colon should be used to set off an introductory phrase from the rest of the sentence.

> After the trip to the raceway; we realized that we should have brought ear plugs. (incorrect)
>
> After the trip to the raceway: we realized that we should have brought ear plugs. (incorrect)
>
> After the trip to the raceway, we realized that we should have brought ear plugs. (correct)

DID YOU KNOW?

Exclamation points should be used sparingly or not at all in formal writing.

The **comma** is a complicated piece of punctuation that can serve many different purposes within a sentence. Many times comma placement is an issue of style, not mechanics, meaning there is not necessarily one correct way to write the sentence. There are, however, a few important hard-and-fast comma rules to be followed.

1. Commas should be used to separate two independent clauses along with a coordinating conjunction.

    > George ordered the steak, but Bruce preferred the ham.

2. Commas should be used to separate coordinate adjectives (two different adjectives that describe the same noun).

    > The shiny, regal horse ran majestically through the wide, open field.

3. Commas should be used to separate items in a series. The comma before the conjunction is called the Oxford or serial comma, and is optional.

    > The list of groceries included cream, coffee, donuts, and tea.

4. Commas should be used to separate introductory words, phrases, and clauses from the rest of the sentence.

> Slowly, Nathan became aware of his surroundings after the concussion.
>
> Within an hour, the authorities will descend on the home.
>
> After Alice swam the channel, nothing intimidated her.

5. Commas should be used to set off non-essential information and appositives.

> Estelle, our newly elected chairperson, will be in attendance.
>
> Ida, my neighbor, watched the children for me last week.

6. Commas should be used to set off titles of famous individuals.

> Charles, Prince of Wales, visited Canada several times in the last ten years.

7. Commas should be used to set off the day and month of a date within a text.

> My birthday makes me feel quite old because I was born on February 16, 1958, in Minnesota.

8. Commas should be used to set up numbers in a text of more than four digits.

> We expect 25,000 visitors to the new museum.

Quotation marks are used for many purposes. First, quotation marks are used to enclose direct quotations within a sentence. Terminal punctuation that is part of the quotation should go inside the marks, and terminal punctuation that is part of the larger sentence goes outside:

> She asked him menacingly, "Where is my peanut butter?"
>
> What is the original meaning of the phrase "king of the hill"?

In American English, commas are used to set quotations apart from the following text and are placed inside the marks:

> "Although I find him tolerable," Arianna wrote, "I would never want him as a roommate."

Additionally, quotation marks enclose titles of short, or relatively short, literary works such as short stories, chapters, and poems. (The titles of longer works, like novels and anthologies, are italicized.) Writers also use quotation marks to set off words used in special sense or for a non-literary purpose:

> The shady dealings of his Ponzi scheme earned him the ironic name "Honest Abe."

Apostrophes, sometimes referred to as single quotation marks, show possession; replace missing letters, numerals, and signs; and form plurals of letters, numerals, and signs in certain instances.

1. To signify possession by a singular noun not ending in *s*, add *'s*.
   boy → boy's

2. To signify possession by a singular noun ending in *s*, add *'s*.
   class → class's

3. To signify possession by an indefinite pronoun not ending in *s*, add *'s*.
   someone → someone's

4. To signify possession by a plural noun not ending in *s*, add *'s*.
   children → children's

5. To signify possession by a plural noun ending in *s*, add only the apostrophe.
   boys → boys'

6. To signify possession by singular, compound words and phrases, add *'s* to the last word in the phrase.
   everybody else → everybody else's

7. To signify joint possession, add *'s* only to the last noun.
   John and Mary's house

8. To signify individual possession, add *'s* to each noun.
   John's and Mary's houses

9. To signify missing letters in a contraction, place the apostrophe where the letters are missing.
   do not → don't

10. To signify missing numerals, place the apostrophe where the numerals are missing.
    1989 → '89

11. There are differing schools of thought regarding the pluralization of numerals and dates, but be consistent within the document with whichever method you choose.
    1990's/1990s; A's/As

Other marks of punctuation include:

DID YOU KNOW?

If a quotation is within another quotation, then the inner quotation uses single quotation marks.

- ▸ **en dash** (–) to indicate a range of dates
- ▸ **em dash** (—) to indicate an abrupt break in a sentence and emphasize the words within the em dashes
- ▸ **parentheses** ( ) to enclose insignificant information
- ▸ **brackets** [ ] to enclose added words to a quotation and to add insignificant information within parentheses
- ▸ **slash** (/) to separate lines of poetry within a text or to indicate interchangeable terminology

▶ **ellipses** (...) to indicate information removed from a quotation, to indicate a missing line of poetry, or to create a reflective pause

SAMPLE QUESTIONS

6) Which of the following is the correct version of the underlined portion of the sentence below?

Fred's brother wanted the following items for <u>Christmas a</u> red car a condo and a puppy.

- A.   Christmas a
- B.   Christmas, a
- C.   Christmas. A
- D.   Christmas: a
- E.   Christmas' a

Answers:

- A.   Incorrect. The sentence needs punctuation to introduce the list.
- B.   Incorrect. A comma should not be used to introduce a list.
- C.   Incorrect. Adding a period creates a sentence fragment (A red car, a condo, and a puppy).
- **D.   Correct.** A semicolon can be used to introduce a list.
- E.   Incorrect. *Christmas* should not be possessive in this sentence.

7) Which of the following sentences contains a comma usage error?

- A.   On her way home she stopped to pick up groceries, pay her electric bill, and buy some flowers.
- B.   I used to drink coffee every morning but my office took away the coffee machine.
- C.   Elizabeth will order the cake for the party after she orders the hats.
- D.   My cousin, who lives in Indiana, is coming to visit this weekend.
- E.   Before you go to the store you need to make a list.

Answers:

- A.   Incorrect. The commas are used correctly in this series.
- **B.   Correct.** This compound sentence requires a comma before the conjunction *but*.
- C.   Incorrect. This complex sentence does not require a comma.
- D.   Incorrect. The appositive phrase *who lives in Indiana* is appropriately set apart by commas.
- E.   Incorrect. A comma could be added after the dependent clause *Before you go to the store*, but it is not an error to omit it.

Avoiding Common Usage Errors

Errors in Agreement

Some of the most common grammatical errors are those involving agreement between subjects and verbs, and between nouns and pronouns. While it is impossible to cover all possible errors, the lists below include the most common agreement rules to look for on the test.

SUBJECT/VERB AGREEMENT

1. Single subjects agree with single verbs; plural subjects agree with plural verbs.

   The <u>girl walks</u> her dog.

   The <u>girls walk</u> their dogs.

2. Compound subjects joined by *and* typically take a plural verb unless considered one item.

   <u>Correctness and precision are required</u> for all good writing.

   <u>Macaroni and cheese makes</u> a great snack for children.

3. Compound subjects joined by *or* or *nor* agree with the nearer or nearest subject.

   Neither <u>I nor my friends are </u>looking forward to our final exams.

   Neither <u>my friends nor I am</u> looking forward to our final exams.

4. For sentences with inverted word order, the verb will agree with the subject that follows it.

   Where <u>are Bob and his friends going</u>? Where <u>is Bob going</u>?

5. All single, indefinite pronouns agree with single verbs.

   <u>Neither</u> of the students <u>is</u> happy about the play.

   <u>Each</u> of the many cars <u>is</u> on the grass.

   Every <u>one</u> of the administrators <u>speaks</u> highly of Trevor.

6. All plural, indefinite pronouns agree with plural verbs.

   <u>Several</u> of the students <u>are</u> happy about the play.

   <u>Both</u> of the cars <u>are</u> on the grass.

   <u>Many</u> of the administrators <u>speak</u> highly of Trevor.

7. Collective nouns agree with singular verbs when the collective acts as one unit. Collective nouns agree with plural verbs when the collective acts as individuals within the group.

   The <u>band plans</u> a party after the final football game.

   The <u>band play</u> their instruments even if it rains.

   The <u>jury announces</u> its decision after sequestration.

   The <u>jury make</u> phone calls during their break time.

8. The linking verbs agree with the subject and the predicate.

   My <u>favorite is</u> strawberries and apples.

   My <u>favorites are</u> strawberries and apples.

9. Nouns that are plural in form but singular in meaning will agree with singular verbs.

   <u>Measles is</u> a painful disease.

   <u>Sixty dollars is</u> too much to pay for that book.

10. Singular verbs come after titles, business corporations, and words used as terms.

    <u>"Three Little Kittens" is</u> a favorite nursery rhyme for many children.

    <u>General Motors is</u> a major employer for the city.

> **HELPFUL HINT**
>
> Ignore words between the subject and the verb to help make conjugation clearer:
>
> The new <u>library</u> ~~with its many books and rooms~~ <u>fills</u> a long-felt need.

PRONOUN/ANTECEDENT AGREEMENT

1. Antecedents joined by *and* typically require a plural pronoun.

   The <u>children and their dogs</u> enjoyed <u>their</u> day at the beach.

2. For compound antecedents joined by *or*, the pronoun agrees with the nearer or nearest antecedent.

   Either the resident mice <u>or the manager's cat</u> gets <u>itself</u> a meal of good leftovers.

3. When indefinite pronouns function in a sentence, the pronoun must agree with the number of the pronoun.

   <u>Neither</u> student finished <u>his or her</u> assignment.

   <u>Both</u> of the students finished <u>their</u> assignments.

4. When collective nouns function as antecedents, the pronoun choice will be singular or plural depending on the function of the collective.

   The <u>audience</u> was cheering as <u>it</u> rose to <u>its</u> feet in unison.

   Our <u>family</u> are spending <u>their</u> vacations in Maine, Hawaii, and Rome.

5. When *each* and *every* precede the antecedent, the pronoun agreement will be singular.

   <u>Each and every man, woman, and child</u> brings unique qualities to <u>his or her</u> family.

   <u>Every creative writer, technical writer, and research writer</u> is attending <u>his or her</u> assigned lecture.

ERRORS IN SENTENCE CONSTRUCTION

Errors in parallelism occur when items in a series are not put in the same form. For example, if a list contains two nouns and a verb, the sentence should be rewritten so that all three items are the same part of speech. Parallelism should be maintained in words, phrases, and clauses:

> The walls were painted <u>green</u> and <u>gold</u>.
>
> Her home is <u>up the hill</u> and <u>beyond the trees</u>.
>
> <u>If we shop on Friday</u> and <u>if we have enough time</u>, we will then visit the aquarium.

Sentence errors fall into three categories: fragments, comma splices (comma fault), and fused sentences (run-on). A **fragment** occurs when a group of words does not have both a subject and verb as needed to construct a complete sentence or thought. Many times a writer will mirror conversation and write down only a dependent clause, for example, which will have a subject and verb but will not have a complete thought grammatically.

> Why are you not going to the mall? Because I do not like shopping. (incorrect)
>
> Because I do not like shopping, I will not plan to go to the mall. (correct)

A **comma splice** (comma fault) occurs when two independent clauses are joined together with only a comma to "splice" them together. To fix a comma splice, a coordinating conjunction should be added, or the comma can be replaced by a semicolon:

> My family eats turkey at Thanksgiving, we eat ham at Christmas. (incorrect)
>
> My family eats turkey at Thanksgiving, and we eat ham at Christmas. (correct)
>
> My family eats turkey at Thanksgiving; we eat ham at Christmas. (correct)

Fused (run-on) sentences occur when two independent clauses are joined with no punctuation whatsoever. Like comma splices, they can be fixed with a comma and conjunction or with a semicolon:

> My sister lives nearby she never comes to visit. (incorrect)
>
> My sister lives nearby, but she never comes to visit. (correct)
>
> My sister lives nearby; she never comes to visit. (correct)

COMMONLY CONFUSED WORDS

a, an: *A* is used before words beginning with consonants or consonant sounds; *an* is used before words beginning with vowels or vowel sounds.

affect, effect: *Affect* is most often a verb; *effect* is usually a noun. (*The experience affected me significantly* OR *The experience had a significant effect on me.*)

among, amongst, between: *Among* is used for a group of more than two people; *amongst* is archaic and not commonly used in modern writing; *between* is reserved to distinguish two people, places, things, or groups.

amount, number: *Amount* is used for non-countable sums; *number* is used with countable nouns. (*She had a large amount of money in her purse, nearly fifty dollars.*)

cite, site: *Cite* is a verb used in documentation to credit an author of a quotation, paraphrase, or summary; *site* is a location.

elicit, illicit: *Elicit* means to draw out a response from an audience or a listener; *illicit* refers to illegal activity.

every day, everyday: *Every day* is an indefinite adjective modifying a noun—*each day* could be used interchangeably with *every day*; *everyday* is a one-word adjective to imply frequent occurrence. (*Our visit to the Minnesota State Fair is an everyday activity during August.*)

fewer, less: *Fewer* is used with a countable noun; *less* is used with a non-countable noun. (*Fewer parents are experiencing stress since the new teacher was hired; parents are experiencing less stress since the new teacher was hired.*)

firstly, secondly: These words are archaic; today, *first* and *second* are more commonly used.

good, well: *Good* is always the adjective; *well* is always the adverb except in cases of health. (*She felt well after the surgery.*)

implied, inferred: *Implied* is something a speaker does; *inferred* is something the listener does after assessing the speaker's message. (*The speaker implied something mysterious, but I inferred the wrong thing.*)

irregardless, regardless: *Irregardless* is non-standard usage and should be avoided; *regardless* is the proper usage of the transitional statement.

its, it's: *Its* is a possessive case pronoun; *it's* is a contraction for *it is*.

moral, morale: *Moral* is a summative lesson from a story or life event; *morale* is the emotional attitude of a person or group of people.

principal, principle: *Principal* is the leader of a school in the noun usage; *principal* means *main* in the adjectival usage; *principle* is a noun meaning *idea* or *tenet*. (*The principal of the school spoke on the principal meaning of the main principles of the school.*)

quote, quotation: *Quote* is a verb and should be used as a verb; *quotation* is the noun and should be used as a noun.

reason why: *Reason why* is a redundant expression—use one or the other. (*The reason we left is a secret. Why we left is a secret.*)

should of, should have: *Should of* is improper usage, likely resulting from misunderstood speech—*of* is not a helping verb and can therefore cannot complete the verb phrase; *should have* is the proper usage. (*He should have driven.*)

than, then: *Than* sets up a comparison of some kind; *then* indicates a reference to a point in time. (*When I said that I liked the hat better than the gloves, my sister laughed; then she bought both for me.*)

their, there, they're: *Their is* the possessive case of the pronoun *they*. *There* is the demonstrative pronoun indicating location, or place. *They're* is a contraction of the words *they are*, the third-person plural subject pronoun and third-person plural, present-tense conjugation of the verb *to be*. These words are very commonly confused in written English.

to lie (to recline), to lay (to place): *To lie* is the intransitive verb meaning *to recline*, so the verb does not take an object; *to lay* is the transitive verb meaning *to place something*. (*I lie out in the sun; I lay my towel on the beach.*)

to try and: *To try and* is sometimes used erroneously in place of *to try to*. (*She should try to succeed daily.*)

unique: *Unique* is an ultimate superlative. The word *unique* should not be modified technically. (*The experience was ~~very~~ unique.*)

who, whom: *Who* is the subject relative pronoun. (*My son, who is a good student, studies hard.*) Here, the son is carrying out the action of studying, so the pronoun is a subject pronoun (*who*). *Whom* is the object relative pronoun. (*My son, whom the other students admire, studies hard.*) Here, *son* is the object of the other students' admiration, so the pronoun standing in for him, *whom*, is an object pronoun.

your, you're: *Your* is the possessive case of the pronoun *you*. *You're* is a contraction of the words *you are*, the second-person subject pronoun and the second-person singular, present-tense conjugation of the verb *to be*. These words are commonly confused in written English.

SAMPLE QUESTIONS

8) **Which sentence does NOT contain an error?**

   A. My sister and my best friend lives in Chicago.

   B. My parents or my brother is going to pick me up from the airport.

   C. Neither of the students refuse to take the exam.

   D. The team were playing a great game until the rain started.

   E. The store, which sells magazines and books, close early on Mondays.

Answers:

A.   Incorrect. Because the sentence reads <u>My</u> sister and <u>my</u> best friend, the subject is plural and needs a plural verb (*live*).

B.   Correct. The verb agrees with the closest subject—in this case, the singular *brother*.

C.   Incorrect. *Neither* is a singular, indefinite pronoun, so the agreement is singular. *Neither refuses*

D.   Incorrect. In the context of a game, the *team* is functioning as a singular, so it should take a singular verb. *The team was*

E.   Incorrect. The subject of the sentence is the *store*, which needs the plural verb *closes*.

9)   **Which sentence does NOT contain an error?**

A.   The grandchildren and their cousins enjoyed their day at the beach.

B.   Most of the grass has lost their deep color.

C.   The jury was cheering as their commitment came to a close.

D.   Every boy and girl must learn to behave themselves in school.

E.   My siblings have his or her own rooms.

Answers:

A.   **Correct.** *Grandchildren and cousins/their*

B.   Incorrect. *Most of the grass has lost <u>its</u> deep color.*

C.   Incorrect. *The jury was cheering as <u>its</u> commitment came to a close.*

D.   Incorrect. *Every boy and girl must learn to behave himself or herself in school.*

E.   Incorrect. *Siblings* is plural, so it requires the plural pronoun *their*.

10)   **Which of the following sentences contains a comma splice?**

A.   Since she went to the store.

B.   The football game ended in a tie, the underdog caught up in the fourth quarter.

C.   If we get rid of the bookcase, we'll have enough room for a couch.

D.   When the players dropped their gloves, a fight broke out on the ice hockey rink floor.

E.   The teacher bought balloons, hats, and cupcakes for the party.

Answers:

A.   Incorrect. The group of words in A is not a complete thought and would be classified as a fragment.

B.   **Correct.** The sentence in B joins two complete thoughts with only a comma and would therefore be classified as a comma splice.

C.   Incorrect. This sentence correctly joins a dependent and independent clause using a comma.

D.   Incorrect. The sentence in D is punctuated properly and constructed correctly.

E.   Incorrect. This sentence correctly uses commas to join three items in a list.

EVALUATING SOURCES

Research is a process of gathering sources containing documented facts that answer specific questions and provide information about an issue. In the twenty-first century, locating sources is easy; however, finding and determining quality sources involves careful evaluation.

It is best to begin by evaluating the credibility of a source's author. Consideration should be given to the author's motivation—the purpose or reason he or she had for writing the text. Next, research involves identifying the author's background and expertise. Although educational credentials are significant, firsthand experience offers equally reliable information.

Questions a researcher should be able to answer about a source include:

▶   Is it current or written fairly recently?

▶   If it is secondary, is it based on both primary as well as other secondary sources?

▶   Is the author an expert in the area of study? Does he or she include or cite relevant information from other authorities on the topic? Are the conclusions based on scientific evidence? How well does the scientifically gathered evidence explain the topic?

▶   Is the purpose of the source clear? Is there any bias?

▶   What does the author assume is true?

▶   Does the author present several viewpoints on issues?

▶   Does the content agree with what other reliable sources on the topic indicate?

Evaluating a website entails determining who the site's intended audience is and if the site has an agenda, such as selling something or promoting a belief system. If the site is educational, researchers should verify whether it was created by authoritative authors and authors that have identified themselves. Grammatically correct content on the site is a helpful indicator. Plus, the site's address should work and be relatively current. (Typing "javascript:alert(document.lastModified)" in the address bar provides a site's most recent modification date.)

SAMPLE QUESTIONS

11) **What legitimizes the claims made in a source?**

   A.   Similar information and conclusions are apparent in other sources.

   B.   The background of the writer is clear.

   C.   The publisher of the source is a respected organization.

   D.   A journalist or an admired writer has written the source.

   E.   The perspective of the author is clear.

   Answers:

   A.   **Correct.** The content is in agreement with what other reliable sources on the topic indicate.

   B.   Incorrect. The writer's background may be clear, but that background is not the subject of the source.

   C.   Incorrect. A respected organization is unrelated to scholarly research, an author's qualifications, or the use of verifiable data.

   D.   Incorrect. The writer may be a journalist or admired, but that does not mean the writer is knowledgeable about the subject of the text or has collected data that supports the ideas of the source.

   E.   Incorrect. Although the perspective should be clear, it has to be supported by reliable data.

12) **A quality source**

   A.   is free of the clutter of citations, quotations, footnotes, and a works-cited page.

   B.   is peer-reviewed by scholars who have credentials in a wide variety of areas, not just the subject of the source article.

   C.   has remained in publication for decades.

   D.   includes accurate, well-documented information.

   E.   provides relevant explanations from one popular perspective.

   Answers:

   A.   Incorrect. A quality source has citations, quotations, footnotes, and a works-cited page.

   B.   Incorrect. A peer-reviewed source has been assessed by scholars who have credentials in the same area as the author of the source.

   C.   Incorrect. A quality source may be a recent publication.

   D.   **Correct.** The author of a quality source is an expert in the source's area of study and will have included or cited relevant information from other authorities on the topic.

   E.   Incorrect. Although the idea of providing relevant explanations is good, providing explanations from only a popular perspective is not good. A perspective must be based on verifiable fact.

TYPES OF SOURCES

Which sources a researcher uses depends on his or her purpose. If the purpose is to analyze, interpret, or critique an historical event, a creative work, or a natural phenomenon, the researcher will use a **primary**, or **original**, **source**. Examples of primary sources include:

- ▶ letters and e-mails
- ▶ autobiographies, diaries, and memoirs
- ▶ firsthand or eyewitness accounts or descriptions of events
- ▶ interviews, questionnaires, and surveys
- ▶ speeches and lectures
- ▶ photographs, drawings, and paintings
- ▶ news stories written at the time of the event

The written analysis or interpretation of a primary source is considered a **secondary source**. These sources are written by people who do not have firsthand experience of the topic being described. Instead, authors of secondary sources examine primary sources in order to draw conclusions or make generalizations about people, events, and ideas. Examples of secondary sources include:

- ▶ literary criticism and interpretation essays
- ▶ biographies
- ▶ historical criticism
- ▶ political analyses
- ▶ essays on ethics and social policies

To research a problem or question that has not been researched before, an analysis of the relevant primary documents is recommended. In addition, researchers can conduct their own observations, interviews, surveys, or experiments.

If the purpose is to report on, explain, or summarize what is known about a topic, the researcher will use texts written by other researchers or secondary sources. Of note, most primary research studies begin with a review of literature, which summarizes what secondary sources are saying about a topic.

Research on topics of interest usually begins with a critical analysis of existing research; researchers draw conclusions from secondary sources that deal with their specific topic. Initially, thought should be given to searching databases. Annotated bibliographies are helpful in locating the most relevant sources for a topic. Web pages created by associations, government agencies, and institutions have a wealth of source material. Although print sources continue to be helpful, most researchers use the Internet to locate digital versions of print sources. Reports by research agencies are often available, particularly in areas concerning the environment. If scholarly sources are required—that is, texts written by those who are highly educated in a particular field—instead of a web search, Google Scholar and databases like JSTOR, EBSCO, and GALE can be more helpful. Public libraries are the best places to avoid the cost of subscription-based databases like JSTOR.

SAMPLE QUESTIONS

13) **A secondary source**

   A.   summarizes or evaluates an original source or research study.

   B.   is written by a person who conducted an original study or wrote an original text.

   C.   must be peer reviewed.

   D.   is published by the government or a private publisher.

   E.   is based on interviews and survey responses.

   Answers:

   A.   **Correct.** A secondary source is a written analysis or interpretation of a primary source. Examples include literary and historical criticism.

   B.   Incorrect. This option describes a primary source.

   C.   Incorrect. This is a possibility, but it does not define what a secondary source is.

   D.   Incorrect. These are possibilities, but they don't explain what a secondary source is.

   E.   Incorrect. This option is more applicable to a primary source; however, secondary sources may refer to interviews or surveys reported in primary sources.

14) **What kind of source is a political speech?**

   A.   a secondary source

   B.   an authoritative source

   C.   a confusing source

   D.   a narrative source

   E.   a primary source

   Answers:

   A.   Incorrect. A secondary source is a written analysis or interpretation of a primary source. Examples include literary and historical criticism.

   B.   Incorrect. The speaker may not be authoritative, or even knowledgeable.

   C.   Incorrect. This is possible but hopefully not true.

   D.   Incorrect. Some political speeches may include an anecdote or follow a narrative structure. However, this option does not define or categorize a political speech.

E.   **Correct.** Primary sources are firsthand accounts of a topic. They are created by authors who have direct experience with the subject and are usually created at the time the authors are involved with the subject. A political speech is written or given by a person who is directly involved with the issues presented in the speech.

RESEARCH STRATEGIES

Research begins with curiosity about a specific topic, then moves from curiosity to a research question. Doing preliminary reading on the topic refines that question and gains the researcher an overview. A search of *available sources related to the question* is also wise. For example:

- ▶ **Research topic**: Emily Dickinson and feminism
- ▶ **Question**: What feminist ideas did Emily Dickinson express?
- ▶ **Preliminary sources**: Literary criticism on Emily Dickinson, especially feminist interpretations of Dickinson's poetry

Next, the researcher will need to decide which primary sources and critical essays to use. After skim-reading these sources, a preliminary *organizational plan* should be determined. Some considerations include: What basic background information does the reader (also considered the audience) need in order to understand the topic? What is the basis of the ideas to be presented? In other words, what topics need to be explained first so other topics can be understood by the reader? What is the most logical way to present the information that has been located? The reader prefers one topic to lead to the next. Organizational plans detail the characteristics, causes, effects, sequences of events, similarities, and contrasts.

A sample organizational plan for the Emily Dickinson research example could involve presenting in the first section a historical account of the nineteenth-century women's rights movement and a definition of the concept of feminism during Dickinson's life. The next sections could delve into the main feminist ideas Dickinson expressed in her poetry.

Once an organizational plan is outlined, the researcher should start taking *notes* from the sources gathered. Most important, each note must include identifying information about the source, including publication details and page numbers. In addition, the section of the outline that corresponds with the source information noted must be designated above each note. This way, the notes are categorized according to the outline, or organizational plan.

Notes come in four different forms. A **direct quotation** is three or more consecutive words copied precisely from a source. It must be designated by quotation marks or by block indentation if the quotation is longer than four lines of prose or three lines of poetry. A quotation can be a definition or a well-worded or authoritative statement that will amplify a main point. A **paraphrase** is a reworded version of any sentence in a source. Typically, a sentence with complex or sophisticated wording needs to be paraphrased. The main thoughts are pulled apart and the language is simplified, but the original meaning is retained. A **summary** is a shortened version of a section of a source, containing only the main points or events of the original. Any type of descriptive, detailed, or narrative text, such as news stories, fictional stories, or chronicles of events needs to be summed up. An **idea and list**—the most common form of notes—consists of the key idea of a section of text followed by a bulleted list of related details. Again, all notes should be marked with corresponding outline sections, so it will be easy to put the notes in the order of the outline and use the information to compose the paper.

The following are sample notes for research on feminist ideas expressed by Emily Dickinson:

Cooper, Susan Fenimore. "Female Suffrage: A Letter to the Christian Women of America." *Harper's New Weekly Magazine* XLI (June–November 1870): 594 – 600.

Outline Section I

Three Reasons Women Remain in a Subordinate Position:

1. They are physically weaker and depend on men for protection.

2. They are intellectually inferior.

   ▶ This claim is considered debatable.

   ▶ Why women have not educated themselves is of concern.

3. Christianity teaches that men are the head of the household.

   ▶ But protects her more than other systems

Figure 2.2a. A Primary Source

Dickinson, Emily. "My Life had stood – a Loaded Gun." Stanzas 1 – 3.

Outline Section I

My Life had stood—a Loaded Gun—
In Corners—till a Day
The Owner passed—identified—
And carried Me away—

And now We roam in Sovereign Woods—
And now We hunt the Doe—
And every time I speak for Him—
The Mountains straight reply—
And do I smile, such cordial light
Upon the Valley glow—
It is as a Vesuvian face
Had let its pleasure through—

Figure 2.2b. A Primary Source

Rich, Adrienne. "Vesuvius at Home: The Power of Emily Dickinson." Reprinted in *Literary Theories in Praxis*. Edited by Shirley F. Staton. Philadelphia: University of Pennsylvania Press, 1987. pp. 258–59.

Outline Section I

Speaking of Emily Dickinson's poem "My Life had stood – a Loaded Gun," Adrienne Rich explains, "But I think that for us, at this time, it is a central poem in understanding Emily Dickinson, and ourselves, and the condition of the woman artist, particularly in the nineteenth century. It seems likely that the nineteenth-century woman poet, especially, felt the medium of poetry as dangerous....Poetry is too much rooted in the unconscious; it presses too close against the barriers of repression; and the nineteenth-century woman had much to repress."

Paraphrase of the above quotation:

Nineteenth-century women had to repress many of their thoughts. In other words, they pushed these thoughts into their unconscious minds and weren't aware of them. Since the unconscious mind is the source of poetic expression, writing poetry was dangerous for a nineteenth-century woman; in doing so, she gave expression to these repressed thoughts and feelings.

Figure 2.3. A Secondary Source, Literary Criticism

SAMPLE QUESTIONS

15)   **Which of the following is an example of a secondary source for an article on local highways?**

A.   an online opinion column promoting tax incentives for those who carpool

B.   photographs of traffic accidents

C.   data from the city's transportation department

D.   an autobiography of a city official who led efforts to improve local infrastructure

E.   e-mails about highway congestion sent to the mayor

Answers:

A.   Correct. Only this option describes a secondary source, since it offers analysis of a topic, not firsthand experience of it.

B.   Incorrect. Photographs are a primary source.

C.   Incorrect. The analysis or interpretation of data could be considered a secondary source, but the data itself is a primary source.

D.   Incorrect. An autobiography is a primary source.

E.   Incorrect. Emails are a primary source.

16) **What is a good reason for a writer of a research paper to include a short section of text copied word for word from a source?**

A.   The text is a secondary source.

B.   The vocabulary is sophisticated.

C.   The text is well worded.

D.   The information relates to several areas of the research.

E.   The section of text would take a significant amount of time to paraphrase.

Answers:

A.   Incorrect. The type of source does not affect whether a direct quote should be included in a research paper.

B.   Incorrect. Sophisticated vocabulary is not a good enough reason to quote text; the text should be still be paraphrased.

C.   Correct. Quoting a statement with wording that is emphatic or memorable can be an especially effective way to amplify an argument in a research paper.

D.   Incorrect. Ideally all the information in a research paper is relevant, so this is not a reason to include direct quotations.

E.   Incorrect. The amount of work it would take to write the research paper is not a factor in whether to include direct quotes.

CITATIONS

In general, any ideas or details that are not original to the writer must be documented. Specifically, this includes any information quoted, paraphrased, or summarized from sources.

Information taken from sources is documented with **in-text citations**, **internal documentation**, or **parenthetical references**. These terms are used interchangeably to mean that the source information—usually the author's last name or the first main words of the title plus the page, line, or section number—is put in parentheses right after the paraphrase, quotation, or summary. If the source of the information is introduced in the text with the author's name, the writer puts just the page, line, or section number in the parentheses.

Writing the Essay

egardless of the format or topic, a high-scoring essay can be written by following several simple rules. First, identify the type of essay to be written: if the essay doesn't correctly address the prompt, it will always receive a low score. Second, determine what the main point and organizational structure of the essay will be. It is much easier to write using a clear outline than to haphazardly organize along the way. Third, make sure that the essay uses sound evidence while maintaining a style that's appropriate to the test. A good essay doesn't have to be complicated; it just needs to have a clear, well-reasoned position. Finally, all of this must be accomplished within a limited time frame. Fortunately, the essay graders will understand that a first draft written under test conditions does not need to be as polished as a final essay in a classroom assignment.

TYPES OF ESSAYS

It is important to note that essays do not follow a single format. Rather, the format is determined by the intended purpose of each essay. For example, an essay may attempt to inform or persuade the reader, or perhaps describe or narrate a scene. It is important to use the appropriate type of essay for a given task.

PERSUASIVE

A **persuasive essay** is meant to convince the reader of the author's point of view on a particular issue. Typically, such an essay will also include a call to action. Thus, a persuasive essay should cause the reader to feel and act in a particular way.

A persuasive essay can be written on any topic on which people can have a difference of opinion. For example, an essay may argue that social media is harmful to teenagers or that a noise ordinance should be adopted in a community. These both seek to sway the reader's opinion to that of the author's. In contrast, essays describing the social media habits of teenagers or telling the story of a neighborhood's attempt to pass local noise ordinances are not persuasive because they do not present a specific opinion.

In writing a persuasive essay, it is vital to take a clear stance on an issue. The reader should be left with no doubt as to which side of an issue the writer supports. In addition, a persuasive essay must include facts and logical reasoning to show that the ideas put forth by the author are superior to other ideas on the topic. This type of essay should be written with a specific audience in mind to tailor the arguments and language to the intended readers.

When writing persuasive essays in an exam setting, keep in mind that the actual stance taken in the essay is not important. The graders don't care about the specific opinion expressed in the essay; they only care that the opinion is well written and supported by logically relevant evidence.

PERSUASIVE ESSAY EXAMPLE

PROMPT: Technology has launched us into a new era and, with it, a new way of living with and relating to one another. It has opened doors and allowed us to accomplish things that would have been impossible in the past: we are able to keep up closely with a large number of people in an easy and comfortable way. As it continues to develop, social media technology will, time and again, offer us new and better ways of staying in touch with one another and, because of it, will make our lives and our relationships fuller and more meaningful.

Discuss the extent to which you agree or disagree with this opinion. Support your position with specific reasoning and examples from your experience, observations, and reading.

One would be foolish to argue that technology has not had a real and pervasive impact on our daily lives. Many of us rely daily on cell phones, tablets, and computers that allow us to reach family, friends, and business associates with little to no trouble. However, this ease of access does not necessarily mean our relationships are improving: the impersonal and anonymous nature of social media and other communication technologies make it even more difficult for us to make meaningful, lasting connections with the people around us.

Social media is, by nature, impersonal. Though we are able to build personal profiles that reflect whom we want the world to see, these profiles do little to improve our connection and communication with others. In fact, it is these very tools that are distancing us from our fellow humans. Birthday notifications, for example, remind social media users every day of the "friends" who are celebrating that day. While this tool seems, in theory, to be a great way to keep up with others, it actually desensitizes us. In truth, when I receive birthday notifications via social media, I end up either ignoring them altogether or sending an impersonal "Happy Birthday" just to be able to say I did. In fact, I never send birthday notes via social media to friends and family whose birthdays I actually care about because I do so in a more personal way—via a phone call or in person. Furthermore, I don't need an app to remember those birthdays. Though it may seem more useful or convenient to be able to stay in touch through social media, the relationships that rely on it are, in my experience, rarely very meaningful. By allowing us to stay in touch with larger numbers of people, social media also makes our connections shallower.

In addition to being impersonal, social media and other communication technologies can also be anonymous, creating a world of users that are disconnected from the things they post and read and, ultimately, from each other. Cyberbullying has been a significant concern of the twenty-first century, with numerous incidents leading to depressing outcomes, like teenage suicide. Through the lens of social media, bullies are able to disregard the humanity of the person on the other end and say things that they might never say in real life. A similar effect is clear during important political events: people post, with aggressive fervor, in favor of their own beliefs and respond, with equally aggressive insults, to anyone they disagree with. While this may, on the surface, seem to encourage open dialogue, social media and other communication technologies fail to have any effect on the quality of the conversation itself. Rather than learning to interact with one another respectfully, a tactic that may actually lead to increased understanding and greater acceptance of others, social media users learn that what they say has little to no consequence in real life.

The sense of community created by social media is deceptive. The ease with which people can "connect" often makes those connections meaningless. The friend who "Likes" a photo you post isn't putting any real energy into that friendship—he just clicked once and moved on. Similarly, people can use the anonymity of the internet to just as easily create enemies. One angry comment (that would never be said face-to-face) can launch a hundred nasty replies. These types of relationships don't make our lives fuller or more meaningful. They make our lives empty and shallow.

EXPOSITORY

An **expository essay** is one in which the author tells the reader something in a straightforward manner. This essay type is meant to explain, inform, or clarify a topic for which the reader may have no prior knowledge. It is also a chance for the writer to display his or her own understanding of a topic. Subjects for an expository essay might include many different sides, but an expository essay doesn't dive into these controversies. Instead, it simply explains a topic with as much neutrality as possible.

To compose a successful expository essay, the author must present facts from verifiable sources and arrange the information in a logical sequence. Language should be clear and precise, and relevant context should be provided since the reader may not be familiar with the topic. It is important that the essay remains objective and does not include the author's opinion.

DID YOU KNOW?

The word *expository* is related to the word *expose*, which means to show.

EXPOSITORY ESSAY EXAMPLE

PROMPT: Following the Second World War, the United States and the Soviet Union emerged as the dominant world powers, ushering in the Cold War and a "bipolar world." Only a few years before, however, European powers like England and France controlled colonial empires around the world, dominating world affairs; in fact, the Soviet Union itself was only a few decades old.

Using your knowledge of world history, explain how the two superpowers were able to rapidly dominate world affairs following World War II.

The United States and the Soviet Union—victorious allies in the Second World War—were not able to maintain a strong relationship for long. Despite losses in the millions, the Soviet Union still had an enormous and powerful military and, in violation of the agreements made at Yalta, Stalin later occupied several Eastern European countries, preventing free elections. The US-led West formed NATO as a result; in response, the USSR organized the Warsaw Pact. This rapid rise in the prominence of the United States and the USSR was a result of both countries' advanced industrial capabilities, large resource reserves, and expanded global military presence.

In the United States, the New Deal and mobilization for the war had strengthened the national economy. At the end of the war, the United States had proven its weapons capacity by using the nuclear bomb: this technology, on the heels of its military domination of Europe and the Pacific, made it an undisputed global superpower.

At the same time, the Soviet Union dominated land throughout Europe, Central, and East Asia. The Soviet Union's Five Year Plans of the 1920s had sped up industrialization, and their wealth included vast mineral, petroleum, timber, and other natural resources. They also developed nuclear weapons and a military with a global reach.

Furthermore, both countries extended their global reach diplomatically and militarily to spread their respective ideologies—communism and democratic capitalism—in order to ensure global security. By promulgating the Marshall Plan and supporting the establishment of the Bretton Woods institutions (the World Bank and the International Monetary Fund), the United States found ways to promote global capitalism. At the same time, the Soviet Union supported Marxist independence movements worldwide in colonies and resistance movements in former colonies; many Cold War battles were fought as proxy wars between the superpowers in Africa, Asia, and Latin America. Each country also had a global presence with bases, officers, diplomats, and military personnel in nearly every country in the world.

Since the European empires had collapsed in the wake of the Second World War, the Soviet Union and the United States dominated the global stage in a way no other country could match. Each used their natural and industrial resources, alongside a growing military and diplomatic presence, to quickly fill the void left by the fall of European powers.

WRITING A THESIS STATEMENT

The thesis, or **thesis statement**, is central to the structure and meaning of an essay: it presents the writer's argument or position on an issue. In other words, it tells readers specifically what the author is going to say in the essay. A strong, direct thesis statement is key to the organization of any essay. It introduces both the central idea of the essay and the main points that will be used to support that idea. Thus, the thesis will mirror the organization of the essay as a whole: each paragraph can elaborate on each supporting point.

In writing a thesis statement, it is important to respond to the prompt provided. The author must identify keywords in the prompt and think about what the prompt is asking. For example, the prompt may be asking for a clear stance to be taken a particular issue, or it may require a detailed explanation of a topic. Once a clear understanding of the task is reached, the author must develop a central idea along with supporting points from relevant sources, including any provided documents and personal knowledge or experience. The central idea and supporting points can then be concisely packaged into a one or two sentence statement. Generally, a thesis statement is no more than two sentences.

> **HELPFUL HINT**
>
> Find an op-ed article in the newspaper. Read it carefully and try to identify the thesis and supporting points.

THESIS STATEMENT EXAMPLES

PROMPT: Many high schools have begun to adopt 1:1 technology programs, meaning that each school provides every student with a computing device, such as a laptop or tablet. Educators who support these initiatives say that the technology allows for more dynamic collaboration and that students need to learn technology skills to compete in the job market. On the other hand, opponents cite increased distraction and the dangers of cyberbullying or unsupervised internet use as reasons not to provide students with such devices.

In your essay, take a position on this question. You may write about either one of the two points of view given, or you may present a different point of view on this question. Use specific reasons and examples to support your position.

Possible thesis statements:

1)   Providing technology to every student is good for education because it allows students to learn important skills such as typing, web design, and video editing, and it also gives students more opportunities to work cooperatively with their classmates and teachers.

2)   I disagree with the idea that schools should provide technology to students because most students will simply be distracted by the free access to games and websites when they should be studying or doing homework.

3)   By providing each student with a laptop or tablet, schools can help students apply technology to work more effectively with other students,

communicate with teachers and classmates, and conduct research for class projects.

STRUCTURING THE ESSAY

There are a lot of different ways to organize an essay. In the limited timeframe of an exam, however, it is best to stick to a basic five-paragraph essay that includes an introduction, body, and conclusion. This structure can be used to discuss nearly any topic and will be easy for graders to follow.

INTRODUCTIONS

The purpose of an **introduction** is to set the stage for the essay. This is accomplished by capturing the reader's interest, introducing and providing context for the topic, and stating the central idea and main points of the essay. Usually the introductory paragraph ends with a thesis statement, which clearly sets forth the position or point the essay will argue.

INTRODUCTION EXAMPLE

Technology has changed massively in recent years, but today's generation barely notices—high school students are already experienced with the internet, computers, apps, cameras, cell phones, and more. It's inevitable that these technologies will be begin to make their way into classrooms. Opponents of 1:1 technology programs might argue that students will be distracted or misuse the technology, but that is exactly why schools must teach them to use it. Students need to know how to navigate technology safely and effectively, and schools have a responsibility to ensure they learn these skills. By providing each student with a laptop or tablet, schools can help students learn how to apply technology to work more effectively with other students, communicate with teachers and classmates, and conduct research for class projects.

> **Explanation**: This introduction *introduces* the topic in the first sentence. It then provides context by discussing why technology in the classroom is an important—and controversial—topic. The paragraph closes with a thesis statement that takes a firm stance and introduces the supporting ideas that the essay will be organized around.

THE BODY PARAGRAPHS

The body of the essay should consist of two to four paragraphs, each of which is focused on a single supporting idea. The body of an essay can be organized in a number of ways:

▶ Body paragraphs can explain each supporting detail given in the thesis statement.

- Body paragraphs can describe a problem then discuss the pros and cons of a solution in separate paragraphs.
- Body paragraphs can tell a story, with the story broken into two to four logical parts.
- Body paragraphs can compare and contrast the merits of two arguments, possibly drawing a conclusion about which is better at the end.

Each paragraph should be structurally consistent, beginning with a topic sentence to introduce the main idea, followed by supporting ideas and examples. No extra ideas unrelated to the paragraph's focus should appear. Transition words and phrases can be used to connect body paragraphs and to improve the flow and readability of the essay.

QUICK REVIEW

Which essay structure would be better suited to a persuasive essay? What about an expository essay?

BODY PARAGRAPH EXAMPLE

Technology can be a powerful tool for collaboration. When all of the students in a classroom have access to reliable laptops or tablets, they are able to more effectively share information and work together on projects. Students can communicate quickly via email, share files through a cloud service, and use a shared calendar for scheduling. They also have the opportunity to teach each other new skills since each student may bring to the group unique knowledge about particular apps or programs. When the availability of technology is limited or inconsistent, these opportunities are lost.

Explanation: This body paragraph discusses a supporting detail given the thesis (*schools can help students apply technology to work more effectively with other students*). It introduces the topic, then provides concrete examples of how technology makes it easier to work with other students. The final sentence reemphasizes the paragraph's main idea.

CONCLUSIONS

To end an essay smoothly, the author must compose a conclusion that reminds the reader of the importance of the topic and then restates the essay's thesis and supporting details. The writer should revisit the ideas in the introduction and thesis statement, but these ideas should not be simply repeated word-for-word. Rather, a well-written conclusion will reinforce the argument using wording that differs from the thesis statement but conveys the same idea. The conclusion should leave the reader with a strong impression of the essay's main idea and provide the essay with a sense of closure.

CONCLUSION EXAMPLE

As technology continues to change and become more incorporated into everyday life, students will need to adapt to it. Schools already teach young people a myriad of academic and life skills, so it makes sense that they would teach students how to use technology appropriately, too. When technology is incorporated into schoolwork, students will learn to collaborate, communicate, and research more effectively. Providing students with their own devices is one part of this important task, and schools that do so should be supported.

> **Explanation:** This conclusion reminds the reader why the topic is important and then restates the thesis and supporting ideas. It ends with a strong, clear statement of the writer's stance on the issue.

SUPPORTING EVIDENCE

An essay's arguments are made up of claims, which in turn are backed by supporting evidence. This evidence can be drawn from a number of sources. Some essay prompts will include texts from which to draw supporting evidence. Other essays will require the writer to use his or her own background knowledge of the issue. For some essay prompts, it may be appropriate to use personal anecdotes and experiences. Regardless of the source of the evidence, it is important that it be conveyed in a clear, specific, and accurate manner.

PROVIDING SPECIFIC EXAMPLES

In body paragraphs, general statements should be followed with specific examples that will help to convince the reader that the argument has merit. These specific examples do not bring new ideas to the paragraph; rather, they explain or defend the general ideas that have already been stated. A poorly written essay will be full of general claims supported by little to no evidence or specific examples. Conversely, successful essays will use multiple specific examples to back up general claims.

EXAMPLES OF GENERAL AND SPECIFIC STATEMENTS

The following are some examples of general statements, followed by examples of specific statements that provide more detailed support of an idea.

General: Students may get distracted online or access harmful websites.

Specific: Some students spend too much time using chat features or social media, or they get caught up in online games. Others spend time reading websites that have nothing to do with an assignment.

Specific: Teens often think they are hidden behind their computer screens. However, providing personal information online can lead to danger in the real world.

General: Schools can teach students how to use technology appropriately and expose them to new tools.

Specific: Schools can help students learn how to use technology to work on class projects, communicate with classmates and teachers, and carry out research for classwork.

Specific: Providing students with laptops or tablets will allow them to get lots of practice using technology and programs at home, and only school districts can ensure that these tools are distributed widely, especially to students who may not have access to them otherwise.

INCORPORATING SOURCES

Providing evidence from outside sources is an excellent way to provide support for the claims in an essay. Some essay prompts will include texts that may be cited in the essay, or writers may want to cite sources from memory. In either case, this supporting evidence should be incorporated smoothly into the essay. Context should be provided for the quote, and the quote should always be followed by a discussion of its importance or relevance to the essay.

> **HELPFUL HINT**
>
> In an essay, a quote never speaks for itself; the writer must always explain where it came from and why it is important.

When using outside sources, it is vital to credit the author or source within the text. Usually a full citation isn't needed—it can simply be sufficient to note the author's name in the text. And, as always, the writer must make sure to place direct quotations in quotation marks.

> **INCORPORATING SOURCES EXAMPLE**
>
> In addition to helping students work better with each other, technology can also help students communicate more effectively with teachers. A recent study from the University of Montana showed that over 75 percent of students have at some point been too intimidated to speak up in class, even if they thought they had something valuable to contribute (Higgins, 2015). But what if technology could provide a way to make speaking up easier? Private online messaging, comment boards for questions, and online tutorials are all made possible by introducing technology to the classroom. A well-trained teacher will be able to use these resources to encourage more effective classroom communication. In my personal experience, I have seen numerous students respond effectively when given the chance to communicate in the privacy of an online interaction.
>
> **Explanation**: This first-person paragraph incorporates two sources: a scientific study and a personal anecdote from the author.

WRITING WELL

Although the content of an essay is of primary importance, the writing itself will also factor into the essay's final score. Writing well means that the language and tone are appropriate for the purpose and audience of the essay, the flow of ideas and the relationships among them are logical and clear, and the sentences are varied enough to keep the reader interested.

TRANSITIONS

Transitions are words, phrases, and ideas that help connect ideas throughout a text both between sentences and between paragraphs. Transitions can be used to imply a range of relationships, including cause and effect, sequence, contradictions, and continuance of an idea. Consistent and creative use of transitions will help the essay flow logically from one idea to the next and will make the essay easy for the reader to follow.

HELPFUL HINT

Common transitions include *then, next, in other words, as well, in addition to, another, because, first, finally, in conclusion, however, in fact, therefore,* and *on the other hand.*

Transitions between paragraphs can also be polished by starting paragraphs with references to ideas mentioned in previous paragraphs or by ending them with a transition to the next topic. Such guideposts will guide the reader from one paragraph to the next.

EXAMPLES OF TRANSITIONS

Teens often think they are hidden behind their computer screens. <u>However</u>, providing personal information online can lead to danger in the real world.

<u>In addition to</u> helping students work better with each other, technology can also help students communicate more effectively with teachers.

They <u>also</u> have the opportunity to teach each other new skills.

SYNTAX

A variety of well-written sentences will help maintain the reader's interest in the essay. To create this theme, a writer can use sentences that differ in length and that begin with varying words, rather than repeating the same word at the start of each new sentence. It is also important for the writer to use a mix of different sentence structures, including simple, complex, compound, and compound-complex sentences.

SYNTAX EXAMPLE

Technology can be a powerful tool for collaboration. When all of the students in a classroom have access to reliable laptops or tablets, they are able to more effectively share information and work together on projects. Students can communicate quickly via email, share files through a cloud service, and use a shared calendar for scheduling. They also have the opportunity to teach each other new skills since each student may bring to the group unique knowledge about particular apps or programs. When the availability of technology is limited or inconsistent, these opportunities are lost.

> **Explanation**: This paragraph starts with a short, simple sentence and follows with a longer, more complex sentence. The next sentence is also long, but it is a simple sentence with a single clause. The second-to-last sentence is complicated with multiple clauses, but it is immediately followed with a short, easy-to-read statement that ends the paragraph.

WORD CHOICE AND TONE

The words a writer chooses influence the reader's assessment of the essay. When writing essays, it is always necessary to choose words that are appropriate to the task.

For instance, a formal essay on an academic topic may benefit from complex sentences and an expansive vocabulary. However, a first-person essay on a personal topic may use a more casual vocabulary and organization. In general, when writing for exam graders, it is best to use clear, direct vocabulary and avoid using vague, general words such as good, bad, very, or a lot. Showing variety in word choice can also help improve an essay's score. However, it is better to use more familiar vocabulary than to try to impress the exam grader with unfamiliar words or words that do not fit the context of the essay.

WORD CHOICE EXAMPLES

Technology has changed massively in recent years, but today's generation barely notices—high school students are already experienced with the internet, computers, apps, cameras, cell phones, and more. It is inevitable that these technologies will be begin to make their way into classrooms. Opponents of 1:1 technology programs might argue that students will be distracted or misuse the technology, but that is exactly why schools must teach them to use it. Students need to know how to navigate technology safely and effectively, and schools have a responsibility to ensure they learn these skills. By providing each student with a laptop or tablet, schools can help students apply technology to work more effectively with other students, communicate with teachers and classmates, and conduct research for class projects.

Technology is everywhere in modern life. We've all walked into a coffee shop full of laptops or have seen people walking with their phones in front of their faces. I know I've often looked up from my tablet to realize I've missed a whole conversation. With technology everywhere, it seems obvious that we would start using it in classrooms. Opponents of 1:1 technology programs say that technology will be too distracting or will be abused by students, but it seems like that's an even more important reason for students to learn how to use it. Schools are where students learn all kinds of life skills, and technology is just another skill to learn. By giving students laptops or tablets, schools can help students work better with each other, work better with teachers, and learn to do better research.

Explanation: The two paragraphs above discuss the same topic. The first has a word choice and tone for an academic essay; the second is written in a more relaxed, personal style.

Managing Time

When working on an essay under time constraints, it is important to manage time wisely. Simply launching into the introduction will likely result in a hurried, unorganized essay and a low score. Instead, the writer should take a few minutes to plan.

HELPFUL HINT

Underline key words in the prompt so you can refer to them while writing the essay. This can help keep you and your essay focused.

As a first step, the writer should thoroughly read the prompt and any accompanying texts, and then determine the type of essay that is required. Next, the writer must decide on a thesis and what kind of supporting evidence to use. Once the thesis is clear, it is a good idea for the writer to create a brief outline of the essay. This whole process should only take a few minutes, leaving the bulk of the time for writing. However, it is always a good idea to leave a few minutes at the end to proofread and revise as necessary.

Example Essays

PROMPT: The rise in popularity of e-cigarettes has reduced the overall smoking rate according to the Centers for Disease Control and Prevention. Many hail the new technology for helping smokers quit traditional tobacco cigarettes. However, others raise concerns about the appeal of e-cigarettes to young people and advocate FDA regulation of e-cigarettes to prevent negative side effects of their use on a new generation of smokers.

In your essay, take a position on this question. You may write about either one of the two points of view given, or you may present a different point of view on this question. Use specific reasons and examples to support your position.

EXAMPLE ESSAY ONE

For decades, youth smoking was a major concern for both parents and public health advocates. With education campaigns informing youth of the dangers of smoking and legal action taken against tobacco producers for their advertising tactics, the number of youth smoking traditional cigarettes has never been lower. But new technology is threatening to overturn that progress as electronic cigarettes (e-cigarettes) have skyrocketed in popularity among both adults and youth. E-cigarettes should be regulated by the FDA to prevent youth from smoking since the long-term effects of e-cig use are unknown, youth are still becoming addicted to nicotine, and e-cigs could be a gateway to traditional smoking.

Smoking has long been a way for young people to feel cool or sophisticated. Popular culture, including film and television, glamorized smoking and led generations of Americans to pick up the habit. Although traditional smoking is no longer considered cool, the use of e-cigarettes, or vaping, threatens to take the same position in popular culture. Companies which produce traditional cigarettes have long been banned from advertising their products on television, but because e-cigarettes are not regulated by the FDA, there are no restrictions on their advertisement. This allows e-cig companies to reach youth through a wide range of media. Furthermore, the gadget-like design of e-cigs and the variety of candy-like flavors make them especially appealing to youth—a tactic that seems designed to hook a new generation on smoking.

This is particularly concerning as the long-term effects of vaping are not yet known for either adults or youth. The technology is too new to have been studied adequately. The FDA must study a drug for years before it can become available to the general public. Yet a device that delivers a highly-addictive substance remains unregulated. It is true that e-cigarettes are healthier for smokers than traditional cigarettes, but we cannot yet know the impact on youth who would have otherwise not smoked but for the easy access to these drug-delivery devices.

In addition, we do know that nicotine is a highly-addictive drug and that once this habit is established, it is very difficult to quit. If nothing else, this is a wasteful way for young people to spend their money. But even more concerning is the danger that nicotine use could alter the brain chemistry of young people and potentially make them prone to other addictions. Even if vaping does not become a gateway to hard drug use, it does make the leap to traditional smoking much more likely, and we know how harmful cigarettes have been.

The FDA has a responsibility to protect the public's health, and it is clear that regulation is needed to stop the momentum of the e-cigarette industry from getting youth addicted to their products. Although long-term health effects of vaping are unknown at this time, we must be cautious and err on the side of safety. At the very least, youth can be spared from an expensive, addictive habit; at best, an entire generation can live longer, healthier lives.

Explanation: This response provides good context for the discussion of the topic and takes a clear stance on the issue raised in the prompt. Strong examples and sound reasoning support the thesis. The essay is cohesive, and strong transitions connect ideas. Vocabulary and tone are appropriate, and the conclusion leaves the reader with a sense of the importance of the issue. Overall, this response would receive a high score.

EXAMPLE ESSAY TWO

Everyone knows smoking is bad for you. So, it's good that lots of people are quitting, and I think e-cigarettes, or vapes as they are also called, are helping people quit. Even though I don't use them, I know some people who use vapes, and they seem pretty healthy. It may be true that e-cigarettes have harmful side effects, but it will be too far into the future before we know. The FDA should be studying this so that we do know if vapes are safe to use, especially for kids. No one wants kids to get hooked on drugs or to be unhealthy.

If they do start smoking, it is better for the kids to use e-cigarettes. They are less harmful because they don't use real tobacco or produce the terrible smelling smoke that normal cigarettes do. Some of my friends vape, and I don't even mind being in the same room. They actually smell pretty sweet. I don't think it's good to vape too much, but once in a while is fine, and I hope people make good choices about smoking.

Explanation: This response does not sufficiently address the prompt. The writer seems to disagree with the position of FDA regulation of e-cigarettes but does not develop this into a clear thesis. The writer's position is further confused by stating that the FDA should be studying the matter. The response is short and lacks adequate supporting detail. Although some personal examples are used, they are weak and a divergence from the main point. Although free of most errors, the language is simplistic, personal pronouns are overused, and the tone is not appropriate for academic writing. Overall, this response would receive a low score.

Part III: Mathematics

4

Numbers and Operations

This chapter provides a review of the basic yet critical components of mathematics such as manipulating fractions, comparing numbers, and using units. These concepts will provide the foundation for more complex mathematical operations in later chapters.

TYPES OF NUMBERS

Numbers are placed in categories based on their properties.

▶ A **natural number** is greater than 0 and has no decimal or fraction attached. These are also sometimes called counting numbers {1, 2, 3, 4, ...}.

▶ **Whole numbers** are natural numbers and the number 0 {0, 1, 2, 3, 4, ...}.

▶ **Integers** include positive and negative natural numbers and 0 {..., –4, –3, –2, –1, 0, 1, 2, 3, 4, ...}.

▶ A **rational number** can be represented as a fraction. Any decimal part must terminate or resolve into a repeating pattern. Examples include –12, $-\frac{4}{5}$, 0.36, $7.\overline{7}$, $26\frac{1}{2}$, etc.

▶ An **irrational number** cannot be represented as a fraction. An irrational decimal number never ends and never resolves into a repeating pattern. Examples include $-\sqrt{7}$, π, and 0.34567989135...

▶ A **real number** is a number that can be represented by a point on a number line. Real numbers include all the rational and irrational numbers.

▶ An **imaginary number** includes the imaginary unit i, where $i = \sqrt{-1}$ Because $i^2 = -1$, imaginary numbers produce a negative value when squared. Examples of imaginary numbers include $-4i$, $0.75i$, $i\sqrt{2}$ and $\frac{8}{3}i$.

▶ A **complex number** is in the form $a + bi$, where a and b are real numbers. Examples of complex numbers include $3 + 2i$, $-4 + i$, $\sqrt{3} - i\sqrt[3]{5}$ and $\frac{5}{8} - \frac{7i}{8}$. All imaginary numbers are also complex.

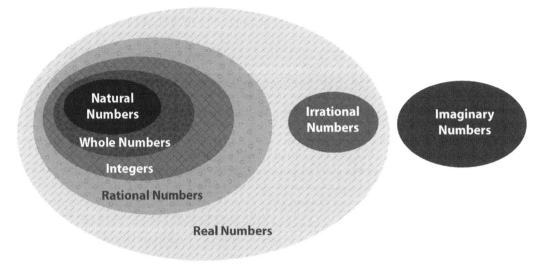

Figure 4.1. Types of Numbers

The **factors** of a natural number are all the numbers that can multiply together to make the number. For example, the factors of 24 are 1, 2, 3, 4, 6, 8, 12, and 24. Every natural number is either prime or composite. A **prime number** is a number that is only divisible by itself and 1. (The number 1 is not considered prime.) Examples of prime numbers are 2, 3, 7, and 29. The number 2 is the only even prime number. A **composite number** has more than two factors. For example, 6 is composite because its factors are 1, 6, 2, and 3. Every composite number can be written as a unique product of prime numbers, called the **prime factorization** of the number. For example, the prime factorization of 90 is $90 = 2 \times 3^2 \times 5$. All integers are either even or odd. An even number is divisible by 2; an odd number is not.

> **HELPFUL HINT**
>
> If a real number is a natural number (e.g., 50), then it is also a whole number, an integer, and a rational number.

PROPERTIES OF NUMBER SYSTEMS

A system is **closed** under an operation if performing that operation on two elements of the system results in another element of that system. For example, the integers are closed under the operations of addition, subtraction, and multiplication but not division. Adding, subtracting, or multiplying two integers results in another integer. However, dividing two integers could result in a rational number that is not an integer $\left(-2 \div 3 = \frac{-2}{3}\right)$.

▶ The rational numbers are closed under all four operations (except for division by 0).

▶ The real numbers are closed under all four operations.

▶ The complex numbers are closed under all four operations.

▶ The irrational numbers are NOT closed under ANY of the four operations.

The **commutative property** holds for an operation if order does not matter when performing the operation. For example, multiplication is commutative for integers: $(-2)(3) = (3)(-2)$.

The **associative property** holds for an operation if elements can be regrouped without changing the result. For example, addition is associative for real numbers: $-3 + (-5 + 4) = (-3 + -5) + 4$

The **distributive property** of multiplication over addition allows a product of sums to be written as a sum of products: $a(b + c) = ab + ac$. The value a is distributed over the sum $(b + c)$. The acronym FOIL (First, Outer, Inner, Last) is a useful way to remember the distributive property.

When an operation is performed with an **identity element** and another element a, the result is a. The identity element for multiplication on real numbers is $1(a \times 1 = a)$, and for addition is $0(a + 0 = a)$.

An operation of a system has an **inverse element** if applying that operation with the inverse element results in the identity element. For example, the inverse element of a for addition is $-a$ because $a + (-a) = 0$. The inverse element of a for multiplication is $\frac{1}{a}$ because $a \times \frac{1}{a} = 1$.

SAMPLE QUESTIONS

1) Classify the following numbers as natural, whole, integer, rational, or irrational. (The numbers may have more than one classification.)

   A. 72
   B. $-\frac{2}{3}$
   C. $\sqrt{5}$

   Answers:

   A. The number is **natural**, **whole**, an **integer**, and **rational** (72 can be written as the fraction $\frac{72}{1}$).

   B. The fraction is **rational**.

   C. The number is **irrational**. (It cannot be written as a fraction, and written as a decimal is approximately 2.2360679... Notice this decimal does not terminate nor does it have a repeating pattern.)

2) Determine the real and imaginary parts of the following complex numbers.

    A.   20

    B. $10 - i$

    C. $15i$

    Answers:

    A complex number is in the form of $a + bi$, where a is the real part and b is the imaginary part.

    A. $20 = 20 + 0i$

          The real part is 20, and there is no imaginary part. (The imaginary part is 0.)

    B. $10 - i = 10 - 1i$

          The real part is 10, and −1 is the imaginary part.

    C. $15i = 0 + 15i$

          The real part is 0, and the imaginary part is 15.

3) Answer True or False for each statement:

    A.   The natural numbers are closed under subtraction.

    B.   The sum of two irrational numbers is irrational.

    C.   The sum of a rational number and an irrational number is irrational.

    Answers:

    A.   **False.** Subtracting the natural number 7 from 2 results in $2 - 7 = -5$, which is an integer, but not a natural number.

    B.   **False.** For example, $(5 - 2\sqrt{3}) + (2 + 2\sqrt{3}) = 7$. The sum of two irrational numbers in this example is a whole number, which is not irrational. The sum of a rational number and an irrational number is sometimes rational and sometimes irrational.

    C.   **True.** Because irrational numbers have decimal parts that are unending and with no pattern, adding a repeating or terminating decimal will still result in an unending decimal without a pattern.

4) Answer True or False for each statement:

    A.   The associative property applies for multiplication in the real numbers.

    B.   The commutative property applies to all real numbers and all operations.

    Answers:

    A.   **True.** For all real numbers, $a \times (b \times c) = (a \times b) \times c$. Order of multiplication does not change the result.

    B.   **False.** The commutative property does not work for subtraction or division on real numbers. For example, $12 - 5 = 7$, but $5 - 12 = -7$ and $10 \div 2 = 5$, but $2 \div 10 = \frac{1}{5}$.

SCIENTIFIC NOTATION

Scientific notation is a method of representing very large and small numbers in the form $a \times 10^n$, where a is a value between 1 and 10, and n is a nonzero integer. For example, the number 927,000,000 is written in scientific notation as 9.27×10^8. Multiplying 9.27 by 10 eight times gives 927,000,000. When performing operations with scientific notation, the final answer should be in the form $a \times 10^n$.

65000000.
7 6 5 4 3 2 1

6.5×10^7

.0000987
-1 -2 -3 -4 -5

9.87×10^{-5}

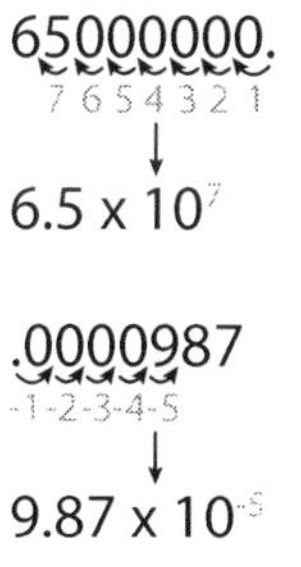

Figure 4.2. Scientific Notation

When adding and subtracting numbers in scientific notation, the power of 10 must be the same for all numbers. This results in like terms in which the a terms are added or subtracted and the 10^n remains unchanged. When multiplying numbers in scientific notation, multiply the a factors, and then multiply that answer by 10 to the sum of the exponents. For division, divide the a factors and subtract the exponents.

SAMPLE QUESTIONS

5) Simplify: $(3.8 \times 10^3) + (4.7 \times 10^2)$

Answer:

$(3.8 \times 10^3) + (4.7 \times 10^2)$	
$3.8 \times 10^3 = 3.8 \times 10 \times 10^2 = 38 \times 10^2$	To add, the exponents of 10 must be the same. Change the first number so the power of 10 is 2.
$38 \times 10^2 + 4.7 \times 10^2 = 42.7 \times 10^2$	Add the a terms together.
$= \mathbf{4.27 \times 10^3}$	Write the number in proper scientific notation.

6) Simplify: $(8.1 \times 10^{-5})(1.4 \times 10^7)$

Answer:

$(8.1 \times 10^{-5})(1.4 \times 10^7)$	
$= 11.34 \times 10^2$	Multiply the a factors and add the exponents on the base of 10.

$$= 1.134 \times 10^3$$

Write the number in proper scientific notation by placing the decimal so that the first number is between 1 and 10 and adjusting the exponent accordingly.

POSITIVE AND NEGATIVE NUMBERS

Positive numbers are greater than 0, and **negative numbers** are less than 0. Both positive and negative numbers can be shown on a **number line**.

Figure 4.3. Number Line

The **absolute value** of a number is the distance the number is from 0. Since distance is always positive, the absolute value of a number is always positive. The absolute value of a is denoted $|a|$. For example, $|-2| = 2$ since -2 is two units away from 0.

Positive and negative numbers can be added, subtracted, multiplied, and divided. The sign of the resulting number is governed by a specific set of rules shown in the table below.

Table 4.1. Operations with Positive and Negative Numbers

Adding Real Numbers		Subtracting Real Numbers*	
Positive + Positive = Positive	$7 + 8 = 15$	Negative – Positive = Negative	$-7 - 8 =$ $-7 + (-8) =$ -15
Negative + Negative = Negative	$-7 + (-8) =$ -15	Positive – Negative = Positive	$7 - (-8) =$ $7 + 8 = 15$
Negative + Positive OR Positive + Negative = Keep the sign of the number with larger absolute value and subtract the absolute values of the numbers	$-7 + 8 = 1$ $7 + -8 = -1$	Negative – Negative = Keep the sign of the number with larger absolute value and subtract the absolute values of the numbers	$-7 - (-8) =$ $-7 + 8 = 1$ $-8 - (-7) =$ $-8 + 7 = -1$
Positive × Positive = Positive	$8 \times 4 = 32$	Positive ÷ Positive = Positive	$8 \div 4 = 2$

*Always change the subtraction to addition and change the sign of the second number; then use addition rules.

Multiplying Real Numbers		Dividing Real Numbers	
Negative × Negative = Positive	$-8 \times (-4) =$ 32	Negative ÷ Negative = Positive	$-8 \div (-4) = 2$
Positive × Negative OR Negative × Positive = Negative	$8 \times (-4) =$ -32 $-8 \times 4 = -32$	Positive ÷ Negative OR Negative ÷ Positive = Negative	$8 \div (-4) = -2$ $-8 \div 4 = -2$

SAMPLE QUESTIONS

7)   Add or subtract the following real numbers:

   A. $-18 + 12$

   B. $-3.64 + (-2.18)$

   C. $9.37 - 4.25$

   D. $86 - (-20)$

   Answers:

   A.   Since $|-18| > |12|$, the answer is negative: $|-18| - |12| = 6$. So the answer is **−6**.

   B.   Adding two negative numbers results in a negative number. Add the values: **−5.82**.

   C.   The first number is larger than the second, so the final answer is positive: **5.12**.

   D.   Change the subtraction to addition, change the sign of the second number, and then add: $86 - (-20) = 86 + 20 = $ **106**.

8)   Multiply or divide the following real numbers:

   A. $\left(\frac{10}{3}\right)\left(-\frac{9}{5}\right)$

   B. $\frac{-64}{-10}$

   C. $(2.2)(3.3)$

   D. $-52 \div 13$

   Answers:

   A.   Multiply the numerators, multiply the denominators, and simplify: $\frac{-90}{15}$ = **−6**.

   B.   A negative divided by a negative is a positive number: **6.4**.

   C.   The parentheses indicate multiplication: **7.26**.

   D.   Dividing a negative by a positive number gives a negative answer: **−4**.

ORDER OF OPERATIONS

The **order of operations** is simply the order in which operations are performed. **PEMDAS** is a common way to remember the order of operations:

- ▶ Parentheses
- ▶ Exponents
- ▶ Multiplication
- ▶ Division
- ▶ Addition
- ▶ Subtraction

Multiplication and division, and addition and subtraction, are performed together from left to right. So, performing multiple operations on a set of numbers is a four-step process:

1. P: Calculate expressions inside parentheses, brackets, braces, etc.
2. E: Calculate exponents and square roots.
3. MD: Calculate any remaining multiplication and division in order from left to right.
4. AS: Calculate any remaining addition and subtraction in order from left to right.

Always work from left to right within each step when simplifying expressions.

SAMPLE QUESTIONS

9)   Simplify: $2(21 - 14) + 6 \div (-2) \times 3 - 10$

Answer:

$2(21 - 14) + 6 \div (-2) \times 3 - 10$	
$= 2(7) + 6 \div (-2) \times 3 - 10$	Calculate expressions inside parentheses.
$14 + 6 \div (-2) \times 3 - 10$ $= 14 + (-3) \times 3 - 10$ $= 14 + (-9) - 10$	There are no exponents or radicals, so perform multiplication and division from left to right.
$5 - 10 = \mathbf{-5}$	Perform addition and subtraction from left to right.

10)   Simplify: $-(3)^2 + 4(5) + (5 - 6)^2 - 8$

Answer:

$-(3)^2 + 4(5) + (5 - 6)^2 - 8$	
$-(3)^2 + 4(5) + (-1)^2 - 8$	Calculate expressions inside parentheses.
$= -9 + 4(5) + 1 - 8$	Simplify exponents and radicals.

$= -9 + 20 + 1 - 8$	Perform multiplication and division from left to right.
$= 11 + 1 - 8 = 12 - 8$ $= \mathbf{4}$	Perform addition and subtraction from left to right.

11) **Simplify:** $\dfrac{(7 - 9)^3 + 8(10 - 12)}{4^2 - 5^2}$

Answer:

$\dfrac{(7 - 9)^3 + 8(10 - 12)}{4^2 - 5^2}$	
$= \dfrac{(-2)^3 + 8(-2)}{4^2 - 5^2}$	Calculate expressions inside parentheses.
$= \dfrac{-8 + (-16)}{16 - 25}$	Simplify exponents and radicals.
$= \dfrac{-24}{-9}$	Perform addition and subtraction from left to right.
$= \dfrac{\mathbf{8}}{\mathbf{3}}$	Simplify.

UNITS OF MEASUREMENT

The standard units for the metric and American systems are shown below, along with the prefixes used to express metric units.

Table 4.2. Units and conversion factors

Dimension	American	SI
length	inch/foot/yard/mile	meter
mass	ounce/pound/ton	gram
volume	cup/pint/quart/gallon	liter
force	pound-force	newton
pressure	pound-force per square inch	pascal
work and energy	cal/British thermal unit	joule
temperature	Fahrenheit	kelvin
charge	faraday	coulomb

Go on →

Table 4.3. Metric Prefixes

Prefix	Symbol	Multiplication Factor
tera	T	1,000,000,000,000
giga	G	1,000,000,000
mega	M	1,000,000
kilo	k	1,000
hecto	h	100
deca	da	10
base unit	--	--
deci	d	0.1
centi	c	0.01
milli	m	0.001
micro	μ	0.0000001
nano	n	0.0000000001
pico	p	0.0000000000001

Units can be converted within a single system or between systems. When converting from one unit to another unit, a conversion factor (a numeric multiplier used to convert a value with a unit to another unit) is used. The process of converting between units using a conversion factor is sometimes known as dimensional analysis.

Table 4.4. Conversion Factors

1 in. = 2.54 cm	1 lb. = 0.454 kg
1 yd. = 0.914 m	1 cal = 4.19 J
1 mi. = 1.61 km	$1°F = \frac{5}{9}(°F - 32°C)$
1 gal. = 3.785 L	$1 cm^3 = 1$ mL
1 oz. = 28.35 g	1 hr = 3600 s

SAMPLE QUESTIONS

12)   **Convert the following measurements in the metric system.**

    A.   4.25 kilometers to meters

    B.   8 m^2 to mm^2

Answers:

A.   4.25 km $\left(\frac{1000 \text{ m}}{1 \text{ km}}\right)$ = **4250 m** (because m is a smaller unit than km, multiply by 1000)

B. $\frac{8 \text{ m}^2}{\square} \times \frac{1000 \text{ mm}}{1 \text{ m}} \times \frac{1000 \text{ mm}}{1 \text{ m}}$ = **8,000,000 mm²**

Since the units are square units (m²), multiply by the conversion factor twice, so that both meters cancel (and mm × mm = mm²).

13) **Convert the following measurements in the American system.**

A.   12 feet to inches

B.   7 yd² to ft²

Answers:

A.   12 ft$\left(\frac{12 \text{ in}}{1 \text{ ft}}\right)$ = **144 in** (since inches is a smaller unit, multiply by 12 inches to get feet)

B.   7 yd²$\left(\frac{9 \text{ ft}^2}{1 \text{ yd}^2}\right)$ = **63 ft²**

Since the units are square units (ft²), multiply by the conversion factor twice: $\left(\frac{3 \text{ ft}}{1 \text{ yd}}\right) \times \left(\frac{3 \text{ ft}}{1 \text{ yd}}\right) = \left(\frac{9 \text{ ft}^2}{1 \text{ yd}^2}\right)$. Yards squared cancel, leaving square feet.

14) **Convert the following measurements in the metric system to the American system.**

A.   23 meters to feet

B.   10 m² to yd²

Answers:

A.   23 m((3.28 ft)/(1 m)) = **75.44 ft**

B. $\frac{10 \text{ m}^2}{\square} \times \frac{1.094 \text{ yd}}{1 \text{ m}} \times \frac{1.094 \text{ yd}}{1 \text{ m}}$ = **11.97 yd²**

15) **Convert the following measurements in the American system to the metric system.**

A.   8 in³ to milliliters

B.   16 kilograms to pounds

Answers:

A.   8 in³ $\left(\frac{16.39 \text{ ml}}{1 \text{ in}^3}\right)$ = **131.12 mL**

Because the conversion factor already has cubic units in it, it only needs to be multiplied once.

B.   16 kg$\left(\frac{2.2 \text{ lb}}{1 \text{ kg}}\right)$ = **35.2 lb**

Decimals and Fractions

Decimals

A **decimal** is a number that contains a decimal point. A decimal number is an alternative way of writing a fraction. The place value for a decimal includes **tenths** (one place after the decimal), **hundredths** (two places after the decimal), **thousandths** (three places after the decimal), etc.

Table 4.5. Place Values

1,000,000	10^6	millions
100,000	10^5	hundred thousands
10,000	10^4	ten thousands
1,000	10^3	thousands
100	10^2	hundreds
10	10^1	tens
1	10^0	ones
.		decimal
$\frac{1}{10}$	10^{-1}	tenths
$\frac{1}{100}$	10^{-2}	hundredths
1/1000	10^{-3}	thousandths

Decimals can be added, subtracted, multiplied, and divided:

▶ To add or subtract decimals, line up the decimal point and perform the operation, keeping the decimal point in the same place in the answer.

▶ To multiply decimals, first multiply the numbers without the decimal points. Then, add the number of decimal places to the right of the decimal point in the original numbers and place the decimal point in the answer so that there are that many places to the right of the decimal.

▶ When dividing decimals move the decimal point to the right in order to make the divisor a whole number and move the decimal the same number of places in the dividend. Divide the numbers without

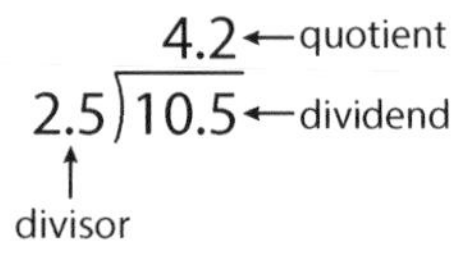

> **HELPFUL HINT**
>
> To determine which way to move the decimal after multiplying, remember that changing the decimal should always make the final answer smaller.

$$4.2 \leftarrow \text{quotient}$$
$$2.5\overline{)10.5} \leftarrow \text{dividend}$$
$$\uparrow$$
$$\text{divisor}$$

Figure 4.4. Division Terms

regard to the decimal. Then, place the decimal point of the quotient directly above the decimal point of the dividend.

SAMPLE QUESTIONS

16) Simplify: $24.38 + 16.51 - 29.87$

Answer:

$24.38 + 16.51 - 29.87$	
$\begin{aligned} 24.38 \\ + \underline{16.51} \\ = 40.89 \end{aligned}$	Align the decimals and apply the order of operations left to right.
$\begin{aligned} 40.89 \\ - \underline{29.87} \\ = \mathbf{11.02} \end{aligned}$	

17) Simplify: $(10.4)(18.2)$

Answer:

$(10.4)(18.2)$	
$104 \times 182 = 18{,}928$	Multiply the numbers ignoring the decimals.
$18{,}928 \rightarrow 189.28$	The original problem includes two decimal places (one in each number), so move the decimal point in the answer so that there are two places after the decimal point.

Estimating is a good way to check the answer: $10.4 \approx 10, 18.2 \approx 18$, and $10 \times 18 = 180$.

18) Simplify: $80 \div 2.5$

Answer:

$80 \div 2.5$	
$\begin{aligned} 80 \rightarrow 800 \\ 2.5 \rightarrow 25 \end{aligned}$	The divisor is 2.5. Move the decimal one place to the right (multiply 2.5 by 10) so that the divisor is a whole number. Since the decimal point of the divisor was moved one place to the right, the decimal point in the dividend must be moved one place right (multiplying it by 10 as well).

$$800 \div 25 = 32 \qquad\qquad \text{Divide normally.}$$

FRACTIONS

A **fraction** is a number that can be written in the form $\frac{a}{b}$, where b is not equal to 0. The *a* part of the fraction is the **numerator** (top number) and the *b* part of the fraction is the **denominator** (bottom number).

If the denominator of a fraction is greater than the numerator, the value of the fraction is less than 1 and it is called a **proper fraction** (for example, $\frac{3}{5}$ is a proper fraction). In an **improper fraction**, the denominator is less than the numerator and the value of the fraction is greater than 1 (example: $\frac{8}{3}$ is an improper fraction). An improper fraction can be written as a mixed number. A **mixed number** has a whole number part and a proper fraction part. Improper fractions can be converted to mixed numbers by dividing the numerator by the denominator, which gives the whole number part, and the remainder becomes the numerator of the proper fraction part. (For example, the improper fraction $\frac{25}{9}$ is equal to mixed number $2\frac{7}{9}$ because 9 divides into 25 two times, with a remainder of 7.)

Conversely, mixed numbers can be converted to improper fractions. To do so, determine the numerator of the improper fraction by multiplying the denominator by the whole number, and then adding the numerator. The final number is written as the (now larger) numerator over the original denominator.

HELPFUL HINT

To convert mixed numbers to improper fractions:
$$a\frac{m}{n} = \frac{n \times a + m}{n}$$

Fractions with the same denominator can be added or subtracted by simply adding or subtracting the numerators; the denominator will remain unchanged. To add or subtract fractions with different denominators, find the **least common denominator (LCD)** of all the fractions. The LCD is the smallest number exactly divisible by each denominator. (For example, the least common denominator of the numbers 2, 3, and 8 is 24.) Once the LCD has been found, each fraction should be written in an equivalent form with the LCD as the denominator. To do this, each fraction can be multiplied by 1 in the form $\frac{a}{a}$, where *a* is the value necessary to convert the denominator to the LCD. Once all fractions have the same denominator, the numerators can be added and the fractions reduced if necessary.

HELPFUL HINT

$$\frac{a}{b} \pm \frac{c}{b} = \frac{a \pm c}{b}$$
$$\frac{a}{b} \times \frac{c}{d} = \frac{ac}{bd}$$
$$\frac{a}{b} \div \frac{c}{d} = \left(\frac{a}{b}\right)\left(\frac{d}{c}\right) = \frac{ad}{bc}$$

To multiply fractions, the numerators are multiplied together and denominators are multiplied together. If there are any mixed numbers, they should first be changed to improper fractions. Then, the numerators are multiplied together and the denominators are multiplied together. The fraction can then be reduced if necessary. To divide fractions, multiply the first fraction by the reciprocal of the second.

Any common denominator can be used to add or subtract fractions. The quickest way to find a common denominator of a set of values is simply to multiply all the values together. The result might not be the least common denominator, but it will get the job done.

SAMPLE QUESTIONS

19) Simplify: $2\frac{3}{5} + 3\frac{1}{4} - 1\frac{1}{2}$

Answer:

$2\frac{3}{5} + 3\frac{1}{4} - 1\frac{1}{2}$	
$= 2\frac{12}{20} + 3\frac{5}{20} - 1\frac{10}{20}$	Change each fraction so it has a denominator of 20, which is the LCD of 5, 4, and 2.
$2 + 3 - 1 = 4$ $\frac{12}{20} + \frac{5}{20} - \frac{10}{20} = \frac{7}{20}$	Add and subtract the whole numbers together and the fractions together.
$4\frac{7}{20}$	Combine to get the final answer (a mixed number).

20) Simplify: $\frac{7}{8} \times 3\frac{1}{3}$

Answer:

$\frac{7}{8} \times 3\frac{1}{3}$	
$3\frac{1}{3} = \frac{10}{3}$	Change the mixed number to an improper fraction.
$\frac{7}{8}\left(\frac{10}{3}\right) = \frac{7 \times 10}{8 \times 3}$ $= \frac{70}{24}$	Multiply the numerators together and the denominators together.
$= \frac{35}{12}$ $= 2\frac{11}{12}$	Reduce the fraction.

21) Simplify: $4\frac{1}{2} \div \frac{2}{3}$

Answer:

$4\frac{1}{2} \div \frac{2}{3}$	
$4\frac{1}{2} = \frac{9}{2}$	Change the mixed number to an improper fraction.

$\frac{9}{2} \div \frac{2}{3}$ $= \frac{9}{2} \times \frac{3}{2}$ $= \frac{27}{4}$	Multiply the first fraction by the reciprocal of the second fraction.
$= 6\frac{3}{4}$	Simplify.

CONVERTING BETWEEN FRACTIONS AND DECIMALS

A fraction is converted to a decimal by using long division until there is no remainder and no pattern of repeating numbers occurs.

A decimal is converted to a fraction using the following steps:

▸ Place the decimal value as the numerator in a fraction with a denominator of 1.

▸ Multiply the fraction by $\frac{10}{10}$ for every digit in the decimal value, so that there is no longer a decimal in the numerator.

▸ Reduce the fraction.

SAMPLE QUESTIONS

22) **Write the fraction $\frac{7}{8}$ as a decimal.**

Answer:

$$
\begin{array}{r}
0.875 \\
8\overline{)7000} \\
-64 \\
\hline
60 \\
-56 \\
\hline
40
\end{array}
$$

Divide the denominator into the numerator using long division.

23) **Write the fraction 5/11 as a decimal.**

Answer:

$$
\begin{array}{r}
0.\overline{4545} \\
11\overline{)50000} \\
-44 \\
\hline
60 \\
-55 \\
\hline
50 \\
-44 \\
\hline
60
\end{array}
$$

Dividing using long division yields a repeating decimal.

24) **Write the decimal 0.125 as a fraction.**

Answer:

0.125	
$= \frac{0.125}{1}$	Create a fraction with 0.125 as the numerator and 1 as the denominator.
$\frac{0.125}{1} \times \frac{10}{10} \times \frac{10}{10} \times \frac{10}{10} = \frac{125}{1000}$	Multiple by 1 in the form 10/10 three times (one for each numeral after the decimal).
$= \frac{1}{8}$	Simplify.

Alternatively, recognize that 0.125 is read "one hundred twenty-five thousandths" and can therefore be written in fraction form as 125/1000.

ROUNDING AND ESTIMATION

Rounding is a way of simplifying a complicated number. The result of rounding will be a less precise value with which it is easier to write or perform operations. Rounding is performed to a specific place value, for example the thousands or tenths place.

The rules for rounding are as follows:

1. Underline the place value being rounded to.

2. Locate the digit one place value to the right of the underlined value. If this value is less than 5, then keep the underlined value and replace all digits to the right of the underlined value with 0. If the value to the right of the underlined digit is greater than 5, then increase the underlined digit by one and replace all digits to the right of it with 0.

HELPFUL HINT

Estimation can often be used to eliminate answer choices on multiple-choice tests without having to work the problem to completion.

Estimation is when numbers are rounded and then an operation is performed. This process can be used when working with large numbers to find a close, but not exact, answer.

SAMPLE QUESTIONS

25) **Round the number 138,472 to the nearest thousands.**

Answer:

138,472

138,472 ≈ **138,000**

The 8 is in the thousands place, and the number to its right is 4. Because 4 is less than 5, the 8 remains and all numbers to the right become 0.

26) The populations of five local towns are 12,341, 8975, 9431, 10,521, and 11,427. Estimate the total population to the nearest 1000 people.

Answer:

12,341 ≈ 12,000 8975 ≈ 9000 9431 ≈ 9000 10,521 ≈ 11,000 11,427 ≈ 11,000	Round each value to the thousands place.
12,000 + 9000 + 9000 + 11,000 + 11,000 = **52,000**	Add.

RATIOS

A **ratio** is a comparison of two numbers and can be represented as $\frac{a}{b}$, $a:b$, or a to b. The two numbers represent a constant relationship, not a specific value: for every a number of items in the first group, there will be b number of items in the second. For example, if the ratio of blue to red candies in a bag is 3:5, the bag will contain 3 blue candies for every 5 red candies. So, the bag might contain 3 blue candies and 5 red candies, or it might contain 30 blue candies and 50 red candies, or 36 blue candies and 60 red candies. All of these values are representative of the ratio 3:5 (which is the ratio in its lowest, or simplest, terms).

To find the *whole* when working with ratios, simply add the values in the ratio. For example, if the ratio of boys to girls in a class is 2:3, the *whole* is five: 2 out of every 5 students are boys, and 3 out of every 5 students are girls.

SAMPLE QUESTIONS

27) There are 10 boys and 12 girls in a first-grade class. What is the ratio of boys to the total number of students? What is the ratio of girls to boys?

Answer:

number of boys: 10 number of girls: 12 number of students: 22	Identify the variables.
number of boys : number of students $= 10 : 22$ $= \frac{10}{22}$ $= \frac{5}{11}$	Write out and simplify the ratio of boys to total students.
number of girls : number of boys $= 12 : 10$ $= \frac{12}{10}$ $= \frac{6}{5}$	Write out and simplify the ratio of girls to boys.

28) A family spends $600 a month on rent, $400 on utilities, $750 on groceries, and $550 on miscellaneous expenses. What is the ratio of the family's rent to their total expenses?

Answer:

rent $= 600$ utilities $= 400$ groceries $= 750$ miscellaneous $= 550$ total expenses $= 600 + 400 + 750 + 550 = 2300$	Identify the variables.
rent : total expenses $= 600 : 2300$ $= \frac{600}{2300}$ $= \frac{6}{23}$	Write out and simplify the ratio of rent to total expenses.

PROPORTIONS

A **proportion** is an equation which states that two ratios are equal. A proportion is given in the form $\frac{a}{b} = \frac{c}{d}$, where the a and d terms are the extremes and the b and c terms are the means. A proportion is solved using cross-multiplication ($ad = bc$) to create an equation with no fractional components. A proportion must have the same units in both numerators and both denominators.

SAMPLE QUESTIONS

29) Solve the proportion for x: $\frac{3x-5}{2} = \frac{x-8}{3}$.

Answer:

$\frac{(3x-5)}{2} = \frac{(x-8)}{3}$	
$3(3x-5) = 2(x-8)$	Cross-multiply.
$9x - 15 = 2x - 16$	
$7x - 15 = -16$	
$7x = -1$	Solve the equation for x.
$x = -\frac{1}{7}$	

30) A map is drawn such that 2.5 inches on the map equates to an actual distance of 40 miles. If the distance measured on the map between two cities is 17.25 inches, what is the actual distance between them in miles?

Answer:

$\frac{2.5}{40} = \frac{17.25}{x}$	Write a proportion where x equals the actual distance and each ratio is written as inches : miles.
$2.5x = 690$	
$x = 276$	Cross-multiply and divide to solve for x.
The two cities are **276 miles apart**.	

31) A factory knows that every 4 out of 1000 parts made will be defective. If in a month there are 125,000 parts made, how many of these parts will be defective?

Answer:

$\frac{4}{1000} = \frac{x}{125,000}$	Write a proportion where x is the number of defective parts made and both ratios are written as defective : total.
$1000x = 500,000$	
$x = 500$	Cross-multiply and divide to solve for x.
There are **500 defective parts** for the month.	

PERCENTAGES

A **percent** (or percentage) means per hundred and is expressed with a percent symbol (%). For example, 54% means 54 out of every 100. A percent can be converted to a decimal by removing the % symbol and moving the decimal point two places to the left, while a decimal can be converted to a percent by moving the decimal point two places to the right and attaching the % sign. A percent can be converted to a fraction by writing the percent as a fraction with 100 as the denominator and reducing. A fraction can be converted to a percent by performing the indicated division, multiplying the result by 100, and attaching the % sign.

The equation for finding percentages has three variables: the part, the whole, and the percent (which is expressed in the equation as a decimal). The equation, as shown below, can be rearranged to solve for any of these variables.

▶ $part = whole \times percent$

▶ $percent = \dfrac{part}{whole}$

▶ $whole = \dfrac{part}{percent}$

This set of equations can be used to solve percent word problems. All that's needed is to identify the part, whole, and/or percent, and then to plug those values into the appropriate equation and solve.

SAMPLE QUESTIONS

32) **Change the following values to the indicated form:**

   A.   18% to a fraction

   B. $\frac{3}{5}$ to a percent

   C.   1.125 to a percent

   D.   84% to a decimal

   Answers:

   A.   The percent is written as a fraction over 100 and reduced: $\frac{18}{100} = \frac{9}{50}$.

   B.   Dividing 3 by 5 gives the value 0.6, which is then multiplied by 100: **60%**.

   C.   The decimal point is moved two places to the right: $1.125 \times 100 = $ **112.5%**.

   D.   The decimal point is moved two places to the left: $84 \div 100 = $ **0.84**.

33) **In a school of 650 students, 54% of the students are boys. How many students are girls?**

Answer:

Percent of students who are girls = 100% − 54% = 46% percent = 46% = 0.46 whole = 650 students part = ?	Identify the variables.
part = whole × percent = 650 x 0.46 = 299 **There are 299 girls.**	Plug the variables into the appropriate equation.

PERCENT CHANGE

Percent change problems involve a change from an original amount. Often percent change problems appear as word problems that include discounts, growth, or markups. In order to solve percent change problems, it's necessary to identify the percent change (as a decimal), the amount of change, and the original amount. (Keep in mind that one of these will be the value being solved for.) These values can then be plugged into the equations below:

▶ amount of change = original amount × percent change

▶ percent change = $\dfrac{\text{amount of change}}{\text{original amount}}$

▶ original amount = $\dfrac{\text{amount of change}}{\text{percent change}}$

SAMPLE QUESTIONS

34) An HDTV that originally cost $1,500 is on sale for 45% off. What is the sale price for the item?

Answer:

original amount = $1,500 percent change = 45% = 0.45 amount of change = ?	Identify the variables.
amount of change = original amount × percent change = 1500 × 0.45 = 675	Plug the variables into the appropriate equation.
1500 − 675 = 825 **The final price is $825.**	To find the new price, subtract the amount of change from the original price.

35) A house was bought in 2000 for $100,000 and sold in 2015 for $120,000. What was the percent growth in the value of the house from 2000 to 2015?

Answer:

original amount = $100,000 amount of change = 120,000 − 100,000 = 20,000 percent change = ?	Identify the variables.
percent change = $\frac{\text{amount of change}}{\text{original amount}}$ $= \frac{20,000}{100,000}$ $= 0.20$	Plug the variables into the appropriate equation.
$0.20 \times 100 =$ **20%**	To find the percent growth, multiply by 100.

EXPONENTS AND RADICALS

EXPONENTS

An expression in the form b^n is in an exponential notation where b is the **base** and n is an **exponent**. To perform the operation, multiply the base by itself the number of times indicated by the exponent. For example, 2^3 is equal to $2 \times 2 \times 2$ or 8.

Table 4.6. Operations with Exponents

Rule	Example	Explanation
$a^0 = 1$	$5^0 = 1$	Any base (except 0) to the 0 power is 1.
$a^{-n} = \frac{1}{a^n}$	$5^{-3} = \frac{1}{5^3}$	A negative exponent becomes positive when moved from numerator to denominator (or vice versa).
$a^m a^n = a^{m+n}$	$5^3 5^4 = 5^{3+4} = 5^7$	Add the exponents to multiply two powers with the same base.
$(a^m)^n = a^{m \times n}$	$(5^3)^4 = 5^{3(4)} = 5^{12}$	Multiply the exponents to raise a power to a power.
$\frac{a^m}{a^n} = a^{m-n}$	$\frac{5^4}{5^3} = 5^{4-3} = 5^1$	Subtract the exponents to divide two powers with the same base.
$(ab)^n = a^n b^n$	$(5 \times 6)^3 = 5^3 6^3$	Apply the exponent to each base to raise a product to a power.
$\left(\frac{a}{b}\right)^n = \frac{a^n}{b^n}$	$\left(\frac{5}{6}\right)^3 = \frac{5^3}{6^3}$	Apply the exponent to each base to raise a quotient to a power.

Table 4.6. Operations with Exponents (continued)

Rule	Example	Explanation
$\left(\frac{a}{b}\right)^{-n} = \left(\frac{b}{a}\right)^{n}$	$\left(\frac{5}{6}\right)^{-3} = \left(\frac{6}{5}\right)^{3}$	Invert the fraction and change the sign of the exponent to raise a fraction to a negative power.
$\frac{a^m}{b^n} = \frac{b^n}{a^m}$	$\frac{5^3}{6^4} = \frac{6^{-4}}{5^{-3}}$	Change the sign of the exponent when moving a number from the numerator to denominator (or vice versa).

SAMPLE QUESTIONS

36) Simplify: $\frac{(10^2)^3}{(10^2)^{-2}}$

Answer:

$\frac{(10^2)^3}{(10^2)^{-2}}$	
$= \frac{10^6}{10^{-4}}$	Multiply the exponents raised to a power.
$= 10^{6-(-4)}$	Subtract the exponent in the denominator from the one in the numerator.
$= 10^{10}$ $= \mathbf{10{,}000{,}000{,}000}$	Simplify.

37) Simplify: $\frac{(x^{-2}y^2)^2}{x^3y}$

Answer:

$\frac{(x^{-2}y^2)^2}{x^3y}$	
$= \frac{x^{-4}y^4}{x^3y}$	Multiply the exponents raised to a power.
$= x^{-4-3}y^{4-1}$ $= x^{-7}y^3$	Subtract the exponent in the denominator from the one in the numerator.
$= \frac{y^3}{x^7}$	Move negative exponents to the denominator.

RADICALS

Radicals are expressed as $\sqrt[b]{a}$, where b is called the **index** and a is the **radicand**. A radical is used to indicate the inverse operation of an exponent: finding the base which can be raised to b to yield a. For example, $\sqrt[3]{125}$ is equal to 5 because $5 \times 5 \times 5$ equals 125. The same operation can be expressed using a fraction exponent, so $\sqrt[b]{a} = \dfrac{1}{a^b}$. Note that when no value is indicated for b, it is assumed to be 2 (square root). When b is even and a is positive, $\sqrt[b]{a}$ is defined to be the positive real value n such that $n^b = a$ (example: $\sqrt{16} = 4$ only, and not –4, even though $(-4)(-4) = 16$). If b is even and a is negative, $\sqrt[b]{a}$ will be a complex number (example: $\sqrt{-9} = 3i$). Finally if b is odd, $\sqrt[b]{a}$ will always be a real number regardless of the sign of a. If a is negative, $\sqrt[b]{a}$ will be negative since a number to an odd power is negative (example: $\sqrt[5]{-32} = -2$ since $(-2)^5 = -32$).

$\sqrt[n]{x}$ is referred to as the nth root of x.

- ▸ $n = 2$ is the square root
- ▸ $n = 3$ is the cube root
- ▸ $n = 4$ is the fourth root
- ▸ $n = 5$ is the fifth root

The following table of operations with radicals holds for all cases EXCEPT the case where b is even and a is negative (the complex case).

Table 4.7. Operations with Radicals

Rule	Example	Explanation
$\sqrt[b]{ac} = \sqrt[b]{a}\,\sqrt[b]{c}$	$\sqrt[3]{81} = \sqrt[3]{27}\,\sqrt[3]{3} = 3\sqrt[3]{3}$	The values under the radical sign can be separated into values that multiply to the original value.
$\sqrt[b]{\dfrac{a}{c}} = \dfrac{\sqrt[b]{a}}{\sqrt[b]{c}}$	$\sqrt{\dfrac{4}{81}} = \dfrac{\sqrt{4}}{\sqrt{81}} = \dfrac{2}{9}$	The b-root of the numerator and denominator can be calculated when there is a fraction under a radical sign.
$\sqrt[b]{a^c} = (\sqrt[b]{a})^c = a^{\frac{c}{b}}$	$\sqrt[3]{6^2} = (\sqrt[3]{6})^2 = 6^{\frac{2}{3}}$	The b-root can be written as a fractional exponent. If there is a power under the radical sign, it will be the numerator of the fraction.
$\dfrac{c}{\sqrt[b]{a}} \dfrac{\sqrt[b]{a^{b-1}}}{\sqrt[b]{a^{b-1}}} = \dfrac{c\sqrt[b]{a^{b-1}}}{a}$	$\dfrac{5}{\sqrt{2}} \dfrac{\sqrt{2}}{\sqrt{2}} = \dfrac{5\sqrt{2}}{2}$	To rationalize the denominator, multiply the numerator and denominator by the radical in the denominator until the radical has been canceled out.
$\dfrac{c}{b - \sqrt{a}} \dfrac{b + \sqrt{a}}{b + \sqrt{a}}$ $= \dfrac{c(b + \sqrt{a})}{b^2 - a}$	$\dfrac{4}{3 - \sqrt{2}} \dfrac{3 + \sqrt{2}}{3 + \sqrt{2}}$ $= \dfrac{4(3 + \sqrt{2})}{9 - 2} = \dfrac{12 + 4\sqrt{2}}{7}$	To rationalize the denominator, the numerator and denominator are multiplied by the conjugate of the denominator.

SAMPLE QUESTIONS

38) Simplify: $\sqrt{48}$

Answer:

$\sqrt{48}$	
$= \sqrt{16 \times 3}$	Determine the largest square number that is a factor of the radicand (48) and write the radicand as a product using that square number as a factor.
$= \sqrt{16}\,\sqrt{3}$ $= \mathbf{4\sqrt{3}}$	Apply the rules of radicals to simplify.

39) Simplify: $\dfrac{6}{\sqrt{8}}$

Answer:

$\dfrac{6}{\sqrt{8}}$	
$= \dfrac{6}{\sqrt{4}\,\sqrt{2}}$ $= \dfrac{6}{2\sqrt{2}}$	Apply the rules of radicals to simplify.
$= \dfrac{6}{2\sqrt{2}}\left(\dfrac{\sqrt{2}}{\sqrt{2}}\right)$ $= \mathbf{\dfrac{3\sqrt{2}}{2}}$	Multiply by $\dfrac{\sqrt{2}}{\sqrt{2}}$ to rationalize the denominator.

5

Algebra

Algebra, meaning "restoration" in Arabic, is the mathematical method of finding the unknown. The first algebraic book in Egypt was used to figure out complex inheritances that were to be split among many individuals. Today, algebra is just as necessary when dealing with unknown amounts.

ALGEBRAIC EXPRESSIONS

The foundation of algebra is the **variable**, an unknown number represented by a symbol (usually a letter such as x or a). Variables can be preceded by a **coefficient**, which is a constant (i.e., a real number) in front of the variable, such as $4x$ or $-2a$. An **algebraic expression** is any sum, difference, product, or quotient of variables and numbers (for example $3x^2$, $2x + 7y - 1$, and $\frac{5}{x}$ are algebraic expressions). **Terms** are any quantities that are added or subtracted (for example, the terms of the expression $x^2 - 3x + 5$ are x^2, $3x$, and 5). A **polynomial expression** is an algebraic expression where all the exponents on the variables are whole numbers. A polynomial with only two terms is known as a **binomial**, and one with three terms is a **trinomial**. A **monomial** has only one term.

> **HELPFUL HINT**
>
> Simplified expressions are ordered by variable terms alphabetically with highest exponent first then down to constants.

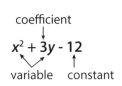

Figure 5.1. Polynomial Expression

Evaluating expressions is another way of saying "find the numeric value of an expression if the variable is equal to a certain number." To evaluate the expression, simply plug the given value(s) for the variable(s) into the equation and simplify. Remember to use the order of operations when simplifying:

- ▶ Parentheses
- ▶ Exponents
- ▶ Multiplication
- ▶ Division
- ▶ Addition
- ▶ Subtraction

SAMPLE QUESTION

1) If $m = 4$, find the value of the following expression:
$5(m-2)^3 + 3m^2 - \frac{m}{4} - 1$

Answer:

$5(m-2)^3 + 3m^2 - \frac{m}{4} - 1$	
$= 5(4-2)^3 + 3(4)^2 - \frac{4}{4} - 1$	Plug the value 4 in for m in the expression.
$= 5(2)^3 + 3(4)^2 - \frac{4}{4} - 1$	Calculate all the expressions inside the parentheses.
$= 5(8) + 3(16) - \frac{4}{4} - 1$	Simplify all exponents.
$= 40 + 48 - 1 - 1$	Perform multiplication and division from left to right.
$= \mathbf{86}$	Perform addition and subtraction from left to right.

OPERATIONS WITH EXPRESSIONS

ADDING AND SUBTRACTING

Expressions can be added or subtracted by simply adding and subtracting **like terms**, which are terms with the same variable part (the variables must be the same, with the same exponents on each variable). For example, in the expressions $2x + 3xy - 2z$ and $6y + 2xy$, the like terms are $3xy$ and $2xy$. Adding the two expressions yields the new expression $2x + 5xy - 2z + 6y$. Note that the other terms did not change; they cannot combine because they have different variables.

SAMPLE QUESTION

2) If $a = 12x + 7xy - 9y$ and $b = 8x - 9xz + 7z$, what is $a + b$?

Answer:

$a + b = (12x + 8x) + 7xy - 9y - 9xz + 7z$ $= \mathbf{20x + 7xy - 9y - 9xz + 7z}$	The only like terms in both expressions are $12x$ and $8x$, so these two terms will be added, and all other terms will remain the same.

DISTRIBUTING AND FACTORING

Often simplifying expressions requires distributing and factoring. Distributing and factoring can be seen as two sides of the same coin. **Distribution** multiplies each term in the first factor by each term in the second factor to clear off parentheses. **Factoring** reverses this process, taking a polynomial in standard form and writing it as a product of two or more factors.

When distributing a monomial through a polynomial, the expression outside the parentheses is multiplied by each term inside the parentheses. (coefficients are multiplied, exponents are added, following the rules of exponents). The first step in factoring a polynomial is always to "undistribute" or factor out the **greatest common factor (GCF)** among the terms. The GCF is multiplied by, in parentheses, the expression that remains of each term when the GCF is divided out of each term. Factoring can be checked by multiplying the GCF factor through the parentheses again.

> **HELPFUL HINT**
>
> Operations with polynomials can always be checked by evaluating equivalent expressions for the same value.

When simplifying two polynomials, each term in the first polynomial must multiply each term in the second polynomial. A binomial (two terms) multiplied by a binomial, will require 2×2 or 4 multiplications. For the binomial × binomial case, this process is sometimes called **FOIL**, which stands for *first*, *outer*, *inner*, and *last*. These terms refer to the placement of each term of the expression: multiply the first term in each expression, then the outside terms, then the inside terms, and finally the last terms. A binomial (two terms) multiplied by a trinomial (three terms), will require 2×3 or 6 products to simplify. The first term in the first polynomial multiplies each of the three terms in the second polynomial, then the second term in the first polynomial multiplies each of the three terms in the second polynomial. A trinomial (three terms) by a trinomial will require 3×3 or 9 products, etc.

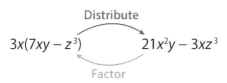

Figure 5.2. Distribution and Factoring

Factoring is the reverse of distributing: the first step is always to remove ("undistribute") the GCF of all the terms, if there is a GCF (besides 1). The GCF is the product of any constants and/or variables that EVERY term shares. (For example, the GCF of $12x^3$, $15x^2$ and $6xy^2$ is $3x$ because $3x$ evenly divides all three terms). This shared factor can be taken out of each term and moved to the outside of the parentheses, leaving behind a polynomial where each term is the original term divided by the GCF. (The remaining terms for the terms in the example would be $4x^2$, $5x$, and $2xy$.) It may be possible to factor the polynomial in the parentheses further, depending on the problem.

FACTORING TRINOMIALS

If the leading coefficient is $a = 1$, the trinomial is in the form $x^2 + bx + c$ and can often be rewritten in the factored form, as a product of two binomials: $(x + m)(x + n)$. Recall that the product of two binomials can be written in expanded form $x^2 + mx + nx + mn$. Equating this expression with $x^2 + bx + c$, the constant term c would have to equal the product mn. Thus, to work backward from the trinomial to the factored form, consider all the numbers m and n that multiply to make c. For example, to factor $x^2 + 8x + 12$, consider all the pairs that multiply to be 12 ($12 = 1 \times 12$ or 2×6 or 3×4). Choose the pair that will make the coefficient of the middle term (8) when added. In this example 2 and 6 add to 8, so making $m = 2$ and $n = 6$ in the expanded form gives:

$x^2 + 8x + 12 = x^2 + 2x + 6x + 12$	
$= (x^2 + 2x) + (6x + 12)$	Group the first two terms and the last two terms.
$= x(x + 6) + 2(x + 6)$	Factor the GCF out of each set of parentheses.
$= (x + 6)(x + 2)$	The two terms now have the common factor $(x + 6)$, which can be removed, leaving $(x + 2)$ and the original polynomial is factored.

In general:

$x^2 + bx + c = x^2 + mx + nx + mn$, where $c = mn$ and $b = m + n$	
$= (x^2 + mx) + (nx + mn)$	Group.
$= x(x + m) + n(x + m)$	Factor each group.
$= (x + m)(x + n)$	Factor out the common binomial.

Note that if none of the factors of c add to the value b, then the trinomial cannot be factored, and is called **prime**.

If the leading coefficient is not 1 ($a \neq 1$), first make sure that any common factors among the three terms are factored out. If the a-value is negative, factor out -1 first as well. If the a-value of the new polynomial in the parentheses is still not 1, follow this rule: Identify two values r and s that multiply to be ac and add to be b. Then write the polynomial in this form: $ax^2 + bx + c = ax^2 + rx + sx + c$, and proceed by grouping, factoring, and removing the common binomial as above.

There are a few special factoring cases worth memorizing: difference of squares, binomial squared, and the sum and difference of cubes.

- ▶ **Difference of squares** (each term is a square and they are subtracted):
  - ▷ $a^2 - b^2 = (a + b)(a - b)$
  - ▷ Note that a sum of squares is never factorable.

▸ **Binomial squared**:
  ▷ $a^2 + 2ab + b^2 = (a + b)(a + b) = (a + b)^2$
▸ **Sum and difference of cubes**:
  ▷ $a^3 + b^3 = (a + b)(a^2 - ab + b^2)$
  ▷ $a^3 - b^3 = (a - b)(a^2 + ab + b^2)$
  ▷   Note that the second factor in these factorizations will never be able to be factored further.

SAMPLE QUESTIONS

3)   Factor: $16x^2 + 52x + 30$

Answer:

$16x^2 + 52x + 30$	
$= 2(8x^2 + 26x + 15)$	Remove the GCF of 2.
$= 2(8x^2 + 6x + 20x + 15)$	To factor the polynomial in the parentheses, calculate $ac = (8)(15) = 120$, and consider all the pairs of numbers that multiply to be 120: 1×120, 2×60, 3×40, 4×30, 5×24, 6×20, 8×15, and 10×12. Of these pairs, choose the pair that adds to be the b-value 26 (6 and 20).
$= 2[(8x^2 + 6x) + (20x + 15)]$	Group.
$= 2[(2x(4x + 3) + 5(4x + 3)]$	Factor out the GCF of each group.
$= 2[(4x + 3)(2x + 5)]$	Factor out the common binomial.
$\mathbf{2(4x + 3)(2x + 5)}$	

If there are no values r and s that multiply to be ac and add to be b, then the polynomial is prime and cannot be factored.

4)   Expand the following expression: $5x(x^2 - 2c + 10)$

Answer:

$5x(x^2 - 2c + 10)$	
$(5x)(x^2) = 5x^3$	Distribute and multiply the term outside the parentheses to all three terms inside the parentheses.
$(5x)(-2c) = -10xc$	
$(5x)(10) = 50x$	
$\mathbf{= 5x^3 - 10xc + 50x}$	

5) Expand the following expression: $x(5 + z) - z(4x - z^2)$

Answer:

$x(5 + z) - z(4x - z^2)$	
$= 5x + zx - 4zx + z^3$	Distribute for each set of parentheses. Note that $-z$ is distributed and that $(-z)(-z^2) = +z^3$. <u>Not distributing the negative is a very common error.</u> Note that the xz is a like term with zx (commutative property) and the terms can therefore be combined.
$= z^3 - 3xz + 5x$	Combine like terms and place terms in the appropriate order (highest exponents first).

6) Expand the following expression: $(x^2 - 5)(2x - x^3)$

Answer:

$(x^2 - 5)(2x - x^3)$	
$(x^2)(2x) = 2x^3$ $(x^2)(-x^3) = -x^5$ $(-5)(2x) = -10x$ $(-5)(-x^3) = 5x^3$	Apply FOIL: first, outside, inside, and last.
$= 2x^3 - x^5 - 10x + 5x^3$	Combine like terms and put them in order.
$= -x^5 + 7x^3 - 10x$	

7) Factor the expression $16z^2 + 48z$

Answer:

$16z^2 + 48z$ $= 16z(z + 3)$	Both terms have a z, and 16 is a common factor of both 16 and 48. So the greatest common factor is $16z$. Factor out the GCF.

8) Factor the expression $6m^3 + 12m^3n - 9m^2$

Answer:

$6m^3 + 12m^3n - 9m^2$ $= 3m^2(2m + 4mn - 3)$	All the terms share the factor m^2, and 3 is the greatest common factor of 6, 12, and 9. So, the GCF is $3m^2$.

9) Factor the expression $3b^2 - 30b - 72$

Answer:

$3b^2 - 30b - 72$	
$= 3(b^2 - 10b - 24)$	Factor out 3, since all the terms share the factor 3.
$= 3(b^2 - 12b + 2b - 24)$	Factor the remaining trinomial in the parentheses. Identify all the values that can be multiplied to make -24 ($-24 = 1 \times -24, -1 \times 24, 2 \times -12, -2 \times 12, 3 \times -8, -3 \times 8, 4 \times -6, -4 \times 6$). Choose the factors 2 and -12 because these values add up to the b-value -10. Rewrite $-10b$ as $-12b + 2b$.
$= 3[(b^2 - 12b) + (2b - 24)]$	Group the terms.
$= 3[b(b - 12) + 2(b - 12)]$	Factor each group.
$= \mathbf{3(b - 12)(b + 2)}$	Factor the binomial $(b - 12)$ out of each term.

10) Factor $16x^2 + 52x + 30$

Answer:

$16x^2 + 52x + 30$	
$= 2(8x^2 + 26x + 15)$	Remove the GCF of 2.
$= 2(8x^2 + 6x + 20x + 15)$	Factor the polynomial in the parentheses. Calculate $ac = (8)(15) = 120$. Consider all the pairs of numbers that multiply to be 120: 1×120, $2 \times 60, 3 \times 40, 4 \times 30, 5 \times 24, 6 \times 20$, 8×15, and 10×12. Choose the pair that adds up to the b-value 26 (6 and 20).
$= 2[(8x^2 + 6x) + (20x + 15)]$	Group.
$= 2[(2x(4x + 3) + 5(4x + 3)]$	Factor out the GCF of each group.
$= 2[(4x + 3)(2x + 5)]$	Factor out the common binomial.
$= \mathbf{2(4x + 3)(2x + 5)}$	

Linear Equations

An **equation** states that two expressions are equal to each other. Polynomial equations are categorized by the highest power of the variables they contain: the highest power of any exponent of a linear equation is 1, a quadratic equation has a variable raised to the second power, a cubic equation has a variable raised to the third power, and so on.

SAMPLE QUESTION

11) Which of the following is a linear equation?

  A. $x + 5$
  B. $x = x^2$
  C. $\frac{x}{x} = 1$
  D. $2y = 3$

Answer:

  A. Incorrect. This is an expression, not an equation.

  B. Incorrect. This is a quadratic equation (the variable is raised to the second power).

  C. Incorrect. It looks like the highest power is 1. However, the xs in the fraction cancel, meaning the equation has no variable; it simply states that $1 = 1$.

  D. Correct. This is the only answer that has a highest power of one and includes an equal sign.

Solving Linear Equations

Solving an equation means finding the value or values of the variable that make the equation true. To solve a linear equation, it is necessary to manipulate the terms so that the variable being solved for appears alone on one side of the equal sign while everything else in the equation is on the other side.

The way to solve linear equations is to "undo" all the operations that connect numbers to the variable of interest. Follow these steps:

1. Eliminate fractions by multiplying each side by the least common multiple of any denominators.

2. Distribute to eliminate parentheses, braces, and brackets.

3. Combine like terms.

4. Use addition or subtraction to collect all terms containing the variable of interest to one side, and all terms not containing the variable to the other side.

5. Use multiplication or division to remove coefficients from the variable of interest.

Sometimes there are no numeric values in the equation or there are a mix of numerous variables and constants. The goal is to solve the equation for one of the variables in terms of the other variables. In this case, the answer will be an expression involving numbers and letters instead of a numeric value.

SAMPLE QUESTIONS

12) Solve for x: $\frac{100(x+5)}{20} = 1$

Answer:

$\frac{100(x+5)}{20} = 1$	
$(20)\left(\frac{100(x+5)}{20}\right) = (1)(20)$ $100(x+5) = 20$	Multiply both sides by 20 to cancel out the denominator.
$100x + 500 = 20$	Distribute 100 through the parentheses.
$100x = -480$	"Undo" the +500 by subtracting 500 on both sides of the equation to isolate the variable term.
$x = \frac{-480}{100}$	"Undo" the multiplication by 100 by dividing by 100 on both sides to solve for x.
$= -4.8$	

13) Solve for x: $2(x+2)^2 - 2x^2 + 10 = 42$

Answer:

$2(x+2)^2 - 2x^2 + 10 = 42$	
$2(x+2)(x+2) - 2x^2 + 10 = 42$	Simplify the left-hand side of the equation using the order of operations and combining like terms. Begin with the exponent.
$2(x^2 + 4x + 4) - 2x^2 + 10 = 42$	Apply FOIL.
$2x^2 + 8x + 8 - 2x^2 + 10 = 42$	Distribute the 2.
$8x + 18 = 42$	Combine like terms on the left-hand side.

$8x = 24$	Isolate the variable. "Undo" + 18 by subtracting 18 on both sides.
$x = 3$	"Undo" multiplication by 8 by dividing both sides by 8.

14) Solve the equation for *D*: $\frac{A(3B + 2D)}{2N} = 5M - 6$

Answer:

$\frac{A(3B + 2D)}{2N} = 5M - 6$	
$3AB + 2AD = 10MN - 12N$	Multiply both sides by 2*N* to clear the fraction, and distribute the *A* through the parentheses.
$2AD = 10MN - 12N - 3AB$	Isolate the term with the *D* in it by moving 3*AB* to the other side of the equation.
$D = \frac{(10MN - 12N - 3AB)}{2A}$	Divide both sides by 2*A* to get *D* alone on the right-hand side.

GRAPHS OF LINEAR EQUATIONS

The most common way to write a linear equation is **slope-intercept form**, $y = mx + b$. In this equation, *m* is the slope, which describes how steep the line is, and *b* is the *y*-intercept. Slope is often described as "rise over run" because it is calculated as the difference in *y*-values (rise) over the difference in *x*-values (run). The slope of the line is also the rate of change of the dependent variable *y* with respect to the independent variable *x*. The *y*-intercept is the point where the line crosses the *y*-axis, or where *x* equals zero.

> **HELPFUL HINT**
>
> Use the phrase "Begin, Move" to remember that *b* is the *y*-intercept (where to begin) and *m* is the slope (how the line moves).

To graph a linear equation, identify the *y*-intercept and place that point on the *y*-axis. If the slope is not written as a fraction, make it a fraction by writing it over 1 $\left(\frac{m}{1}\right)$. Then use the slope to count up (or down, if negative) the "rise" part of the slope and over the "run" part of the slope to find a second point. These points can then be connected to draw the line. To find the equation of a line, identify the *y*-intercept, if possible, on the graph and use two easily identifiable points to find the slope. If the *y*-intercept is not easily identified, identify the slope by choosing easily identifiable points; then choose one point on the graph, plug the point and the slope values into the equation, and solve for the missing value *b*.

▶ slope: $m = \frac{y_2 - y_1}{x_2 - x_1}$

▶ standard form: $Ax + By = C$

- $m = -\frac{A}{B}$
- $x\text{-intercept} = \frac{C}{A}$
- $y\text{-intercept} = \frac{C}{B}$

Another way to express a linear equation is standard form: $Ax + By = C$. In order to graph equations in this form, it is often easiest to convert them to point-slope form. Alternately, it is easy to find the x- or y-intercept from this form, and once these two points are known, a line can be drawn through them. To find the x-intercept, simply make $y = 0$ and solve for x. Similarly, to find the y-intercept, make $x = 0$ and solve for y.

HELPFUL HINT

slope-intercept form:
$y = mx + b$

SAMPLE QUESTIONS

15) **What is the equation of the following line?**

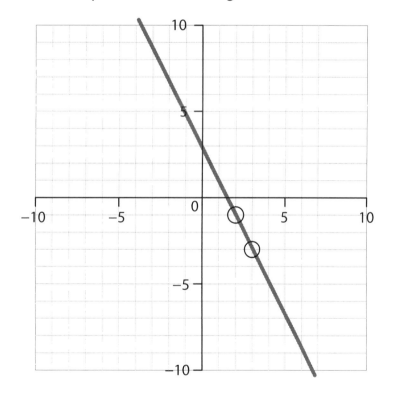

Answer:

$b = 3$

$m = \frac{(-3) - (-1)}{3 - 2} = \frac{-2}{1} = -2$

The y-intercept can be identified on the graph as $(0, 3)$.

To find the slope, choose any two points and plug the values into the slope equation. The two points chosen here are $(2, -1)$ and $(3, -3)$.

| $y = -2x + 3$ | Counting squares and verifying the line goes down 2 and over 1 to get from one point on the line to another point on the line gives the same result. Replace m with -2 and b with 3 in $y = mx + b$ |

16) **What is the equation of the following graph?**

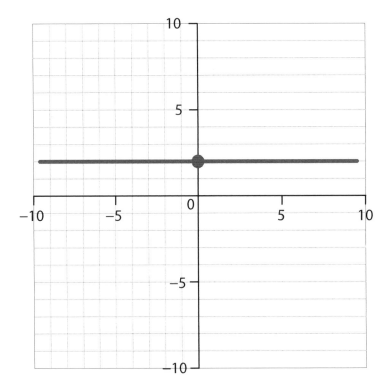

Answer:

| $y = 0x + 2$, or $y = 2$ | The line has a rise of 0 and a run of 1, so the slope is $\frac{0}{1} = 0$. There is no x-intercept. The y-intercept is $(0, 2)$, meaning that the b-value in the slope-intercept form is 2. |

17) **What is the slope of the line whose equation is $6x - 2y - 8 = 0$?**

Answer:

$6x - 2y - 8 = 0$

$-2y = -6x + 8$	Rearrange the equation into slope-intercept form by solving the equation for x. "Undo" $6x$ by subtracting $6x$ on both sides of the equation.
$y = \dfrac{-6x + 8}{-2}$	"Undo" multiplication of -2 by y by dividing both sides by -2.
$y = 3x - 4$	Simplify the fractions.
= 3	The slope is 3, the value attached to x.

18) Write the equation of the line going through the points $(-2, 5)$ and $(-5, 3)$.

Answer:

$(-2, 5)$ and $(-5, 3)$	
$m = \dfrac{3 - 5}{(-5) - (-2)}$ $= \dfrac{-2}{-3}$ $= \dfrac{2}{3}$	Calculate the slope.
$5 = \dfrac{2}{3}(-2) + b$ $5 = \dfrac{-4}{3} + b$ $b = \dfrac{19}{3}$	To find b, plug into the equation $y = mx + b$ the slope for m and a set of points for x and y.
$y = \dfrac{2}{3}x + \dfrac{19}{3}$	Replace m and b to find the equation of the line.

19) The revenue of a company in the year 2010 was $50,000. The revenue five years later was $125,000. Assuming that the revenue grew in a linear manner, what was the rate of change of revenue per year?

Answer:

rate of change = slope $= \dfrac{125{,}000 - 50{,}000}{5 - 0} = \dfrac{75{,}000}{5} = 15{,}000$	The rate of change is just the slope. It is helpful to represent year 2010 as $t = 0$. Then the two points given are $(0, 50000)$ and $(5, 125000)$.
The rate of change of revenue is $15,000 per year.	

Building Equations

In word problems, it is often necessary to translate a verbal description of a relationship into a mathematical equation. No matter the problem, this process can be done using the same steps:

1. Read the problem carefully and identify what value needs to be solved for.

2. Identify the known and unknown quantities in the problem, and assign the unknown quantities a variable.

3. Create equations using the variables and known quantities.

4. Solve the equations.

5. Check the solution: Does it answer the question asked in the problem? Does it make sense?

> **HELPFUL HINT**
>
> Use the acronym STAR to remember word-problem strategies: Search the problem, Translate into an expression or equation, Answer, and Review.

SAMPLE QUESTIONS

20) A school is holding a raffle to raise money. There is a $3 entry fee, and each ticket costs $5. If a student paid $28, how many tickets did he buy?

Answer:

Number of tickets $= x$ Cost per ticket $= 5$ Cost for x tickets $= 5x$ Total cost $= 28$ Entry fee $= 3$	Identify the quantities.
$5x + 3 = 28$	Set up equations. The total cost for x tickets will be equal to the cost for x tickets plus the $3 flat fee.
$5x + 3 = 28$ $5x = 25$ $x = 5$ The student bought **5 tickets**.	Solve for the equation.

21) Kelly is selling shirts for her school swim team. There are two prices: a student price and a nonstudent price. During the first week of the sale, Kelly raised $84 by selling 10 shirts to students and 4 shirts to nonstudents. She earned $185 in the second week by selling 20 shirts to students and 10 shirts to nonstudents. What is the student price for a shirt?

Answer:

Student price = s Nonstudent price = n	Assign variables.
$10s + 4n = 84$ $20s + 10n = 185$	Create two equations using the number of shirts Kelly sold and the money she earned.
$10s + 4n = 84$ $10n = -20s + 185$ $n = -2s + 18.5$ $10s + 4(-2s + 18.5) = 84$ $10s - 8s + 74 = 84$ $2s + 74 = 84$ $2s = 10$ $s = 5$	Solve the system of equations using substitution. Since the question asks for the student price, the goal is to solve for s. Therefore, solve one of the equations for n, so that when the expression is substituted for n, n will be eliminated and s will remain.
The student cost for shirts is **$5**.	

LINEAR INEQUALITIES

An **inequality** shows the relationship between two expressions, much like an equation. However, the equal sign is replaced with an inequality symbol that expresses the following relationships:

- ▸ $<$ less than
- ▸ $\leq$ less than or equal to
- ▸ $>$ greater than
- ▸ $\geq$ greater than or equal to

Inequalities are read from left to right. For example, the inequality $x \leq 8$ would be read as "x is less than or equal to 8," meaning x has a value smaller than or equal to 8. The set of solutions of an inequality can be expressed using a number line.

$x = 5$

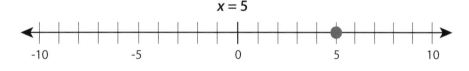

Figure 5.3. Inequalities on a Number Line

The shaded region on the number line represents the set of all the numbers that make an inequality true. One major difference between equations and inequalities is that equations generally have one or two solutions, while inequalities generally have infinitely many solutions (an entire interval on the number line containing infinitely many values).

SOLVING LINEAR INEQUALITIES

Linear inequalities can be solved in the same way as linear equations, with one exception. When multiplying or dividing both sides of an inequality by a negative number, the direction of the inequality sign must reverse—"greater than" becomes "less than" and "less than" becomes "greater than."

SAMPLE QUESTIONS

22) Solve for z: $3z + 10 < -z$

Answer:

Solve the inequality using the same steps used to solve equations.

$3z + 10 < -z$	
$3z < -z - 10$	Collect nonvariable terms to one side.
$4z < -10$	Collect variable terms to the other side.
$\mathbf{z} < -2.5$	Isolate the variable.

−2.5

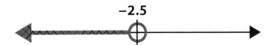

23) Solve for x: $2x - 3 > 5(x - 4) - (x - 4)$

Answer:

$2x - 3 > 5(x - 4) - (x - 4)$	
$2x - 3 > 5x - 20 - x + 4$	Distribute 5 through the parentheses and −1 through the parentheses.
$2x - 3 > 4x - 16$	Combine like terms.
$-2x > -13$	Collect x-terms to one side, and constant terms to the other side.
$x < 6.5$	Divide both sides by −2; since dividing by a negative, reverse the direction of the inequality.

6.5

GRAPHING LINEAR INEQUALITIES IN TWO VARIABLES

Linear inequalities in two variables can be graphed in much the same way as linear equations. Start by graphing the corresponding equation of a line (temporarily replace the inequality with an equal sign, and then graph). This line creates a boundary line of two half-planes. If the inequality is a "greater/less than," the boundary should not be included and a dotted line is used. A solid line is used to indicate that the boundary should be included in the solution when the inequality is "greater/less than or equal to."

HELPFUL HINT

A dotted line is used for "greater/less than" because the solution may approach that line, but the coordinates on the line can never be a solution.

One side of the boundary is the set of all points (x,y) that make the inequality true. This side is shaded to indicate that all these values are solutions. The simplest method to determine which side should be shaded is to choose a point (x,y) on one side of the boundary and evaluate the inequality, plugging in this x- and y- value. If the point makes the inequality true, that side should be shaded; if it does not, it is not a solution, so the other side should be shaded. A second point can be tested as a check. Any point on the shaded side should make the inequality true.

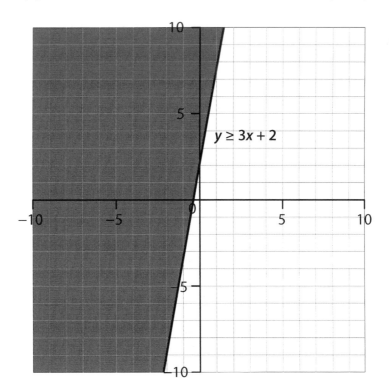

$y \geq 3x + 2$

Figure 5.4. Graphing Inequalities

A set of two or more linear inequalities is a **system of inequalities**. Solutions to the system are all the values of the variables that make every inequality in the system true. Systems of inequalities are solved graphically by graphing all the inequalities in the same plane. The region where all the shaded solutions overlap is the solution to the system.

SAMPLE QUESTIONS

24)   **What is the inequality represented on the graph below?**

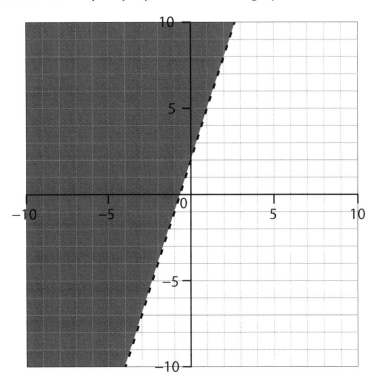

Answer:

	The line crosses the *y*-axis at $y = 2$.
y-intercept: (0,2) slope: 3 $y = 3x + 2$	To arrive at another point on the line, go up 3 (rise) and right 1 (run). Determine the equation of the boundary line.
$y > 3x + 2$	Replace the equal sign with the appropriate inequality: the line is dotted and the shading is above the line, indicating that the symbol should be "greater than." Check a point: for example (1, 5) is a solution since $5 > 3(-1) + 2$.

25)   **Graph the following inequality: $3x + 6y \le 12$**

Answer:

The easiest way to graph this line is to find the *x*- and *y*-intercepts. Find the *y*-intercept by making $x = 0$ and solving for *y*. This gives $(0, 2)$ as the *y*-intercept. Find the *x*-intercept by making $y = 0$ and solving for *x*. This give $(4, 0)$ as the *x*-intercept. Knowing these two points, the line can be drawn. Because the inequality says "or equal to," the boundary line is included and is represented by a solid line. To determine which side to shade, choose a value on one side of the boundary, plug it in, and determine if it is a solution. For example, choosing the origin $(0, 0)$ and plugging it into the inequality gives $3(0) + 6(0)$, which gives 0, which is less than 12, so it must be a solution. Therefore, ALL the solutions lie on the same side as $(0, 0)$. Shade the side that includes $(0, 0)$.

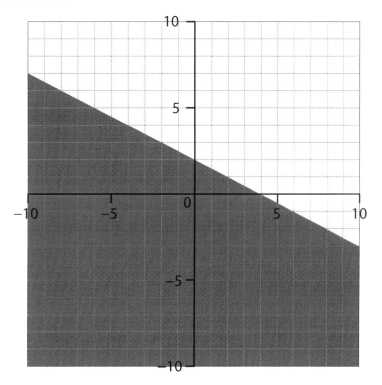

26) **Graph the system of inequalities:** $-x + y \leq 1, x \geq 1, y > 2x - 4$

Answer:

To solve the system, graph all three inequalities in the same plane; then identify the area where the three solutions overlap. All points (x, y) in this area will be solutions to the system since they satisfy all three inequalities. The first inequality is a solid line with slope 1, and the area below that line is shaded. The second inequality is a vertical line and the area to the right of that line is shaded. The third inequality is the dashed line with slope 2 and the area above that line is shaded. The overlapping area is the shaded triangle in the middle. To check the solution, choose one point in that area. It looks like $(0, 0)$ is a solution and plugging that point into each inequality confirms that it is a solution.

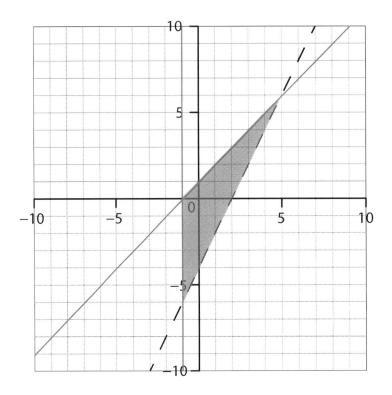

FUNCTIONS

WORKING WITH FUNCTIONS

Functions can be thought of as a process: when something is put in, an action (or operation) is performed, and something different comes out. A **function** is a relationship between two quantities (for example x and y) in which, for every value of the independent variable (usually x), there is exactly one value of the dependent variable (usually y). Briefly, each input has *exactly one* output. Graphically this means the graph passes the **vertical line test**: anywhere a vertical line is drawn on the graph, the line hits the curve at exactly one point. The notation $f(x)$ or $g(t)$, etc., is often used when a function is being considered. This is **function notation.** The

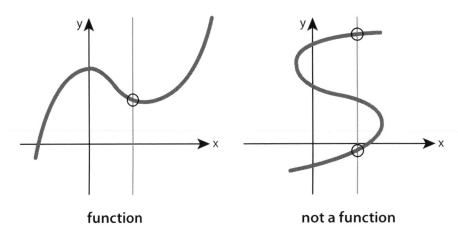

function   not a function

Figure 5.5. Vertical Line Test

input value is *x* and the output value *y* are written as *y* = *f*(*x*). Thus, *f*(2) represents the output value (or *y* value) when *x* = 2, and *f*(2) = 5 means that when *x* = 2 is plugged into the *f*(*x*) function, the output (*y* value) is 5. In other words, *f*(2) = 5 represents the point (2,5) on the graph of *f*(*x*).

Every function has an **input domain** and **output range**. The domain is the set of all the possible *x* values that can be used as input values (these are found along the horizontal axis on the graph), and the range includes all the *y* values or output values that result from applying *f*(*x*) (these are found along the vertical axis on the graph). Domain and range are usually intervals of numbers and are often expressed as inequalities.

A function *f*(*x*) is **even** if *f*(–*x*) = *f*(*x*). Even functions have symmetry across the *y*-axis. An example of an even function is the parent quadratic *y* = *x*², because any value of *x* (for example, 3) and its opposite –*x* (for example, –3) have the same *y* value (for example, 3² = 9 and (–3)² = 9). A function is **odd** if *f*(–*x*) = –*f*(*x*). Odd functions have symmetry about the origin. For example, *f*(*x*) = *x*³ is an odd function because *f*(3) = 27, and *f*(–3) = –27. A function may be even, odd, or neither.

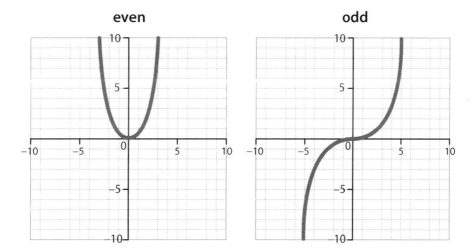

Figure 5.6. Even and Odd Function

SAMPLE QUESTIONS

27) **Evaluate:** *f*(4) *if f*(*x*) = *x*³ − 2*x* + √*x*

Answer:

$f(4)$ if $f(x) = x^3 - 2x + \sqrt{x}$	
$f(4) = (4)^3 - 2(4) + \sqrt{(4)}$	Plug in 4.
$= 64 - 8 + 2$ $= 58$	Follow the PEMDAS order of operations.

28)   What is the domain and range of the following function?

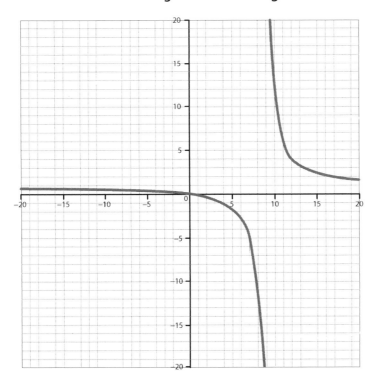

Answer:

This function has an asymptote at $x = 8$, so is not defined there. Exclude 8 from the domain. Otherwise, the function is defined for all other values of x. The proper way to write the domain is:

D: $-\infty < x < \mathbf{8}$ or $\mathbf{8} < x < \infty$

Another way to state the domain is "all real numbers except 8." Sometimes interval notations are used: $(-\infty, 8)$ U $(8, \infty)$. The round brackets indicate that 8 is not included; square brackets [ ] would indicate that the value is included in the domain. The U symbol simply means *or*.

Since the function has a horizontal asymptote at $y = 1$ that it never crosses, the function never takes the value 1, so the range is all real numbers except 1, or **R:** $-\infty < y < 1$ *or* $1 < y < \infty$.

29)   Which of the following represents a function?

A.			B.		
	x	$g(x)$		x	$f(x)$
	0	0		0	1
	1	1		0	2
	2	2		0	3
	1	3		0	4

C.			D.		
	t	*f(t)*		*x*	*f(x)*
	1	1		0	0
	2	2		5	1
	3	3		0	2
	4	4		5	3

Answer:

For a set of numbers to represent a function, every input must generate a unique output. Therefore, if the same input (*x*) appears more than once in the table, determine if that input has two different outputs. If so, then the table does not represent a function.

A. Incorrect. This table is not a function because input value 1 has two different outputs (1 and 3).

B. Incorrect. Table B is not function because 0 is the only input and results in four different values.

C. **Correct.** Each input has one output.

D. Incorrect. This table also has one input going to two different values.

> **HELPFUL HINT**
>
> Put any function into the *y* = part of a calculator and look at the table to get domain and range values. Looking at −100, −10, 0, 10, and 100 give a sense about any function's limitations.

30) **What is the domain and the range of the following graph?**

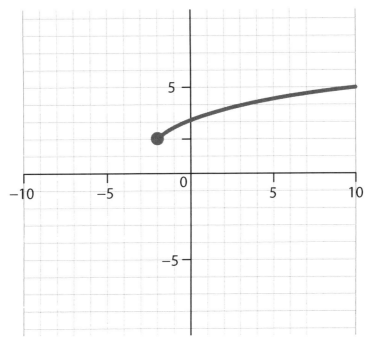

Answer:

For the domain, this graph goes on to the right to positive infinity. Its leftmost point, however, is $x = -2$. Therefore, its domain is all real numbers equal to or greater than -2, **D: $-2 \leq x < \infty$.** In interval notation, write **[$-2, \infty$).**

The lowest range value is $y = 2$. Although it has a decreasing slope, this function continues to rise and there is no reason to think it will stop rising. Therefore, the domain is all real numbers greater than 2, **R: $2 \leq y < \infty$.**

Also notice that this is indeed a graph of a function, since there is no x-value that has more than one y-value. It passes the vertical line test, since any vertical line drawn anywhere in the domain of the function results in hitting the curve only once.

6

Geometry

Geometry is the study of shapes, angles, volumes, areas, lines, points, and the relationships among them. It is normally approached as an axiomatic system; that is, a small number of entities are taken for granted as true, and everything else is derived logically from them.

PROPERTIES OF SHAPES

BASIC DEFINITIONS

The basic figures from which many other geometric shapes are built are points, lines, and planes. A point is a location in a plane. It has no size or shape, but is represented by a dot. It is labeled using a capital letter.

Two points may be connected by a **line** that extends indefinitely in both directions. There are infinitely many points on a line. A line is a one-dimensional figure. Lines are represented by any two points (say, *A* and *B*) on the line and the line symbol: ($\overleftrightarrow{AB}$). For any two points, a line can be defined that goes through the points. Any points on the same line are co-linear. If two lines are parallel, they will never touch. Parallel lines have the exact same slopes. Two lines with different slopes intersect at a point. If two lines are perpendicular, they intersect at 90° angles.

A **line segment** has two endpoints and a finite length. The length of a segment, called the measure of the segment, is the distance from *A* to *B*. A line segment is a subset of a line, and is also denoted with two points, but with a segment symbol: ($\overline{AB}$). The midpoint of a line segment is the point at which the segment is divided into two equal parts. A line, segment, or plane that passes through the midpoint of a segment is called a bisector of the segment, since it cuts the segment into two equal segments.

A **ray** has one endpoint and extends indefinitely in one direction. It is defined by its endpoint, followed by any other point on the ray: ($\overrightarrow{AB}$). It is important that the first letter represents the endpoint. A ray is sometimes called a half line.

Table 6.1. Basic Geometric Figures

Term	Dimensions	Graphic	Symbol
point	zero	●	·A
line segment	one	A ——— B	$\overline{AB}$
ray	one	A ——— B ▸	$\overrightarrow{AB}$
line	one	◂——— ▸	$\overleftrightarrow{AB}$
plane	two	▱	Plane M

A **plane** is a flat sheet that extends indefinitely in two directions (like an infinite sheet of paper). A plane is a two-dimensional (2D) figure. A plane can ALWAYS be defined through any three noncollinear points in three-dimensional (3D) space. A plane is named using any three points that are in the plane (for example, plane **ABC**). Any points lying in the same plane are said to be coplanar. When two planes intersect, the intersection is a line.

SAMPLE QUESTION

1) Which points and lines are not contained in plane *M* in the diagram below?

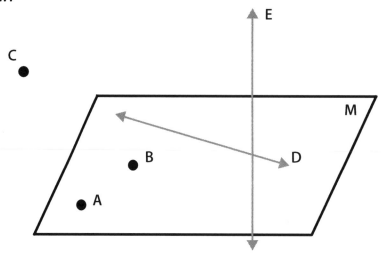

Answer:

Points *A* and *B* and line *D* are all on the same plane, as is the ray beginning at *D*. Point *C* is above the plane, and line *E* cuts through the plane and thus is on a more vertical plane. The point at which line *E* intersects plane *M* is on plane *M* but the line as a whole is not.

ANGLES

Angles are formed when two rays share a common endpoint. They are named using three letters, with the vertex point in the middle (for example ∠*ABC*, where *B* is the vertex). They can also be labeled with a number or named by their vertex alone (if it is clear to do so). Angles are commonly measured in degrees or radians. They are also classified based on their angle measure. A **right angle** has a measure of exactly 90°. **Acute angles** have measures that are less than 90°, whereas **obtuse angles** have measures that are greater than 90°.

Any two angles that add to make 90° are called **complementary angles**. A 30° angle would be complementary to a 60° angle. **Supplementary angles** add up to 180°. A supplementary angle to a 60° angle would be a 120° angle; likewise, 60° is the **supplement** of 120°. Angles that are next to each other and share a common ray are called **adjacent angles**. Angles that are adjacent and supplementary are called a **linear pair** of angles. Their nonshared rays form a line (thus the *linear* pair). Note that angles that are supplementary do not need to be adjacent; their measures simply need to add to 180°.

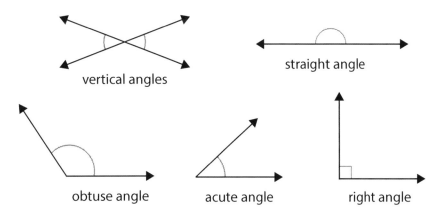

Figure 6.1. Types of Angles

Vertical angles are formed when two lines intersect. Four angles will be formed; the vertex of each angle is at the intersection point of the lines. The vertical angles across from each other will be equal in measure. The angles adjacent to each other will be linear pairs and therefore supplementary.

A ray, line, or segment that divides an angle into two equal angles is called an **angle bisector**.

SAMPLE QUESTIONS

2) How many pairs of supplementary angles are there in the following figure?

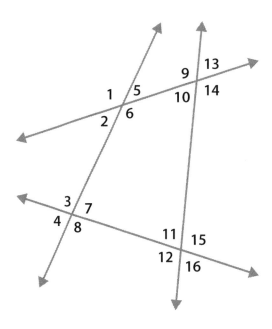

Answers:

Any two angles that are adjacent to one another on a line are supplementary. Therefore, there are **sixteen supplementary pairs** here (∠1 and ∠5, ∠2 and ∠6, ∠5 and ∠6, ∠2 and ∠1, and so on).

3) If angles *M* and *N* are supplementary and ∠*M* is 30° less than twice ∠*N*, what is the degree measurement of each angle?

Answer:

This problem requires a system of equations to solve:

∠*M* + ∠*N* = 180°

∠*M* = 2∠*N* − 30°

Replacing ∠*M* with 2∠*N* − 30° gives:

2∠*N* − 30° + ∠*N* = 180°	Substitute.
3∠*N* − 30° = 180°	Combine like terms.
3∠*N* = 210°	Add 30 to both sides.
∠***N* = 70°**	Divide by 3.

Since ∠*N* and ∠*M* are supplementary, ∠*M* must be 110°. Work can be checked by using the second equation: 110 = 2(70) − 30 verifies the answers.

CIRCLES

Circles are a fundamental shape in geometry. A **circle** is the set of all the points in a plane that are the same distance from a fixed point (called the **center**). The distance from the center to any point on the circle is the **radius** of the circle. The distance around the circle (the perimeter) is called the **circumference**.

The ratio of a circle's circumference to its diameter is a constant value called pi (π), an irrational number which is commonly rounded to 3.14. The formula to find a circle's circumference is $C = 2\pi r$. The formula to find the enclosed area of a circle is $A = \pi r^2$.

Circles have a number of unique parts and properties:

- The **diameter** is the largest measurement across a circle. It passes through the circle's center, extending from one side of the circle to the other. The measure of the diameter is twice the measure of the radius.

- A line that cuts across a circle and touches it twice is called a **secant** line.

- A line that touches a circle or any curve at one point is **tangent** to the circle or the curve. These lines are always exterior to the circle. A line tangent to a circle and a radius drawn to the point of tangency meet at a right angle (90°).

- An **arc** is any portion of a circle between two points on the circle. The **measure** of an arc is in degrees, whereas the **length of the arc** will be in linear measurement (such as centimeters or inches). A **minor arc** is the small arc between the two points (it measures less than 180°), whereas a **major arc** is the large arc between the two points (it measures greater than 180°).

- An angle with its vertex at the center of a circle is called a **central angle**. For a central angle, the measure of the arc intercepted by the sides of the angle (in degrees) is the same as the measure of the angle.

- The part of a secant line that lies within a circle is called a **chord**.

- A **sector** is the part of a circle *and* its interior that is inside the rays of a central angle (its shape is like a slice of pie). The formula for area of a sector using θ in degrees is *sector area* $= \frac{\theta}{360}\pi r^2$ (note that this formula is simply the total area of the circle multiplied by $\frac{\theta}{360}$, the fraction of the complete circle area that the sector contains). If θ is in radians, then *sector area* $= \frac{r^2\theta}{2}$.

- The formula to find the **arc length** (measured in linear units like centimeters, inches, or feet) is *arc length* $= s = \frac{\theta}{360}(2\pi a) = \frac{\theta}{180}(\pi a)$, where

α is the central angle forming the arc, measured in degrees. Again, this is just the fraction of the total circumference. The formula to find the length of the arc if α is measured in radians is *arc length s = rα*.

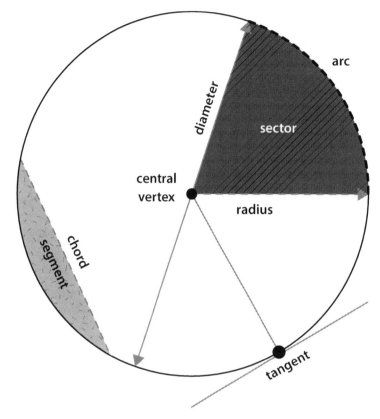

Figure 6.2. Parts of a Circle

▶ An **inscribed angle** has a vertex on the circle and is formed by two chords that share that vertex point. The angle measure of an inscribed angle is one-half the angle measure of the central angle with the same endpoints on the circle (in the diagram below right, $\theta = \frac{\alpha}{2}$).

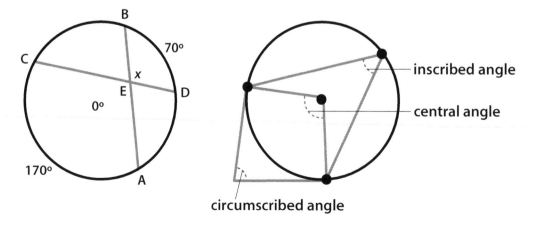

Figure 6.3. Angles in a Circle

▶ A **circumscribed angle** has rays tangent to the circle. The angle lies outside of the circle.

▶ Any angle outside the circle, whether formed by two tangent lines, two secant lines, or a tangent line and a secant line, is equal to half the difference of the intercepted arcs.

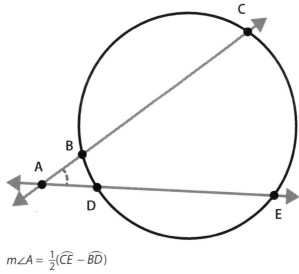

$$m\angle A = \tfrac{1}{2}(\widehat{CE} - \widehat{BD})$$

Figure 6.4. Angles Outside a Circle

▶ Angles are formed within a circle when two chords intersect in the circle. The measure of the smaller angle formed is half the sum of the two smaller arc measures (in degrees). Likewise, the larger angle is half the sum of the two larger arc measures (think: average the arc measures).

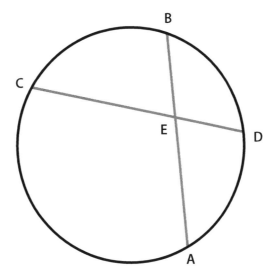

$$m\angle E = \tfrac{1}{2}(\widehat{AC} + \widehat{BD})$$

Figure 6.5. Intersecting Chords

▶ If a chord intersects a line tangent to the circle, the angle formed by this intersection measures one half the measurement of the intercepted arc (in degrees).

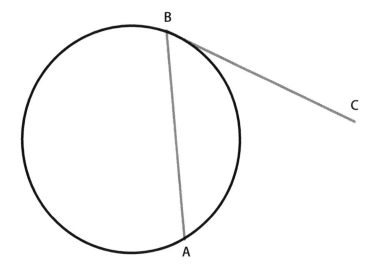

$m\angle ABC = \frac{1}{2}m\widehat{AB}$

Figure 6.6. Intersecting Chord and Tangent

SAMPLE QUESTIONS

4) Find the area of the sector *NHS* of the circle below with center at *H*:

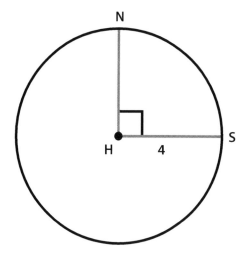

Answer:

$A = \pi 4^2 = 16\pi$	First, determine the area of the entire circle.
$\dfrac{x}{16\pi} = \dfrac{90°}{360°}$	Next, write a proportion.
$\boldsymbol{x = 4\pi}$	Solve.

This answer makes sense because the sector in question is a quarter of the circle, and the area is one quarter of the total area.

5) **In the circle below with center *O*, the minor arc *ACB* measures 5 feet. What is the measurement of *m∠AOB*?**

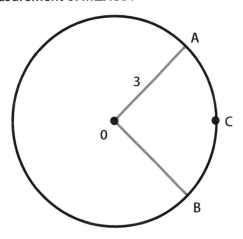

Answer:

The circumference of this circle is $C = 2\pi r = 2\pi(3) = 6\pi$ or 18.84. Now a proportion can be set up, equating the ratio of the arc lengths to the ratio of the angle measures:

$\dfrac{5}{18.84} = \dfrac{x}{360°}$	
$x = 95.54°$	Multiply both sides by 360 to solve.

6) **In the circle below with center *A*, there are two congruent chords. Solve for *x*.**

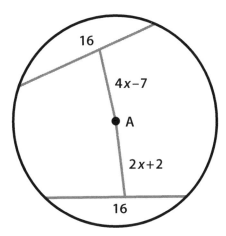

Answer:

A circle's chords are equal only if they are the same distance from the circle. This means that the two segments expressed in terms of *x* are equal. The equation that must be solved is:

$$4x - 7 = 2x + 2$$
$$2x = 9$$
$x = 4.5$

TRIANGLES

Much of geometry is concerned with **triangles** as they are commonly used shapes. A good understanding of triangles allows decomposition of other shapes (specifically polygons) into triangles for study.

Triangles have three sides, and the three interior angles always sum to 180°. The formula for the area of a triangle is $A = \frac{1}{2}bh$ or one-half the product of the base and height (or altitude) of the triangle.

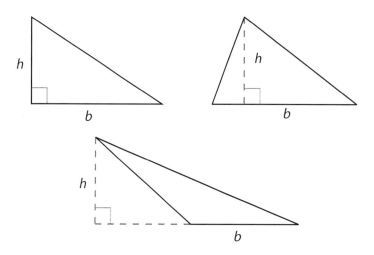

Figure 6.7. Finding the Base and Height of Triangles

Some important segments in a triangle include the angle bisector, the altitude, and the median. The **angle bisector** extends from the side opposite an angle to bisect that angle. The **altitude** is the shortest distance from a vertex of the triangle to the line containing the **base side** opposite that vertex. It is perpendicular to that line and can occur on the outside of the triangle. The **median** extends from an angle to bisect the opposite side.

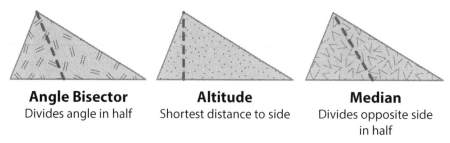

Angle Bisector
Divides angle in half

Altitude
Shortest distance to side

Median
Divides opposite side
in half

Figure 6.8. Important Segments in a Triangle

Triangles have two "centers." The **orthocenter** is formed by the intersection of a triangle's three altitudes. The **centroid** is where a triangle's three medians meet.

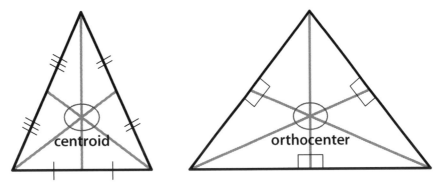

Figure 6.9. Centroid and Orthocenter of a Triangle

Triangles can be classified in two ways: by sides and by angles.

A **scalene triangle** has no equal sides or angles. An **isosceles triangle** has two equal sides and two equal angles, often called **base angles**. In an **equilateral triangle**, all three sides are equal as are all three angles. Moreover, because the sum of the angles of a triangle is always 180°, each angle of an equilateral triangle must be 60°.

Triangles Based on Sides

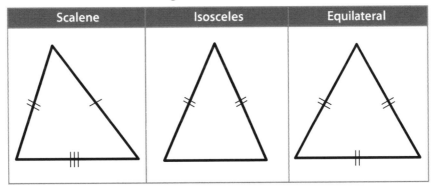

Triangles Based on Angles

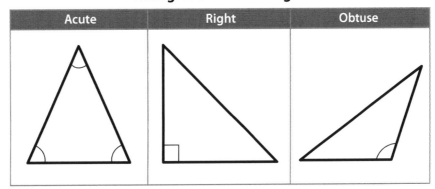

Figure 6.10. Types of Triangles

A **right triangle** has one right angle (90°) and two acute angles. An **acute triangle** has three acute angles (all angles are less than 90°). An **obtuse triangle** has one obtuse angle (more than 90°) and two acute angles.

For any triangle, the side opposite the largest angle will have the longest length, while the side opposite the smallest angle will have the shortest length. The **triangle**

inequality theorem states that the sum of any two sides of a triangle must be greater than the third side. If this inequality does not hold, then a triangle cannot be formed. A consequence of this theorem is the **third-side rule**: if b and c are two sides of a triangle, then the measure of the third side a must be between the sum of the other two sides and the difference of the other two sides: $c - b < a < c + b$.

Solving for missing angles or sides of a triangle is a common type of triangle problem. Often a right triangle will come up on its own or within another triangle. The relationship among a right triangle's sides is known as the **Pythagorean theorem**: $a^2 + b^2 = c^2$, where c is the hypotenuse and is across from the 90° angle. Right triangles with angle measurements of 90° – 45° – 45° and 90° – 60° – 30° are known as *special* right triangles and always have the following relationship between legs and hypotenuse:

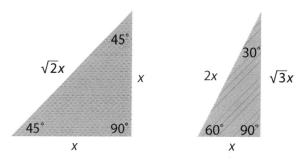

Figure 6.11. Special Right Triangles

SAMPLE QUESTIONS

7)   What are the minimum and maximum values of the third side of the triangle, x, to the nearest hundredth?

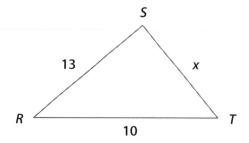

Answers:

The sum of two sides is 23 and their difference is 3. To connect the two other sides and enclose a space, *x* must be less than the sum and greater than the difference (that is, $3 < x < 23$). Therefore, ***x*'s minimum value to the nearest hundredth is 3.01 and its maximum value is 22.99.**

8) Examine and classify each of the following triangles:

1.

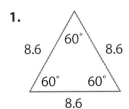

2.

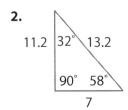

3.

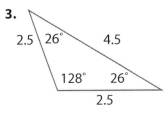

4.

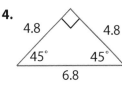

Answers:

Triangle 1 is an equilateral triangle (since all 3 sides are equal, and all 3 angles are equal)

Triangle 2 is a scalene, right triangle (since all 3 sides are different, and there is a 90° angle)

Triangle 3 is an isosceles triangle (since there are 2 equal sides and, consequently, 2 equal angles)

Triangle 4 is a right, isosceles triangle (since there are 2 equal sides and a 90° angle)

9) Given the diagram, if $XZ = 100$, $WZ = 80$, and $XU = 70$, then $WY = ?$

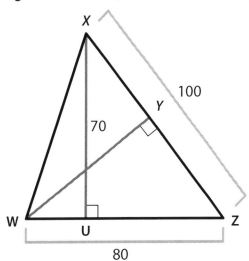

Answer:

WY can be seen as one of the legs of a right triangle, but from the given information it is unclear how that segment divides *XZ* (we cannot assume that it splits in exactly in two since the triangle is not necessarily isosceles). Another approach is required. Since altitude *XU* and base *WZ* are given values, the area of the triangle can be written in two different ways and equated.

$A = \frac{1}{2}(80)(70) = 2800$	The height *XU* = 70 and base *WZ* = 80 give the area of triangle *XWZ*.
$A = \frac{1}{2}(100)(WY)$	The area of triangle *XWZ* can also be written using *XZ* = 100 and height *WY*.
$2800 = \frac{1}{2}(100)(WY)$	Since both these represent the same area, these may be equated, and *WY* can be solved for.

WY = 56

QUADRILATERALS

All closed, four-sided shapes are **quadrilaterals**. The sum of all internal angles in a quadrilateral is always 360°. (Think of drawing a diagonal to create two triangles. Since each triangle contains 180°, two triangles, and therefore the quadrilateral, must contain 360°.) The **area of any quadrilateral** is $A = bh$, where *b* is the base and *h* is the height (or altitude).

A **parallelogram** is a quadrilateral with two pairs of parallel sides. A rectangle is a parallelogram with two pairs of equal sides and four right angles. A **kite** also has two pairs of equal sides, but its equal sides are consecutive. Both a **square** and a **rhombus** have four equal sides. A square has four right angles, while a rhombus has a pair of acute opposite angles and a pair of obtuse opposite angles. A **trapezoid** has exactly one pair of parallel sides.

> **HELPFUL HINT**
>
> All squares are rectangles and all rectangles are parallelograms; however, not all parallelograms are rectangles and not all rectangles are squares.

Table 6.2 Properties of Parallelograms

Term	Shape	Properties
Parallelogram		Opposite sides are parallel. Consecutive angles are supplementary. Opposite angles are equal. Opposite sides are equal. Diagonals bisect each other.

Term	Shape	Properties
Rectangle		All parallelogram properties hold.
		Diagonals are congruent *and* bisect each other.
		All angles are right angles.
Square		All rectangle properties hold.
		All four sides are equal.
		Diagonals bisect angles.
		Diagonals intersect at right angles and bisect each other.
Kite		Kites have exactly one pair of opposite equal angles and two pairs of equal consecutive sides.
		Diagonals meet at right angles.
Rhombus		All four sides are equal.
		Diagonals bisect angles.
		Diagonals intersect at right angles and bisect each other.
Trapezoid		Trapezoids have exactly one pair of parallel sides (called bases).
		Bases have different lengths.
		Isosceles trapezoids have a pair of equal sides (and base angles).

SAMPLE QUESTIONS

10) Figure *WEST* is a parallelogram. Determine each of the following:

$\overline{TW}$ = _____

$\overline{EM} \cong$ _____

$\overline{TM} = \frac{1}{2}$ _____

$\angle STW \cong \angle$ _____

$\angle EST + \angle$ _____ = 180°.

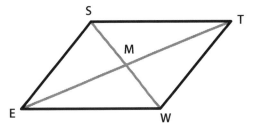

Answer:

Line $\overline{TW}$ is parallel to $\overline{SE}$ (opposite sides are equal); $\overline{EM}$ is congruent to $\overline{TM}$; $\overline{TM}$ is one half of $\overline{TE}$ (since diagonals bisect each other); $\angle STW$ is congruent to $\angle SEW$ (opposite sides are equal); and the sum of angles $\angle EST$ and $\angle STW$ is 180° (consecutive angles are supplementary); $\angle SEW$ would also work.

11) In parallelogram *ABCD*, the measure of the exterior angle at *C* is *m*° = 260°. What is the measure of *n*°?

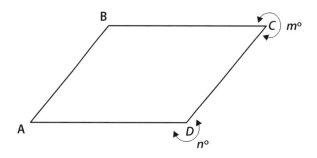

Answers:

The two variables are exterior angles. If these two angles were to be added to the interior angles (*A* and *D*) the sum of each pair would be 360°. Since *ABCD* is a parallelogram, these two consecutive interior angles are supplementary. The problem can be solved with this information:

$260° + m\angle C = 360°$

$m\angle C + m\angle D = 180°$

$m\angle D + n = 360°$

It follows from the first equation that $m\angle C = 100°$. Substituting that value in for $\angle C$ in the second equation yields $m\angle D = 80°$. Substituting 80° in for $m\angle D$ in the third equation gives **$n = 280°$**.

12) A rectangular section of a football field has dimensions of *x* and *y* and an area of 1000 square feet. Three additional lines drawn vertically divide the section into four smaller rectangular areas as seen in the diagram below. If all the lines shown need to be painted, calculate the total number of linear feet, in terms *x*, to be painted.

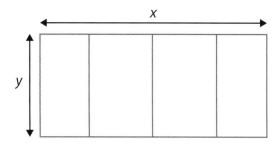

Answer:

Since the area is 1000 square feet, $xy = 1000$. The total perimeter of the larger rectangle is $2x + 2y$. In addition, the three interior lines, each of length *y*, need to be painted for a total of $2x + 2y + 3y$ or $2x + 5y$. To express the total in terms of *x*, solve $xy = 1000$ for *y*, and substitute:

$y = \frac{1000}{x}$	Solve for y.
$P = 2x + 5y$	
$= 2x + 5\left(\frac{1000}{x}\right)$	Solve for the perimeter.
$= 2x + \frac{5000}{x}$	

POLYGONS

Any closed shape made up of three or more line segments is a polygon. In addition to triangles and quadrilaterals, **hexagons** and **octagons** are two common polygons:

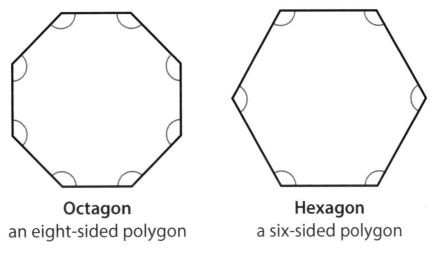

Octagon
an eight-sided polygon

Hexagon
a six-sided polygon

Figure 6.12. Common Polygons

The two polygons depicted above are **regular polygons**, meaning that they are equilateral (all sides having equal lengths) and equiangular (all angles having equal measurements). Angles inside a polygon are **interior angles**, whereas those formed by one side of the polygon and a line extending outside the polygon are **exterior angles**:

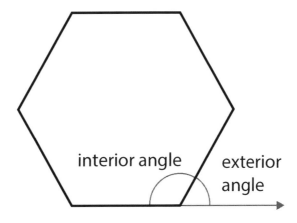

interior angle   exterior angle

Figure 6.13. Interior and Exterior Angles

The sum of the all the exterior angles of a polygon is always 360°. Dividing 360° by the number of a polygon's sides finds the measure of the polygon's exterior angles.

To determine the sum of a polygon's interior angles, choose one vertex and draw diagonals from that vertex to each of the other vertices, decomposing the polygon into multiple triangles. For example, an octagon has six triangles within it, and therefore the sum of the interior angles is 6 × 180° = 1080°. In general, the formula for finding the sum of the angles in a polygon is sum of angles = $(n - 2) \times 180°$, where n is the number of sides of the polygon.

To find the measure of a single interior angle, simply divide the sum of the interior angles by the number of angles (which is the same as the number of sides). So, in the octagon example, each angle is $\frac{1080}{8} = 135°$.

In general, the formula to find the measure of a regular polygon's interior angles is: *interior angle* $= \frac{(n - 2)}{n} \times 180°$ where n is the number of sides of the polygon.

To find the area of a polygon, it is helpful to know the perimeter of the polygon (p), and the **apothem** (a). The apothem is the shortest (perpendicular) distance from the polygon's center to one of the sides of the polygon. The formula for the area is: *regular polygon area* $= \frac{ap}{2}$.

Finally, there is no universal way to find the perimeter of a polygon (when the side length is not given). Often, breaking the polygon down into triangles and adding the base of each triangle all the way around the polygon is the surest way to calculate the perimeter.

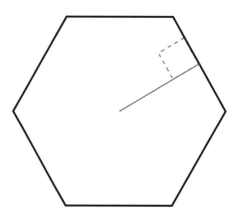

Figure 6.14. Apothem in a Hexagon

SAMPLE QUESTIONS

13)   **What is the measure of an exterior angle and an interior angle of a regular 400-gon?**

Answer:

The sum of the exterior angles is 360°. Dividing this sum by 400 gives $\frac{360°}{400} = \mathbf{0.9°}$. Since an interior angle is supplementary to an exterior angle, all the interior angles have measure 180 – 0.9 = **179.1°**. Alternately, using the formula for calculating the interior angle gives the same result:

interior angle $= \frac{400 - 2}{400} \times 180° = 179.1°$

14) The circle and hexagon below both share center point T. The hexagon is entirely inscribed in the circle. The circle's radius is 5. What is the area of the shaded area?

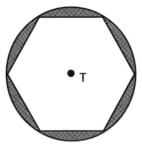

Answer:

The area of the circle (with radius $r = 5$) is:

$A = 5^2\pi = 25\pi = 78.54$

To find the hexagon's area, the perimeter must be calculated. The key is using the interior angle formula to find the measure of the interior angles: $\frac{(6-2)}{6}(180°) = 120°$. Six triangles can be drawn by drawing segments from the center of the hexagon to each vertex. Since these triangles are all the same (congruent), and isosceles, they divide each 120° angle exactly in half. Thus, each of the three angles of each triangle is 60°. Moreover the triangles are, in fact, equilateral. The side length of the hexagon is therefore 5 units, and the perimeter is 30. Drawing a perpendicular to the side and using special triangles to find the side opposite the 60° angle calculates the apothem:

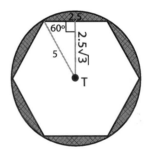

The apothem is $2.5\sqrt{3}$, and the area can now be calculated as $area = \frac{ap}{2}$ $= \frac{(2.5\sqrt{3})(30)}{2} = \frac{75\sqrt{3}}{2} = 64.95$.

The shaded area constitutes only parts of the circle that are not in the polygon. The difference between the circle's area and the polygon's area is $78.54 - 64.95 = $ **13.59**.

THREE–DIMENSIONAL SHAPES

Three-dimensional shapes have depth in addition to width and length. The sides of three-dimensional shapes exist on a flat plane, so questions concerning these shapes require the use of the properties discussed above.

Volume is expressed as the number of cubic units any solid can hold—that is, what it takes to fill it up. Surface area is the sum of the areas of the two-dimensional figures that are found on its surface. Three-dimensional shapes have unique formulas:

Table 6.3. Three–Dimensional Shapes and Formulas

Term	Shape	Formula	Description
Prism		$V = Bh$ $SA = 2lw + 2wh + 2lh$ $SA = 2B + lateral\ area$	B refers to the area of the two-dimensional base, which can be any polygon; h is the height of the prism. For a rectangular prism, the surface area formula can be found to the left, where l is the length, w is the width, and h is the height. The shape of the base changes this formula, where B is the area of the base (top and bottom), and the lateral area is the sum of the areas of all the rectangular sides of the prism.
Cube		$V = s^3$ $SA = 6s^2$ $d^2 = a^2 + b^2 + c^2$	A cube has twelve edges (s) and six faces that are equal. A cube is a type of rectangular prism. Additionally, the super Pythagorean theorem gives the length of the longest diagonal that can be drawn between any rectangular solid's corners by using the solid's three measurements.
Sphere		$V = \frac{4}{3}\pi r^3$ $SA = 4\pi r^2$	A sphere is defined as all the points in a three-dimensional space that are the same distance (measured as the radius) from a center.
Cylinder		$V = Bh = \pi r^2 h$ $SA = 2\pi r^2 + 2\pi rh$	A cylinder can be thought of as a prism with a circular base (with area $B = \pi r^2$).
Cone		$V = \frac{1}{3}\pi r^2 h$	A cone is a special case of a pyramid where the base is a circle, so $B = \pi r^2$. The distance between a point on the circle of the cone's base and the terminating point is the slant height. The formula for calculating the surface area of a cone is beyond the scope of this text.

Term	Shape	Formula	Description
Pyramid		$V = \frac{1}{3}Bh$	A pyramid has a polygon base with area B and comes to a point. The height is the perpendicular distance from the peak point to the base. To find the surface area of a pyramid, find the area of the base and add the areas of all the triangular sides. To do so, finding the slant height of each triangular side will require using the Pythagorean theorem. On the left is an example of a square-based pyramid.

SAMPLE QUESTIONS

15) A sphere has a radius z. If that radius is increased by t, by how much is the surface area increased? Write the answer in terms of z and t.

Answer:

$SA_1 = 4\pi z^2$	The original surface area is:
$SA_2 = 4\pi(z + t)^2$	The increased surface area is:
$= 4\pi(z^2 + 2zt + t^2)$	
$= 4\pi z^2 + 8\pi zt + 4\pi t^2$	
$4\pi z^2 + 8\pi zt + 4\pi t^2 - 4\pi z^2$	To find the difference between the two, subtract the original from the increased surface area:
$= 4\pi t^2 + 8\pi zt$	The surface area increased by $4\pi t^2 + 8\pi zt$.

16) The length of the base of a rectangular pyramid measures 4 feet, and the width of the base is half of the pyramid's height. What is the pyramid's volume in terms of height?

Answer:

The length of the base is $l = 4$. The width of the base is $w = \frac{1}{2}h$.

The base of the pyramid is rectangular and thus has area:

$B = lw = 4\left(\frac{1}{2}h\right) = 2h$

Plugging this information into a pyramid's volume equation provides the answer:

$$V = \tfrac{1}{3}Bh = \tfrac{1}{3}(2h)h = \tfrac{2h^2}{3}$$

17) **A cube with volume 27 cubic meters is inscribed within a sphere and all of the cube's vertices touch the sphere. What is the length of the sphere's radius?**

Answer:

Since the cube's volume is 27, each side length is equal to $\sqrt[3]{27} = 3$. The long diagonal distance from one of the cube's vertices to its opposite vertex will provide the sphere's diameter. Using the super Pythagorean theorem, it is found that:

$$d = \sqrt{3^2 + 3^2 + 3^2} = \sqrt{27} = 5.2$$

This is the diameter of the sphere. Half of this length is the radius, which is **2.6 meters**.

TRANSFORMATIONS OF GEOMETRIC FIGURES

TRANSLATIONS, ROTATIONS, REFLECTIONS, AND CONGRUENCE

Geometric figures are often drawn in the coordinate *xy*-plane, with the vertices or centers of the figures indicated by ordered pairs. Important understandings about the nature of a figure can be examined by performing **transformations**, which are manipulations of the shape in the plane. The original shape is called the **pre-image**, and the shape after a transformation is applied is called the **image**.

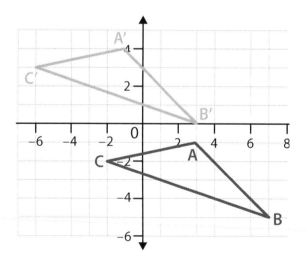

The translation moved triangle ABC left 4 units and up 6 units to produce triangle A'B'C'.

Figure 6.15. Translation

A **translation** transforms a shape by moving it right or left, or up or down. Translations are sometimes called slides. The image under this transformation is identical in size and shape to the pre-image. In other words, the image is **congruent**, or identical in size, to the pre-image. All corresponding pairs of angles are congruent, and all corresponding side lengths are congruent.

Translations are often written with pointy brackets: $\{-x, y\}$. The first number represents the change in the x direction (left/right), while the second number shows the change in the y direction (up/down). The symbol $\cong$ is read "congruent."

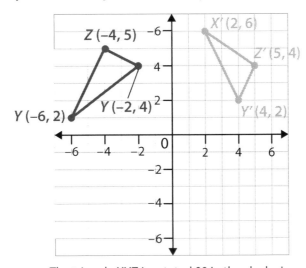

The triangle XYZ is rotated 90 in the clockwise direction about the origin (0, 0).

Figure 6.16. Rotation

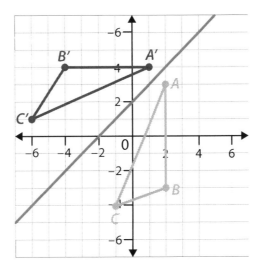

The triangle ABC is reflected over the line to produce the triangle A'B'C'.

Figure 6.17. Reflection

Similarly, rotations and reflections preserve the size and shape of the figure, so congruency is preserved. A **rotation** takes a pre-image and rotates it about a fixed point (often the origin) in the plane. Although the position or orientation of the shape changes, the angles and side lengths remain the same.

A **reflection** takes each point in the pre-image and flips it over a point or line in the plane (often the *x*- or *y*-axis, but not necessarily). The image is congruent to the pre-image. When a figure is flipped across the *y*-axis, the signs of all *x*-coordinates will change. The *y*-coordinates change sign when a figure is reflected across the *x*-axis.

SAMPLE QUESTIONS

18) If quadrilateral *ABCD* has vertices *A* (–6, 4), *B* (–6, 8), *C* (2, 8), and *D* (4, –4), what are the new vertices if *ABCD* is translated 2 units down and 3 units right?

Answer:

Translating two units down decreases each *y*-value by 2, and moving 3 units to the right increases the *x*-value by 3. The new vertices are *A* (–3, 2), *B* (–3, 6), *C* (5, 6), and *D* (7, –6).

19) If quadrilateral *ABCD* has vertices *A* (–6, 4), *B* (–6, 8), *C* (2, 8), and *D* (4, –4), what are the new vertices if *ABCD* is rotated 270° and then reflected across the *x*-axis?

Answer:

When a figure is rotated 270°, the coordinates change: $(a, b) \rightarrow (b, -a)$ (see the summary of rotation coordinate changes in the next section). After the rotation, the new coordinates are (4, 6), (8, 6), (8, –2), and (–4, –4). Reflecting across the *x*-axis requires that every *y*-value is multiplied by –1 to arrive at the completely transformed quadrilateral with vertices of (4, –6), (8, –6), (8, 2), and (–4, 4).

Dilations and Similarity

The last transformations of interest are dilations. A **dilation** increases (or decreases) the size of a figure by some **scale factor**. Each coordinate of the points that make up the figure is multiplied by the same factor. If the factor is greater than 1, multiplying all the factors enlarges the shape; if the factor is less than 1 (but greater than 0), the shape is reduced in size.

In addition to the scale factor, a dilation needs a **center of dilation**, which is a fixed point in the plane about which the points are multiplied. Usually, but not always, the center of dilation is the origin (0,0). For dilations about the origin, the image coordinates are calculated by multiplying each coordinate by the scale factor **k**. Thus, point **(*x*, *y*) → (*kx*,*ky*)**. Although dilations do not result in congruent figures, the orientation of the figure is preserved; consequently, corresponding line segments will be parallel.

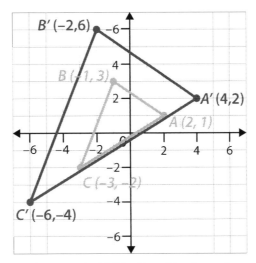

The triangle ABC is dilated by the scale factor 2 to produce triangle A'B'C'.

Fiure 6.18. Dilation

Importantly, dilations do NOT create images that are congruent to the original because the size of each dimension is increased or decreased (the only exception being if the scale factor is exactly 1). However, the shape of the figure is maintained. The corresponding angle measures will be congruent, but the corresponding side lengths will be **proportional**. In other words, the image and pre-image will be **similar** shapes.

Considering congruent and similar shapes as a consequence of transformations is helpful in understanding what is meant by congruence and similarity. Often, however, the fact that two shapes are congruent or similar is given as a fact, unrelated to a transformation. In that case, much information is being given in a single statement. For example, given that $\triangle ABC \sim \triangle PQR$ (~ is read *is similar to*) tells the reader that $\angle A \cong \angle P$, $\angle B \cong \angle Q$, $\angle C \cong \angle R$, and $\frac{AB}{PQ} = \frac{BC}{QR} = \frac{AC}{PR} = k$ (where k is the constant of proportionality).

TRANSFORMING COORDINATES

Transformations in a plane can actually be thought of as functions. An input pair of coordinates, when acted upon by a transformation, results in a pair of output coordinates. Each point is moved to a unique new point (a one-to-one correspondence).

Go on →

Table 6.4. How Coordinates Change for Transformations in a Plane

Type of Transformation	Coordinate Changes
Translation right *m* units and up *n* units	$(x,y) \rightarrow (x + m, y + n)$
Rotations about the origin in positive (counterclockwise) direction	
Rotation 90°	$(x,y) \rightarrow (-y, x)$
Rotation 180°	$(x,y) \rightarrow (-x, -y)$
Rotation 270°	$(x,y) \rightarrow (y, -x)$
Reflections about the	
x-axis	$(x,y) \rightarrow (x, -y)$
y-axis	$(x,y) \rightarrow (-x, y)$
line **y = x**	$(x,y) \rightarrow (y, x)$
Dilations about the origin by a factor of *k*	
0 < k < 1 → size reduced	
k > 1 → size enlarged	$(x,y) \rightarrow (kx, ky)$

SAMPLE QUESTIONS

20) Triangle *ABC* with coordinates (2, 8), (10, 2), and (6, 8) is transformed in the plane as shown in the diagram. What transformations result in the image triangle *A'B'C'*?

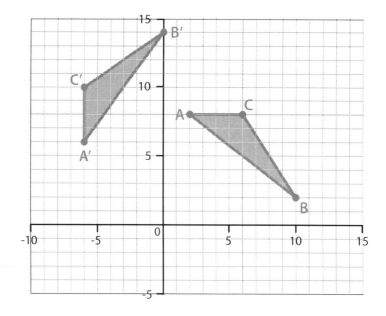

Answer:

Since the orientation of the triangle is different from the original, it must have been rotated. A counterclockwise rotation of 90° about the point *A* (2, 8) results in a triangle with the same orientation. Then the triangle must be translated to move it to the image location. Pick one point, say *A*, and determine the translation necessary to move it to point *A'*. In this case, each point on the pre-image must be translated 8 units left and 2 units down. **This could be written {−8, −2}.** Note that other transformations could also result in the same image. For example, triangle ABC could be rotated clockwise 270° and then translated.

21) If quadrilateral *ABCD* has vertices *A* (−6, 4), *B* (−6, 8), *C* (2, 8), and *D* (4, −4), what are the new vertices if *ABCD* is increased by a factor of 5?

Answer:

Changing coordinates to account for a dilation transformation requires that all the coordinates be multiplied by the scale factor. The new vertices are **A (−30, 20), B (−30, 40), C (10, 40), and D (20, −20).**

TRANSFORMATIONS AND COORDINATE GEOMETRY PROOF

Using transformation and coordinates can be a powerful method of proving geometric theorems. For example, the image of a line in a plane that has been translated within the plane is clearly parallel to its pre-image. This can be proven using transformations.

Consider any line with slope $m = \frac{\Delta y}{\Delta x}$ = $\frac{\text{rise}}{\text{run}}$, as shown in Figure 6.19. The Δy can be represented with a vertical segment, and the Δx with a horizontal segment, which forms a triangle as shown. When the line is shifted vertically down 4 units (or in any direction, really), the triangle representing slope will be congruent to the original slope triangle. Thus, the rise and run are equivalent, and the slopes must be equal. This proves that lines are parallel if and only if they have equal slopes.

Similarly, a rotation transformation can prove that two lines are perpendicular if and only if they have opposite, reciprocal slopes. This is facilitated by using a line that goes through (0,0) and rotating about that point. This can be assumed since any line can be translated to the origin without changing its slope, as seen in the previous example.

If the line with positive slope in this diagram contains points (0,0) and (*a*,*b*), then the slope of this line is $\frac{b}{a}$. When the line is

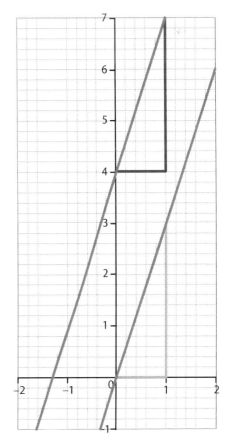

Figure 6.19. Translation of a Line in a Plane

rotated 90° about the origin, point $(a,b) \rightarrow (-b,a)$, according to the rules of rotations. Thus, the image line passes through $(0,0)$ and $(-b,a)$ and has slope $\frac{a}{-b} = -\frac{a}{b}$. Notice that the slope of the image line is the opposite, reciprocal (flip) of the pre-image line. This proves the theorem.

In the Figure 3.20, the slope of the pre-image line is 3, whereas the slope of the perpendicular image line is $-\frac{1}{3}$.

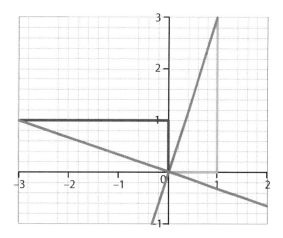

Figure 6.20. Rotation of a Line in a Plane

Another theorem that can be proven using coordinate geometry is that **all circles are similar to one another**. Suppose that circle 1 has radius r_1 and center (h,k), and circle 2 has radius r_2 $(r_2 > r_1)$ and center (a,b). Circle 2 can be re-centered to (h,k) by doing a horizontal translation of $h - a$ and a vertical translation $k - b$. Then a dilation can be performed about the center with a scale factor of $\frac{r_1}{r_2}$. This results in the image of circle 2 landing right on top of circle 1, showing that the circles are similar.

All equations for two-dimensional lines have a slope, a zero slope, or an undefined slope. A horizontal line has zero slope and a vertical line has undefined slope (since its slope would be the opposite, reciprocal of a horizontal line, which would require division by 0).

SAMPLE QUESTIONS

22) **Identify three lines perpendicular to $y = 3x + 3$.**

Answer:

There are an infinite number of lines perpendicular to this line since the line does not stop. Three possibilities are $y = -\frac{1}{3}x + 3$, $y = -\frac{1}{3}x$, and $y = -\frac{1}{3}x - 3$. These four equations are depicted below. The original equation is the only line with a positive slope. Note that all of the lines perpendicular to $y = 3x + 3$ are parallel to one another. Any line with the form $y = -\frac{1}{3}x + b$, where b is any real number, is perpendicular to the original line.

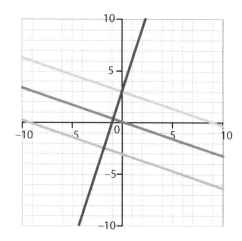

23) If one line has a slope of $\frac{k}{6}$ and a line parallel to that line has a slope of $\frac{k-10}{12}$, what is the slope of a line perpendicular to both these lines?

Answer:

Since the slopes of the two given lines are equal, x can be solved for by setting these two equations equal to one another:

$\frac{k}{6} = \frac{k-10}{12}$

$12k = 6k - 60$

$6k = -60$

$k = -10$

If k is equal to -10, then the slope of these parallel lines is $-\frac{5}{3}$. **A line perpendicular to both of these lines would have a slope of $\frac{3}{5}$.**

Statistics and Probability

The statistics and probability sections below will provide multiple ways to collect, interpret, and display data. **Data** is simply the result of an observation or measurement. Data is often collected when an experiment or survey is performed. Conclusions are drawn from this data using various mathematical formulas.

To collect data, investigators run experiments or observe behavior. In an **experiment**, a treatment is applied to a group (of people, animals, plants, etc.), and the effect of that treatment is observed. In a **randomized experiment**, the subjects are randomly split into two groups (by a flip of a coin or a random number generator, for example). One group is a **control** group and does not receive the treatment, and the other group does receive the treatment. Then measurements are conducted on each group, and results are compared. In an **observational study** no treatment is applied, but researchers observe and measure some variable of interest. An example of an observational study is studying the relationship between left- or right-handedness and industrial accidents. No treatment would be applied to either group in this situation.

Information is frequently used to make statements about an entire population. In these cases, because collecting data from every member of the population is impossible, statisticians collect data from a small, random, but specific subset of the entire population. This random **sample** enables inferences to be made about the entire population. There are a variety of methods of creating a representative sample that are beyond the scope of this text, but it is important to note that statistics are only as good as the experiment and sampling methods used. Too small a sample will not represent the larger population, and a sample that is not representative of the population introduces **bias** into the experiment. For example, if a survey was to be conducted about Americans' feelings on race relations, bias could occur if the sample did not include people of different races, sexes, and geographical locations (including urban, suburban, and rural locations).

Describing Sets of Data

Measures of Central Tendency

If there are more than two measurements of a certain event or phenomenon, central values help identify trends in the entirety of measurements. There are three such **central tendencies** that describe the "center" of the data in different ways. The **mean** is the arithmetic average and is found by dividing the sum of all measurements by the number of measurements. The equation for the mean, can be written as follows:

$$\text{population mean} = \mu = \frac{x_1 + x_2 + \ldots x_N}{N} = \frac{\Sigma x}{N} \qquad \text{sample mean} = \bar{x} = \frac{x_1 + x_2 + \ldots x_n}{n} = \frac{\Sigma x}{n}$$

The data points are represented by xs with subscripts; the sum is denoted using the Greek letter sigma $(\Sigma)x$; N is the number of data points in the entire population; and n is the number of data points in a sample set.

The **median** divides the measurements into two equal halves. The median is the measurement right in the middle of an odd set of measurements (the fifth-largest in nine measurements) or the average of the two middle numbers in an even data set (the average of the fifth- and sixth-largest measurements of ten total measurements). When calculating the median, it is important to order the data values from least to greatest before attempting to locate the middle value. The **mode** is simply the measurement that occurs most often. There can be many modes in a data set, or no mode. Since measures of central tendency describe a *center* of the data, all three of these measures will be between the lowest and highest data values (inclusive).

Unlike the mean, the median is not affected by very large or very small unusual measurements (**outliers**). Notice that in the following sample questions, both have the same data points, but the median is not skewed by the single large value. That is, the median is much closer to the terms in the data set than the mean is. If there is a high outlier, the mean will be greater than the median; if there is a low or negative outlier, the mean will be lower than the median. When outliers are present, the median is a better measure of the center of the data than the mean is.

SAMPLE QUESTIONS

1) **What is the mean of the following data set? {1000, 0.1, 10, 1}**

Answer:

The mean to the nearest hundredth is found as follows:

$\frac{1000 + 0.1 + 10 + 1}{4} = \textbf{252.78}$

2) **What is the median of the following data set? {1000, 10, 1, 0.1}**

Answer:

Since there are an even number of data points in the set, the median will be the mean of the two middle numbers. Order the numbers from least to greatest: 0.1, 1, 10, and 1000. The two middle numbers are 1 and 10, and their mean is:

$$\frac{1 + 10}{2} = \mathbf{5.5}$$

3)   **Josey has an average of 81 on four equally weighted tests she has taken in her statistics class. She wants to determine what grade she must receive on her fifth test so that her mean is 83, which will give her a B in the course, but she does not remember her other scores. What grade must she receive on her fifth test?**

Answer:

Even though Josey does not know her test scores, she knows her average. Therefore it can be assumed that each test score was 81, since four scores of 81 would average to 81. To find the score, x, that she needs:

$$\frac{4(81) + x}{5} = 83$$

$$324 + x = 415$$

$$x = 91$$

Josey must score a 91 on the last test to have a mean score of 83.

Measures of Variation

The values in a data set can be very close together (close to the mean), or very spread out. This is called the **spread** or **dispersion** of the data. Sometimes most of the data is close to the mean, but there are one or more values far from the mean. These are called **outliers**. There are a few **measures of variation** (or **measures of dispersion**) that quantify the spread within a data set. **Range** is the difference between the largest and smallest data points in a set:

R = largest data point – smallest data point

Notice range depends on only two data points, the two extremes. Sometimes these data points are outliers; regardless, for a large data set, relying on only two data points is not an exact tool. The understanding of the data set can be improved by calculating **quartiles**. To calculate quartiles, first arrange the data in ascending order and find the set's median (also called quartile 2 or Q2). Then find the median of the lower half of the data, called quartile 1 (Q1), and the median of the upper half of the data, called quartile 3 (Q3). These three points divide the data into four equal groups of data (thus the word *quartile*). Each quartile contains 25% of the data.

Interquartile range (IQR) provides a more reliable range that is not as affected by extremes. IQR is the difference between the third quartile data point and the first quartile data point:

$$IQR = Q_3 - Q_1$$

The interquartile range gives the spread of the middle 50% of the data.

A measure of variation that depends on the mean is **standard deviation**, which uses every data point in a set and basically calculates the average distance of each data point from the mean of the data. Standard deviation can be computed for an entire population, if the data set is not too large, or for a sample of the population. The formula for standard deviation is slightly different based on whether it is a population standard deviation (denoted by σ or lowercase sigma) or a sample standard deviation (denoted by the letter s):

$$\sigma = \sqrt{\frac{\Sigma(x_i - \mu)^2}{N}} \qquad s = \sqrt{\frac{\Sigma(x_i - \bar{x})^2}{n - 1}}$$

HELPFUL HINT

Standard deviation and variance are also affected by extreme values. Though much simpler to calculate, interquartile range is the more accurate depiction of how the data is scattered when there are outlier values.

Thus, to calculate standard deviation, the difference between the mean μ or $\bar{x}$ or and each data point x_i is calculated. Each of these differences is squared (this is done mostly to make all the differences positive). The average of the squared values is computed by summing the squares and dividing by N or $(n - 1)$. (The reason for dividing by $n - 1$ and not just n is beyond the scope of this text.) Then the square root is taken, to "undo" the previous squaring.

The **variance** of a data set is simply the square of the standard variation:

$$V = \sigma^2 = \frac{1}{N} \sum_{i=1}^{N} (x_i - \mu)^2$$

Variance measures how narrowly or widely the data points are distributed. A variance of zero means every data point is the same; a large variance means there are a relatively small amount of data points near the set's mean.

SAMPLE QUESTIONS

4)   What are the range and interquartile range of the following set? {3, 9, 49, 64, 81, 100, 121, 144, 169}

Answer:

The range is the difference between the largest and smallest data points:

$R = 169 - 3 = 166$

The set's median is 81, which is Q_2. The median of the bottom half of the data is midway between 9 and 49, which, averaging those two numbers, is 29. This is Q_1. The median of the upper half of the data is midway between 121 and 144, which, averaging those two numbers, is 132.5. This is Q_3. Thus, the $IQR = Q_3 - Q_1 = 132.5 - 29 = $ **103.5**.

5)   In a group of 7 people, 1 person has no children, 2 people have 1 child, 2 people have 2 children, 1 person has 5 children, and 1 person has 17 children. To the nearest hundredth of a child, what is the standard deviation in this group? What is the variance?

Answer:

{0, 1, 1, 2, 2, 5, 17}	Create a data set out of this scenario.
$\mu = \dfrac{0 + 1 + 1 + 2 + 2 + 5 + 17}{7} = 4$	Calculate the population mean.
$(0 - 4)^2 = (-4)^2 = 16$ $(1 - 4)^2 = (-3)^2 = 9$ $(1 - 4)^2 = (-3)^2 = 9$ $(2 - 4)^2 = (-2)^2 = 4$ $(2 - 4)^2 = (-2)^2 = 4$ $(5 - 4)^2 = (1)^2 = 1$ $(17 - 4)^2 = (13)^2 = 169$	Find the square of the difference of each term and the mean $(x_i - \mu)^2$.
$\sigma = \sqrt{\dfrac{212}{7}} = \sqrt{30.28} = 5.50$	Plug the sum (Σ) of these squares, 212, into the standard deviation formula.

The standard deviation is 5.50 and the variance is 30.28. Notice that both the mean and the standard deviation are greatly skewed by the outlier value 17. Of the 7 people, 5 have fewer than 3 children, but the mean number of children is 4. Most of the people have within 1 or 2 children of one another, but the deviation is more than 5 children. An outlier seriously skews statistics, especially in a small data set.

6) **What happens to the mean and the standard deviation of a data set if all n values of the data set are increased by the same amount? What if each data value is multiplied by the same value?**

Answer:

When all the members of a data set are increased by the same amount, the sum of the data is increased by the product of that number times the number of values n. For example, if each member of a data set with ten values were increased by 4, the sum would be increased by 40. To calculate the new mean:

$$new\ mean = \frac{3a + 3b + 3c + 3d}{4} = \frac{3(a + b + c + d)}{4} = 3\left(\frac{a + b + c + d}{4}\right) = 3\ (old\ mean)$$

The new mean is just shifted up by the amount each data value is increased. Since each data value is shifted up the same amount, and the mean is also shifted up by that amount, the deviation between each value and the mean will be unchanged.

Thus, when the same value is added to each element of a data set, the mean increases by the same value and the standard deviation is unchanged.

When all the members of a data set are multiplied by the same amount, the sum of the values will be multiplied by that amount due to the distributive property, and the mean will also be multiplied by the same value. Say there are four values, a, b, c, and d, and each is multiplied by 3:

In the standard deviation formula, since each of the differences will also be multiplied by 3, the squares of the difference will be multiplied by 9, so the variance is multiplied by 9. But after the square root of the variance is taken to calculate the standard deviation, standard deviation is changed by a factor of 3.

Thus both the mean and the standard deviation of a data set is changed by the same factor (k) when each value of the data set is multiplied by some factor k.

Box Plots

A **box plot** depicts the median and quartiles along a scaled number line. A box plot is meant to summarize the data in a visual manner and emphasize central trends while decreasing the pull of outlier data. To construct a box plot:

1. Create a number line that begins at the lowest data point and terminates at the highest data point.
2. Find the quartiles of the data: Q_1, the median (Q_2), and Q_3. Create a horizontal rectangle (the "box") whose left border is Q_1 and right border is Q_3.
3. Draw a vertical line within the box to mark the median.
4. Draw a horizontal line going from the left edge of the box to the smallest data value.
5. Draw a horizontal line going from the right edge of the box to the largest data value.

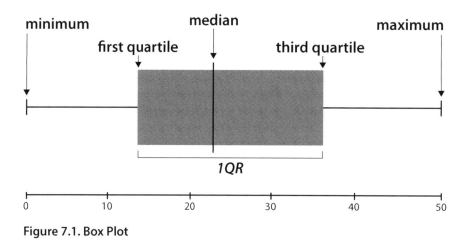

Figure 7.1. Box Plot

When reading a box plot, the following stands out:

▶ The length of the box is the IQR, $Q_3 - Q_1$, hence the middle 50% of the data.

▶ Each of the four pieces (the whiskers and two pieces in the box) represent 25% of the data.

▶ If the median is skewed more toward the right, the second quartile has more data points in it; if the median is skewed more toward the left, the third quartile has more data points in it.

▶ The horizontal lines (whiskers) show by their length whether the data higher or lower than the middle 50% is more or less prominent.

▶ Reading from left to right: the horizontal line (whisker) shows the spread of the first quarter; the box's left compartment shows the spread of the second quarter; the box's right compartment shows the spread of the third quarter; and the right horizontal line (whisker) shows the spread of the fourth quarter.

> **HELPFUL HINT**
>
> Box plots are also known as box-and-whisker plots, because if they are drawn correctly the two horizontal lines look like whiskers.

SAMPLE QUESTION

7)   A recent survey asked 8 people how many pairs of shoes they wear per week. Their answers are in the following data set: {1, 3, 5, 5, 7, 8, 12}. Construct a box plot from this data.

Answer:

Create a number line that begins at 1 and ends at 12. Q_1 is 3, the median (Q_2) is 5, and Q_3 is 8. A rectangle must be drawn whose length is 5 and that borders on Q_1 and Q_3. Mark the median of 5 within the rectangle. Draw a horizontal line going left to 1. Draw a horizontal line going right to 12.

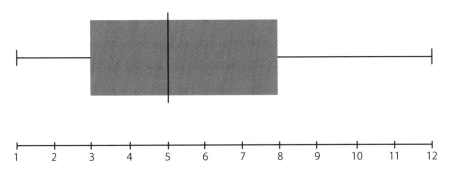

GRAPHS, CHARTS, AND TABLES

PIE CHARTS

Pie charts summarize the prominence of categories in a data set. Appropriate uses of pie charts may include budgets, production breakdowns, population analyses, and data that is best expressed as percentages. A pie chart simply states the proportion of each category within the whole. To construct a pie chart, the categories of a data set must be determined. The frequency of each category must be found and that frequency converted to a percent of the total. To draw the pie chart, determine the angle of each slice by multiplying the percentage by 360°.

SAMPLE QUESTION

8) A firm is screening applicants for a job by education-level attainment. There are 125 individuals in the pool. By the highest level of education attained in the pool, 5 have a doctorate, 20 have a master's degree, 40 have a bachelor's degree, 30 have an associate degree, and the remaining only have a high school degree. Construct a pie chart showing the highest level of education attained by the applicants.

Answer:

The total given to us is 125, meaning there are 30 applicants with just a high school degree. Next, a frequency table must be created. The percent is found by dividing the frequency of a specific category by the total (125). Multiply that percent by 360° to get the angle measure:

Category	Frequency	Percent	Angle Measure
High School	30	24%	86.4
Associate	30	24%	86.4
Bachelor's	40	32%	115.2
Master's	20	16%	57.6
Doctorate	5	4%	14.4

The pie chart below expresses the table's data.

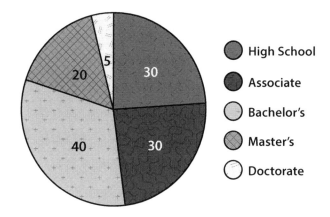

Scatter Plots

A scatter plot is displayed in the first quadrant of the *xy*-plane where all numbers are positive. A scatter plot is an easy way to tell if there is a correlation between two variables in a data set. Data points are plotted as ordered pairs, with one variable along the horizontal axis and the other along the vertical axis. Constructing a scatter plot requires the plotting of every point on a domain and range that includes every data outcome. Often, but not always, the data points will show a linear tendency. There is a **positive correlation** (expressed as a positive slope) if increasing one variable appears to result in an increase in the other variable. A **negative correlation** (expressed as a negative slope) occurs when an increase in one variable causes a decrease in the other. If the scatter plot shows no discernible pattern, then there is no correlation (a zero, mixed, or indiscernible slope). Scatter plots are often used for lab experiments and any attempt to establish a causal link.

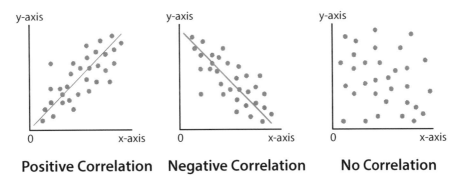

Positive Correlation   Negative Correlation   No Correlation

Figure 7.2. Scatter Plots and Correlation

Working from data points, or using the regression feature of a calculator, a regression equation can be created that encapsulates the directionality of the scatter plot. If the regression equation is graphed, the resulting line (or curve) is known as a regression line (or curve). This is also known as the "line of best fit." To figure out how well the regression line (or curve) fits every data point on a scatter plot, the equation's **correlation coefficient** (r) can be considered. The formula for computing the correlation coefficient is complex, but the calculator will provide this number along with the regression line if the diagnostics feature is on. The value of r is between –1 and 1. The closer r is to 1 (if the line has a positive slope) or –1 (if the line has a negative slope), the better the regression line fits the data. The closer the r value is to 0, the weaker the correlation between the line and the data. Generally, if the absolute value of the correlation coefficient is 0.8 or higher, then it is considered to be a strong correlation, while an |r| value of less than 0.5 is considered a weak correlation.

To determine which curve is the "best fit" for a set of data, **residuals** are calculated. The calculator automatically calculates and saves these values to a list called RESID. These values are all the differences between the actual y-value of data points and the y-value calculated by the best-fit line or curve for that x-value. These values can be plotted on an xy-plane with the x-values along the x-axis and the residuals along the y-axis. This is called a **residual plot**. The residual plot helps determine if a line is the best model for the data. Residual points that are randomly dispersed above and below the horizontal indicate that a linear model is appropriate, while a u shape or upside-down u shape indicate a nonlinear model would be more appropriate.

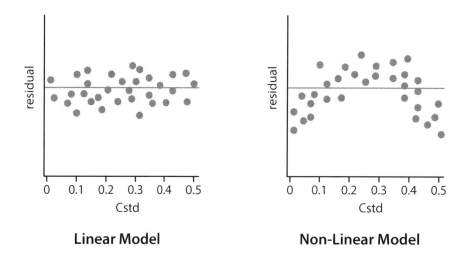

Figure 7.3. Residual Plots

Once a best-fit line (or curve) is established, it can be used to estimate output values given an input value within the domain of the data. For a short extension outside that domain, reasonable predictions may be possible. However, the further from the domain of the data the line is extended, the greater the reduction in the accuracy of the prediction. For example, a model is created from the growth data of a city over a twenty-year period; that model will not be a good predictor of the population of the city in one hundred years.

It is important to note here that just because two variables have a strong positive or negative correlation, it cannot necessarily be inferred that those two quantities have a **causal** relationship—that is, that one variable changing *causes* the other quantity to change. There are often other factors that play into their relationship. For example, a positive correlation can be found between the number of ice cream sales and the number of shark attacks at a beach. It would be incorrect to say that selling more ice cream *causes* an increase in shark attacks. It is much more likely that on hot days more ice cream is sold, and many more people are swimming, so one of them is more likely to get attacked by a shark. Confusing correlation and causation is one of the most common statistical errors people make.

HELPFUL HINT

A graphing calculator can provide the regression line, *r* value, and residuals list.

9) Based on the scatter plot below, where the x-axis represents hours spent studying per week and the y-axis represents the average percent grade on exams during the school year, is there a correlation between the amount of studying for a test and test results?

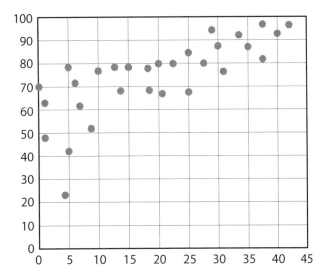

Answer:

There is a somewhat weak positive correlation. As the number of hours spent studying increases, the average percent grade also generally increases.

LINE GRAPHS

Line graphs are used to display a relationship between two variables, such as change over time. Like scatter plots, line graphs exist in quadrant I of the xy-plane. Line graphs are constructed by graphing each point and connecting each point to the next consecutive point by a line. To create a line graph, it may be necessary to consolidate data into single bivariate data points. Thus, a line graph is a function, with each x-value having exactly one y-value, whereas a scatter plot may have multiple y-values for one x-value.

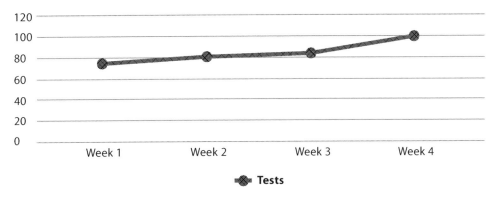

Figure 7.4. Line Graph

SAMPLE QUESTION

10) Create a line graph based on the following survey values, where the first column represents an individual's age and the other represents that individual's reported happiness level on a 20-point scale (0 being the least happy that person has been and 20 being the happiest). Then interpret the resulting graph to determine whether the following statement is true or false: *On average, middle-aged people are less happy than young or older people are.*

Age	Happiness
12	16
13	15
20	18
15	12
40	5
17	17
18	18
19	15
42	7
70	17
45	10
60	12
63	15
22	14
27	15
36	12
33	10
44	8
55	10
80	10
15	13
40	8
17	15
18	17
19	20
22	16
27	15
36	9
33	10
44	6

Answer:

To construct a line graph, the data must be ordered into consolidated categories by averaging the data of people who have the same age so that the data is one-to-one. For example, there are two twenty-two-year-olds who are reporting. Their average happiness level is 15. When all the data has been consolidated and ordered from least to greatest, the table and graph below can be presented.

Age	Happiness
12	16
13	15
15	12.5
17	16
18	17.5
19	17.5
20	18
22	15
27	15
33	10
36	10.5
40	6.5
42	7
44	7
45	10
55	10
60	12
63	15
70	17
80	10

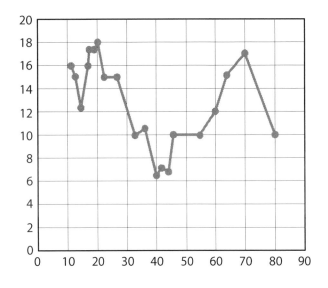

Average Happiness Rating Versus Age

The statement that, on average, middle-aged people are less happy than young or older people appears to be true. According to the graph, people in their thirties, forties, and fifties are less happy than people in their teens, twenties, sixties, and seventies.

BAR GRAPHS

Like line graphs, **bar graphs** compare changes between groups or over time. The data here is grouped into certain ranges and represented by rectangles (a bar graph's rectangles can be vertical or horizontal, depending on whether the dependent variable is placed on the *x*- or *y*-axis). Instead of the *xy*-plane, however, one axis is made up of types of categories. Bar graphs are useful because the differences between categories are easy to see. Reading a bar graph requires understanding that the width or height (depending on vertical or horizontal orientation) of each rectangle indicates the total within that category, and the difference among the rectangles shows the difference year to year.

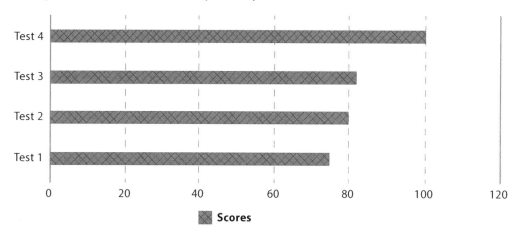

Figure 7.5. Bar Graph

SAMPLE QUESTION

11) A company X had a profit of $10,000 in 2010, $12,000 in 2011, and each of the following two years saw a 30% increase in profits. Create a bar graph displaying the profit from each of these four years.

Answer:

If 2012 saw a 30% increase from 2011, that year's profit is 1.3($12,000) = $15,600; by the same method, the profit in 2013 was $20,280. The bar graph below captures this data:

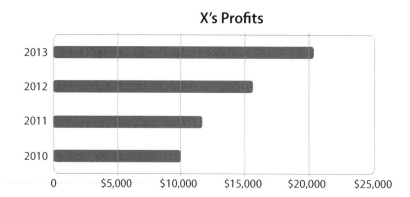

STEM-AND-LEAF PLOTS

Stem-and-leaf plots are ways of organizing large amounts of data by grouping it into classes. All data points are broken into two parts: a stem and a leaf. For instance, the number 512 might be broken into a stem of 5 and a leaf of 12. All data in the

500 range would appear in the same row (this group of data is a class). Usually a simple key is provided to explain how the data is being represented. For instance, 5|12 = 512 would show that the stems are representing hundreds. The advantage of this display is that it shows general density and shape of the data in a compact display, yet all original data points are preserved and available. It is also easy to find medians and quartiles from this display.

Stem	Leaf
0	5
1	6, 7
2	8, 3, 6
3	4, 5, 9, 5, 5, 8, 5
4	7, 7, 7, 8
5	5, 4
6	0

Figure 7.6. Stem and Leaf Plot

SAMPLE QUESTION

12) The table gives the weights of wrestlers (in pounds) for a certain competition. What is the mean, median, and IQR of the data?

2	05, 22, 53, 40
3	07, 22, 29, 45, 89, 96, 98
4	10, 25, 34
6	21

Key: 2|05 = 205 pounds

Answer:

The mean weight is calculated by adding up all data values, and dividing by the number of wrestlers:

$mean = \frac{5281}{15} =$ **353.1 lbs.**

An advantage of this kind of display is that without actually calculating the median, it is clear that it is going to be in the 300 lb. category. A good display helps the reader interpret the data quickly. By counting all the "leaves," the number of data points can be determined. There are 15 wrestlers competing. The median (also called Q_2) will be the eighth data point (leaving seven on either side). Thus, counting eight leaves, **345 is the median weight**. Finding the median of each of the halves requires finding the fourth data point, 240 (Q_1), and the eighth plus fourth, or twelfth data point, 410 (Q_3). Thus, the interquartile range is $Q_3 - Q_1 = 410 - 240 =$ **170.**

FREQUENCY TABLES AND HISTOGRAMS

The frequency of a particular data point is the number of times that data point occurs. Constructing a frequency table requires that the data or data classes be arranged in ascending order in one column and the frequency in another column.

A histogram is used to compare the frequency of specified ranges of data. It is a graphical representation of a frequency table. A histogram is constructed in quadrant 1 of the *xy*-plane, with data in each equal-width class presented as a bar and the height of each bar representing the frequency of that class. Unlike bar graphs, histograms cannot have gaps between bars. A histogram is used to determine the distribution of data among the classes. Examples of histograms include population statistics, arrivals and departures at airports, and ecological studies such as the average temperature over a year.

Histograms can be symmetrical, skewed left or right, or multimodal (data spread around). Note that **skewed left** means the peak of the data is on the *right*, with a tail to the left, while **skewed right** means the peak is on the *left*, with a tail to the right. This seems counterintuitive to many; the "left" or "right" always refers to the tail of the data. This is because a long tail to the right, for example, means there are high outlier values that are skewing the data to the right.

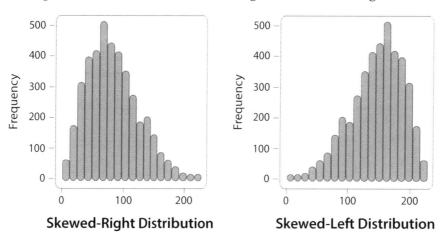

Skewed-Right Distribution   **Skewed-Left Distribution**

Figure 7.7. Histograms

A **two-way frequency table** compares **categorical data** (data in more than one category) of two related variables (bivariate data). Two-way frequency tables are also called **contingency tables** and are often used to analyze survey results. One category is displayed along the top of the table and the other category down along the side. Rows and columns are added and the sums appear at the end of the row or column. The sum of all the row data must equal the sum of all the column data. From a two-way frequency table, the **joint relative frequency** of a particular category can be calculated by taking the number in the row and column of the categories in question and dividing by the total number surveyed. This gives the percent of the total in that particular category. Sometimes the **conditional relative frequency** is of interest. In this case, calculate the relative frequency confined to a single row or column, because a condition was given that restricts the data examined.

Students by Grade and Gender

	9th grade	10th grade	11th grade	12th grade	Total
Male	57	63	75	61	256
Female	54	42	71	60	227
Total	111	105	146	121	483

Figure 7.8. Two-Way Frequency Table

SAMPLE QUESTIONS

13) **A café owner tracked the number of customers he had over a twelve-hour period one day in the frequency table below. Display the data in a histogram and determine what kind of distribution there is in the data.**

Time	Number of Customers
6 a.m. – 8 a.m.	5
8 a.m. – 9 a.m.	6
9 a.m. – 10 a.m.	5
10 a.m. – 12 p.m.	23
12 p.m. – 2 p.m.	24
2 p.m. – 4 p.m.	9
4 p.m. – 6 p.m.	4

Answer:

Since time is the independent variable, it is on the *x*-axis and the number of customers is on the *y*-axis. For the histogram to correctly display data continuously, categories on the *x*-axis must be equal 2-hour segments. The 8 a.m. – 9 a.m. and 9 a.m. – 10 a.m. categories must be combined for a total

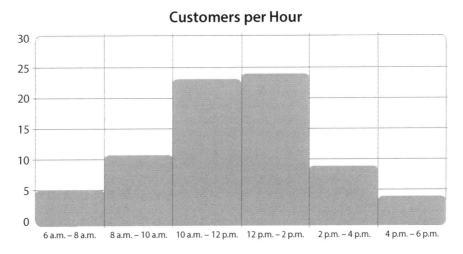

of 11 customers in that time period. The correct graph is displayed below. Although not perfectly symmetrical, the amount of customers peaks in the middle and is therefore considered symmetrical.

14) **In a class of 30 students, 10% got an A, 30% got a B, 30% received a C, 10% received a D, and the remainder received an F on a recent exam (the minimum possible grade recorded was a 50). Create a frequency table summarizing this data. Estimate the average (mean) grade on the exam by using the midpoint of each class of grade.**

Answer:

Frequency tables deal with total frequency. Every percent then must be multiplied by 30 students to figure out the total number of students in each grade category. Additionally, the number of students with an F can be found by multiplying the remaining percent by 30: $(1 - 0.10 - 0.30 - 0.30 - 0.10)$ $(30) = 6$.

Grade	Number of Students
A (90 – 100)	3
B (80 – 89)	9
C (70 – 79)	9
D (60 – 69)	3
F (50 – 59)	6

An estimate of the class average using approximate midpoints of each class and computing the weighted average:

$$\frac{3(95) + 9(85) + 9(75) + 3(65) \; 6(55)}{30} = \frac{2250}{3.0} = \textbf{75}.$$

15) **Cineflix movie theater polled its moviegoers on a weeknight to determine their favorite type of movie. The results are in the two-way frequency table below. How many people were polled? Which of the following statements are true based on the results of the survey in the table?**

Moviegoers	Comedy	Action	Horror	Totals
Male	15	25	21	61
Female	8	18	17	43
Totals	23	43	38	104

A.   Men choose the horror genre more frequently than women do.

B.   Action films are the most popular type of movie offered.

C.   About 1 in 5 moviegoers prefers comedy films.

D.   More than 40% of female moviegoers prefer action films.

Answer:

The total number of people polled can be found in the bottom-right corner of the table. This is the total of the male and female rows, and also the total of the movie-type columns.

Based on this survey, it is not fair to say that men choose horror movies more than women do, so statement A is false. If percentages are calculated, $\frac{21}{61}$ men or 34.4% of men preferred horror movies, while $\frac{17}{43}$ or 39.5% of women chose horror. Notice this differs from the statement, "Of the people who prefer horror, men are more represented," which is asking for the *conditional* relative frequency (the condition being "people who like horror," focusing the attention on the 38 people in the horror column). If this were the case, $\frac{21}{38}$ would be men and $\frac{17}{38}$ would be women, so *of the people who prefer horror,* there would be a higher percentage of men.

Statement B is true, since 43 out of the total 104 moviegoers preferred action movies, the highest total of all the categories. Statement C is also true, since $\frac{23}{104}$ or about 22%, a little more than 1 in 5, preferred comedies.

Statement D is looking at a conditional relative frequency. This statement focuses on the row involving females. There are a total of 43 females. Of those females, 18 prefer action films, so the conditional relative frequency is $\frac{18}{43} = 0.418$, which is more than 40%, making statement D true.

Another way to analyze the data is to make a two-way *relative* frequency table that shows percentages of the total number surveyed in each cell. To do so, divide all totals by the total number surveyed (104 in this case):

Moviegoers	Comedy	Action	Horror	Totals
Male	0.15	0.24	0.20	0.59
Female	0.08	0.17	0.16	0.41
Totals	0.23	0.41	0.36	1.00

COUNTING PRINCIPLES

THE FUNDAMENTAL COUNTING PRINCIPLE

An **outcome** is any possible result of an experiment, such as the outcome "heads" in a coin toss. The set of all possible outcomes for a specific experiment is called the **sample space**. The sample space for tossing a single coin is {H = heads, T = tails}. Any outcome's probability is based on all the unique possibilities that could occur, so being able to calculate all the possible outcomes is critical to finding probabilities. The number of unique possible outcomes for any sequence of events is often calculated by the **fundamental counting principle**. This principle states that the total number of possible outcomes is the product of the total possible number of outcomes in each trial. Suppose a coin is tossed three times. Each toss of the coin is a trial. Each trial has two possible outcomes. By the fundamental counting principle, the total number of possibilities (the number of elements in the sample space) when a coin is tossed three times is $2 \times 2 \times 2 = 8$. They are {HHH, HHT, HTT, HTH, TTH, THH, THT, TTT}.

SAMPLE QUESTIONS

16) **A personal assistant is struggling to pick a shirt, tie, and cufflink set that go together. If his client has 70 shirts, 2 ties, and 5 cufflinks, how many possible combinations does he have to consider?**

Answer:

The formula is always the same. The total number of combinations is (70)(2)(5) = 700. **There are 700 shirt, tie, and cufflink combinations.**

17) **A bank requires a four-digit personal identification number (PIN) for access to an automated teller machine. If only numbers 1 – 9 are allowed, how many different four-digit PIN numbers are there?**

Answer:

Assuming repeat digits are allowed, there are 9 possible numbers for each of the 4 digits (each digit is a "trial"). Thus, there are $9 \times 9 \times 9 \times 9 = $ **6561 possible PIN codes.**

18) **How many ways can four distinct books be arranged on the shelf?**

Answer:

As in the previous problem, there are four slots to be filled. Unlike the previous problem, however, each slot does not have the same number of choices. For the first slot, there are four book choices. Once one book is chosen to be put on the shelf, there are only three book choices for the second slot, two for the third slot, and one for the last. The total number of ways to arrange the four books is $4 \times 3 \times 2 \times 1 = $ **24.**

COMBINATIONS AND PERMUTATIONS

Combinations and permutations are arrangements of a set of objects. In **combinations**, the order of the arrangement or selection does not matter. For **permutations**, the order of the arrangement or selection is important. A "combination lock" is therefore *misnamed*—it really should be a *permutation lock*, since the order in which the numbers are dialed is important. An example of a question calling for a combination would be, "How many ways can a committee of three people be chosen from twelve people?" The order in which the people are chosen is not relevant if all the positions on the committee are exactly the same.

The formulas for calculating the number of permutations or combinations both use factorials. Factorials are expressed by an integer, followed by an exclamation point (!). Recall that a factorial $n!$ is the product of n times $(n - 1)$, times $(n - 2)$, etc., until n is multiplied by 1. For example, $3! = 3 \times 2 \times 1 = 6$. Zero factorial is defined to 1, that is $0! = 1$.

Also recall that factorial expressions, when divided, can be simplified. For example,

$$10! \div 8! = \frac{10 \times 9 \times 8 \times 7 \times 6 \times 5 \times 4 \times 3 \times 2 \times 1}{8 \times 7 \times 6 \times 5 \times 4 \times 3 \times 2 \times 1} = 10 \times 9 = 90$$

since all the number from 8 down to 1 cancel. In the following two formulas, represents the total amount of items or actions and represents the total number of these items that are to be selected or ordered.

Permutation Formula	Combination Formula
$P(n,k) = \dfrac{n!}{(n-k)!}$	$C(n,k) = \dfrac{n!}{(n-k)!\,k!}$

Figure 7.9. Permutation and Combination Formulas

The only difference between the two formulas is the k! in the combination denominator. This is to account for redundancy of data with the same values just in a different order. Dividing by this k! reduces the number of possibilities.

The example from the previous section about ordering four books on a shelf is actually a permutation problem. Since each book is unique, when arranging them, the order matters. Using the permutation formula with $n = 4$ items, all $k = 4$ of which are being ordered, yields $P(4,4) = \frac{4!}{(4-4)!} = \frac{4!}{0!} = \frac{4 \times 3 \times 2 \times 1}{1} = 24$, which is the same answer arrived at before.

SAMPLE QUESTIONS

19) **If there are twenty applicants for three open positions, in how many different ways can a team of three be hired?**

Answer:

In this problem, $n = 20$ and $k = 3$. Since the three positions are presumably identical, the order of hiring is not important, so this is a combination problem. Using the combination formula:

$$C(20,3) = \frac{20!}{(20-3)!\,3!} = \frac{20!}{17!\,3!} = \frac{(20)(19)(18)}{3!} = 1140$$

There are **1140 different three-person teams** that can be hired.

Another way to think about this problem is to calculate all the ways that a three-spot team can be created and then divide by how many ways that team of three can be arranged. For the first spot, 20 people can be chosen; for the second, 19; for the third, 18. This gives $(20)(19)(18) = 6840$ teams of three. But this is too many since the order of those three chosen does not matter, so it is necessary to divide by the number of ways possible to order three people $= 3 \times 2 \times 1 = 6$. Dividing, 6840 by 6 gives 1140.

20) At a sandwich shop, a customer has a choice of ten toppings he can add to his sandwich. If three distinct toppings are added, how many three-topping sandwiches are possible?

Answer:

This question is a combination problem—the order does not matter, only that each item added be distinct. Plugging the appropriate values into the equation, it is found that:

$$C(10, 3) = \frac{10!}{(10 - 3)!\, 3!} = 120$$

There are **120 possible sandwiches** with three toppings added out of ten possible ingredients to add.

21) Calculate the number of unique permutations that can be made out of all the letters in the word *pickle*, the number of unique permutations that can be made out of all the letters in the word *cheese*, and the number of unique permutations that can be made out of all the letters in the word *blueberry*.

Answer:

To find the number of unique permutations of the letters of *pickle*, use the permutation formula with the total number of letters $n = 6$, and the number to be arranged $k = 6$.

$$P(6, 6) = \frac{6!}{(6 - 6)!} = \frac{720}{1} = 720$$

(Or think of it as six slots that need to be filled; in the first there are six choices, the second five choices, etc., giving 6! as the answer.)

There are 720 distinct arrangements of the letters in the word *pickle*.

The word *cheese* has the letter *e* that repeats three times. Thus, some permutations of the six letters will be indistinguishable from others, as the reader will be unable to tell one *e* from another. The number of permutations must be divided by the number of ways the three *e*s can be arranged, 3! = 6. The formula is:

total number of permutations = number of ways to arrange 6 letters/number of ways to arrange 3 letters $= \frac{6!}{3!} = 6 \times 5 \times 4 = 120$

There are 120 distinct arrangements of the letters in the word *cheese*.

The word *blueberry* repeats *b* two times, *e* two times, and *r* two times. To calculate the number of unique arrangements of all nine letters, calculate the number of ways to arrange nine items, and divide by the number of ways the *b*s can be arranged (2!), the *e*s can be arranged (2!), and the *r*s can be arranged (2!):

total number of permutations $= \frac{9!}{2!\, 2!\, 2!} = \frac{9!}{8} = 45,360.$

There are 45,360 distinct arrangements of all the letters in the word *blueberry*.

22) Suppose 7 runners are lining up for a race. 3 runners are women and 4 are men. How many ways can they line up if they can line up in any order? How many ways can they line up if the women must be beside each other, and the men must be grouped together?

Answer:

If all 7 can be arranged in any order, there are 7! = **5040 arrangements**. If the women must stay together, and the men must stay together, there are 2 groups that can be arranged in exactly 2 ways (women on the left and men on the right, or vice-versa). Within these groups, the women can be arranged 3! ways and the men 4! ways. Using the fundamental counting principle:

total number of arrangements with men grouped and women grouped =
$2 \times 3! \times 4! = 2 \times 6 \times 24 = $ **288**.

Probability

Probability of a Single Event

Probability is the likelihood of one or a certain number of specific events occurring. The probability of a single event occurring is the number of outcomes in which that event occurs (called **favorable events**) divided by the number of items in the sample space (total possible outcomes):

$$P \text{ (an event)} = \frac{\textit{number of favorable outcomes}}{\textit{total number of possible outcomes}}$$

The probability of any event occurring will always be a fraction or decimal between 0 and 1. It may also be expressed as a percent. An event with 0 probability will never occur and an event with a probability of 1 is certain to occur. The probability of an event not occurring is referred to as that event's **complement**. The sum of an event's probability and the probability of that event's complement will always be 1.

SAMPLE QUESTIONS

23) In an experiment to see if a certain drug works correctly, it is determined that there are 10 distinct equally likely outcomes that would show the drug works incorrectly and 1 that it does work correctly. All else being equal, what is the probability that the experiment shows the drug in question works correctly?

Answer:

The problem specified there are 11 equally likely possible outcomes: 10 negatives and 1 positive. Therefore, the probability of the 1 positive occurring is:

$P \text{ (drug working correctly)} = \frac{1}{11}$

24) **What is the difference between the probability that when a six-sided die is rolled an even number outcome results and the probability that the die lands on the number 5?**

Answer:

In both of these probabilities, the denominator is 6. There are 3 even numbers possible in the first event. There is just 1 possible favorable outcome in the other. The two probabilities are:

P (rolling even) = $\frac{3}{6}$

P (rolling 5) = $\frac{1}{6}$

The difference then is $\frac{2}{6}$ or **$\frac{1}{3}$**.

25) **Only 20 tickets were issued in a raffle. If someone were to buy 6 tickets, what is the probability that person would not win the raffle?**

Answer:

If 6 tickets were purchased, that means 14 remain. Thus, the probability of not winning the raffle is:

P (not winning) = $\frac{14}{20}$

Notice that the sum of the probability of winning, $\frac{6}{20}$, and the probability of losing, $\frac{14}{20}$, is **1**. Since these events are complements of each other, one of these must occur (the raffle participant either wins or loses).

Probability of Multiple Events

If events are **independent events**, the probability of one occurring does not affect the probability of the other event occurring. If events are **dependent events**, the probability of one occurring changes the probability of the other event occurring. Rolling a die and getting one number does not change the probability of getting any particular number on the next roll. The number of faces has not changed, so these are independent events. When drawing two cards from a deck of cards, it is important to pay attention to whether the card is *replaced* or not. If the cards are drawn *with replacement*, then the second draw of a card is independent of the first draw (assuming the cards are shuffled). If the cards are drawn *without replacement*, then the probability of the second draw is affected by the first draw, and the events are dependent.

The probability of two independent events occurring is the product of the two events' probabilities:

$$P \text{ (}A \text{ and } B\text{)} = P(A) \times P(B)$$

The probability of one event *or* another occurring can be found using the following formula:

$$P \text{ (}A \text{ or } B\text{)} = P(A) + P(B) - P \text{ (}A \text{ and } B\text{)}$$

Notice this is exactly the same as finding in set theory. These topics are closely related. Two events that are **mutually exclusive** *cannot* happen at the same time. This is similar to disjoint sets in set theory. In that case, $P(A \text{ and } B) = 0$ and $P(A \text{ or } B) = P(A) + P(B)$. For example, if a single die is to be rolled one time, event A represents getting an even number, and event B represents getting the number 5, then these events are mutually exclusive and $P(A \text{ and } B) = 0$. Also, the probability of one or the other event occurring is $P(A \text{ or } B) = P(A) + P(B) = \frac{1}{2} + \frac{1}{6} = \frac{4}{6} = \frac{2}{3}$.

Conditional probability is the probability of an event (A) occurring given that another event (B) has occurred. Above, the formula did not specify that an event had already occurred. Conditional probability deals with a fact of past occurrence. The example of calculating the probability of drawing a second card from a deck when the first card was not replaced is an example of conditional probability.

The notation $P(B|A)$ represents the probability that event B occurs, given that event A has already occurred (it is read "probability of B, given A"). For example, suppose 2 cards are drawn from a deck of 10 cards, numbered 1 through 10, without replacement. Let event A be drawing a 7 on the first draw; then $P(A) = \frac{1}{10}$. Let event B be drawing a 5 on the second draw. The probability that a 5 is now drawn given that 7 was already drawn is $P(B|A) = \frac{1}{9}$, since there are now only 9 cards from which to draw. The probability of both events occurring is $P(A \text{ and } B) = \frac{1}{10} \times \frac{1}{9} = P(A) \times P(B|A)$. Note that the $P(B)$ just represents the probability of drawing a 7 out of 10 cards, so it is incorrect to say $P(A \text{ and } B) = P(A) \times P(B)$. The fact that the 7 has already been drawn prior to the second event must be taken into account. In general,

$$P(A \text{ and } B) = P(B|A)P(A) = P(A|B)P(B)$$

This formula can be rearranged to solve for any of the three quantities on the right side, if necessary. If A and B are independent events, then the left side becomes $P(A) \times P(B)$ and the above equation simplifies to:

$$P(B|A) = P(B) \text{ or } P(A|B) = P(A)$$

for A and B independent.

SAMPLE QUESTIONS

26) **A group of ten individuals is drawing straws. There are 30 straws and 2 of them are short. If the straws are not replaced, what is the probability, as a percentage, that none of the first three individuals to draw straws will draw a short straw?**

   Answer:

   Drawing straws in this scenario is a sequence of dependent events. The total number of possible outcomes diminishes after each person draws. Therefore, the first person has a probability of 28 normal-sized straws out of 30 straws. The second person, however, only has 27 normal straws out of 29, since the first person took out, and did not replace, 1 straw. The third person's probability is even lower, at 26 out of the 28. Thus,

P (3 people not drawing short straws) = $\frac{28}{30} \times \frac{27}{29} \times \frac{26}{28} = \frac{117}{145} = 0.81$

There is an **81% chance** that none of the first three people to draw will get a short straw.

27) **A used car dealership is selling 30 cars, and 2 of these cars are defective. One individual buys a car that is defective. What is the probability of the next person at the dealership buying a car that is not defective?**

Answer:

These two events are dependent and conditional since one already occurred. The probability of the first event occurring was $\frac{2}{30}$. Since one of the defective cars was purchased, the probability that the next car purchased is not defective is 28 properly functioning cars over 29 defective and properly functioning cars. The conditional probability is:

P (not defective car | defective car) $= \frac{P \text{ (defective AND 2nd not defective)}}{P \text{ (defective)}} =$

$\frac{\frac{2}{30} \times \frac{28}{29}}{\frac{2}{30}} = \frac{28}{29}$

28) **Alyssa has 2 blue blouses out of 13 total. The likelihood of her wearing blue slacks if she is wearing a blue blouse is $\frac{1}{10}$. What is the likelihood that she wears blue slacks and a blue blouse?**

Answer:

$P(B) = \frac{2}{13}$	Let $P(B)$ stand for the chance of wearing a blue blouse.
$P(S\|B) = \frac{1}{10}$	Let $P(S\|B)$ the probability of her wearing blue slacks, given that she is wearing a blue blouse.
$P(S\|B) = \frac{P(B \text{ and } S)}{P(B)}$ $\frac{1}{10} = \frac{P(B \text{ and } S)}{\frac{2}{13}}$ $P(B \text{ and } S) = \frac{2}{130}$ $= \frac{1}{65}$	Plug what is known into the conditional probability formula.

Thus, the probability of Alyssa wearing blue slacks and a blue blouse is $\frac{1}{65}$.

Part IV: Practice

Practice Test

READING

After reading the passage, choose the best answer to each question.

In recent decades, jazz has been associated with New Orleans and festivals like Mardi Gras, but in the 1920s, jazz was a booming trend whose influence reached into many aspects of American culture. In fact, the years between World War I and the Great Depression were known as the Jazz Age, a term coined by F. Scott Fitzgerald in his famous novel *The Great Gatsby*. Sometimes also called the Roaring Twenties, this time period saw major urban centers experiencing new economic, cultural, and artistic vitality. In the United States, musicians flocked to cities like New York and Chicago, which would became famous hubs for jazz musicians. Ella Fitzgerald, for example, moved from Virginia to New York City to begin her much-lauded singing career, and jazz pioneer Louis Armstrong got his big break in Chicago.

Jazz music was played by and for a more expressive and freed populace than the United States had previously seen. Women gained the right to vote and were openly seen drinking and dancing to jazz music. This period marked the emergence of the flapper, a woman determined to make a statement about her new role in society. Jazz music also provided the soundtrack for the explosion of African American art and culture now known as the Harlem Renaissance. In addition to Fitzgerald and Armstrong, numerous musicians, including Duke Ellington, Fats Waller, and Bessie Smith, promoted their distinctive and complex music as an integral part of the emerging African American culture.

1

What is the main idea of the passage?

A.   People should associate jazz music with the 1920s, not modern New Orleans.

B.   Jazz music played an important role in many cultural movements of the 1920s.

C.   Many famous jazz musicians began their careers in New York City and Chicago.

D.   African Americans were instrumental in launching jazz into mainstream culture.

E.   The Jazz Age was a period of cultural and artistic exuberance, which had little economic or political significance.

2

The passage supports which of the following claims about jazz music?

A.   Jazz music was important to minority groups struggling for social equality in the 1920s.

B.   Duke Ellington, Fats Waller, and Bessie Smith were the most important jazz musicians of the Harlem Renaissance.

C.   Women gained the right to vote with the help of jazz musicians.

D.   Duke Ellington, Fats Waller, and Bessie Smith all supported women's right to vote.

E.   The success of jazz music contributed to a spike in America's economic wealth.

3

The primary purpose of the passage is to

A.   explain the role jazz musicians played in the Harlem Renaissance.

B.   inform the reader about the many important musicians playing jazz in the 1920s.

C.   discuss how jazz influenced important cultural movements in the 1920s.

D.   provide a history of jazz music in the 20th century.

E.   describe how jazz music and the Roaring Twenties are depicted in modern day popular culture.

4

Which of the following is not a fact stated in the passage?

A. The years between World War I and the Great Depression were known as the Jazz Age.

B. Ella Fitzgerald and Louis Armstrong both moved to New York City to start their music careers.

C. Women danced to jazz music during the 1920s to make a statement about their role in society.

D. Jazz music was an integral part of the emerging African American culture of the 1920s.

E. In modern day popular culture, jazz music is most often associated with New Orleans and Mardi Gras.

5

Which conclusion about jazz music is supported by the passage?

A. F. Scott Fitzgerald supported jazz musicians in New York and Chicago.

B. Jazz music is no longer as popular as it once was.

C. Both women and African Americans used jazz music as a way of expressing their newfound freedom.

D. Flappers and African American musicians worked together to produce jazz music.

E. Jazz music was a direct result of the economic wealth the country was experiencing at the time.

It has now been two decades since the introduction of thermonuclear fusion weapons into the military inventories of the great powers, and more than a decade since the United States, Great Britain, and the Soviet Union ceased to test nuclear weapons in the atmosphere. Today our understanding of the technology of thermonuclear weapons seems highly advanced, but our knowledge of the physical and biological consequences of nuclear war is continuously evolving.

6

The passage is primarily concerned with

A. the impact of thermonuclear weapons on the military.

B. the technology of thermonuclear weapons.

C. atmospheric testing of nuclear weapons.

D. the physical and biological consequences of nuclear war.

E. nuclear ceasefire between the United States, Great Britain, and the Soviet Union.

The social and political discourse of America continues to be permeated with idealism. An idealistic viewpoint asserts that the ideals of freedom, equality, justice, and human dignity are the truths that Americans must continue to aspire to. Idealists argue that truth is what should be, not necessarily what is. In general, they work to improve things and to make them as close to ideal as possible.

7

The primary purpose of the passage is to

A. advocate for freedom, equality, justice, and human rights.

B. explain what an idealist believes in.

C. explain what's wrong with social and political discourse in America.

D. persuade readers to believe in certain truths.

E. encourage readers to question the truth.

In Greek mythology, two gods, Epimetheus and Prometheus, were given the work of creating living things. Epimetheus gave good powers to the different animals. To the lion he gave strength; to the bird, swiftness; to the fox, sagacity; and so on. Eventually, all of the good gifts had been bestowed, and there was nothing left for humans. As a result, Prometheus returned to heaven and brought down fire, which he gave to humans. With fire, human beings could protect themselves by making weapons. Over time, humans developed civilization.

8

As used in the passage, *bestowed* most nearly means

A. purchased.

B. forgotten.

C. accepted.

D. given.

E. lost.

It could be said that the great battle between the North and South we call the Civil War was a battle for individual identity. The states of the South had their own culture, one based on farming, independence, and the rights of both man and state to determine their own paths. Similarly, the North had forged its own identity as a center of centralized commerce and manufacturing. This clash of lifestyles was bound to create tension, and this tension was bound to lead to war. But people who try to sell you this narrative are wrong. The Civil War was not a battle of cultural identities—it was a battle about slavery. All other explanations for the war are either a direct consequence of the South's desire for wealth at the expense of her fellow man or a fanciful invention to cover up this sad portion of our nation's history. And it cannot be denied that this time in our past was very sad indeed.

9

As used in the passage, *fanciful* most nearly means

A.   complicated.

B.   imaginative.

C.   successful.

D.   unfortunate.

E.   opulent.

10

The primary purpose of the passage is to

A.   convince readers that slavery was the main cause of the Civil War.

B.   illustrate the cultural differences between the North and the South before the Civil War.

C.   persuade readers that the North deserved to win the Civil War.

D.   demonstrate that the history of the Civil War is too complicated to be understood clearly.

E.   describe the various causes of the American Civil War.

11

What is the main idea of the passage?

A.   The Civil War was the result of cultural differences between the North and South.

B.   The Civil War was caused by the South's reliance on slave labor.

C.   The North's use of commerce and manufacturing allowed it to win the war.

D.   The South's belief in the rights of man and state cost the war.

E.   America's reliance on slave labor in the centuries before the Civil War is a sad and shameful part of the country's history.

After looking at five houses, Robert and I have decided to buy the one on Forest Road. The first two homes we visited didn't have the space we need—the first had only one bathroom, and the second did not have a guest bedroom. The third house, on Pine Street, had enough space inside but didn't have a big enough yard for our three dogs. The fourth house we looked at, on Rice Avenue, was stunning but well above our price range. The last home, on Forest Road, wasn't in the neighborhood we wanted to live in. However, it had the right amount of space for the right price.

Go on

12

What is the author's conclusion about the house on Pine Street?

- A.   The house did not have enough bedrooms.
- B.   The house did not have a big enough yard.
- C.   The house was not in the right neighborhood.
- D.   The house was too expensive.
- E.   The house had the right amount of space for the right price.

As you can see from the graph, my babysitting business has been really successful. The year started with a busy couple of months—several snows combined with a large number of requests for Valentine's Day services boosted our sales quite a bit. The spring months have admittedly been a bit slow, but we're hoping for a big summer once school gets out. Several clients have already put in requests for our services!

Sam's Net Income by Month

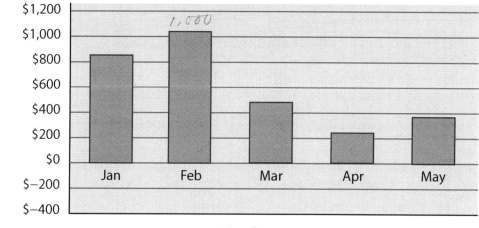

Month

13

Based on the information in the graph, how much more did Sam's Babysitting Service bring in during February than during April?

- A. $200
- B. $900
- C. $1100
- D. $1300
- E. $1800

14

Which of the following best describes the tone of the passage?

A. professional

B. casual

C. concerned

D. neutral

E. disheartened

Taking a person's temperature is one of the most basic and common health care tasks. Everyone from nurses to emergency medical technicians to concerned parents should be able to grab a thermometer to take a patient or loved one's temperature. But what's the best way to get an accurate reading? The answer depends on the situation.

The most common way people measure body temperature is orally. A simple digital or disposable thermometer is placed under the tongue for a few minutes, and the task is done. There are many situations, however, when measuring temperature orally isn't an option. For example, when a person can't breathe through his nose, he won't be able to keep his mouth closed long enough to get an accurate reading. In these situations, it's often preferable to place the thermometer in the rectum or armpit. Using the rectum also has the added benefit of providing a much more accurate reading than other locations can provide.

It's also often the case that certain people, like agitated patients or fussy babies, won't be able to sit still long enough for an accurate reading. In these situations, it's best to use a thermometer that works much more quickly, such as one that measures temperature in the ear or at the temporal artery. No matter which method is chosen, however, it's important to check the average temperature for each region, as it can vary by several degrees.

15

Which statement is NOT a fact from the passage?

A. Taking a temperature in the ear or at the temporal artery is more accurate than taking it orally.

B. If an individual cannot breathe through the nose, taking his or her temperature orally will likely give an inaccurate reading.

C. The standard human body temperature varies depending on whether it's measured in the mouth, rectum, armpit, ear, or temporal artery.

D. The most common way to measure temperature is by placing a thermometer in the mouth.

E. Some patients are unable to sit still long enough for an accurate reading using an oral thermometer.

16

The primary purpose of the passage is to

A. advocate for the use of thermometers that measure temperature in the ear or at the temporal artery.

B. explain the methods available to measure a person's temperature and the situation where each method is appropriate.

C. warn readers that the average temperature of the human body varies by region.

D. discuss how nurses use different types of thermometers depending on the type of patient they are examining.

E. inform readers of the proper procedure for taking a baby's temperature.

17

Which of the following is the best summary of this passage?

A. It's important that everyone know the best way to take a person's temperature in any given situation.

B. The most common method of taking a person's temperature—orally—isn't appropriate in some situations.

C. The most accurate way to take a temperature is placing a digital thermometer in the rectum.

D. There are many different ways to take a person's temperature, and which is appropriate will depend on the situation.

E. Nurses and parents must take special steps when taking the temperatures of fussy babies.

18

According to the passage, why is it sometimes preferable to take a person's temperature rectally?

A. Rectal readings are more accurate than oral readings.

B. Many people cannot sit still long enough to have their temperatures taken orally.

C. Temperature readings can vary widely between regions of the body.

D. Many people do not have access to quick-acting thermometers.

E. People who are ill may not be able to sit still long enough to have their temperatures taken through their ears or temporal arteries.

19

As used in the passage, *agitated* most nearly means

A. obviously upset.

B. quickly moving.

C. violently ill.

D. slightly dirty.

E. physically comfortable.

If life is not always poetical, it is at least metrical. Periodicity rules over the mental experience of man, according to the path of the orbit of his thoughts. Distances are not gauged, ellipses not measured, velocities not ascertained, times not known. Nevertheless, the recurrence is sure. What the mind suffered last week, or last year, it does not suffer now; but it will suffer again next week or next year. Happiness is not a matter of events; it depends upon the tides of the mind.

20

The passage suggests that "periodicity" is significant because it

A. provides examples of the aspects of life that cannot be measured.

B. describes the suffering that some people experience.

C. explains the "ups" and "downs" of a person's state of mind.

D. points to the fact that change is the dominant force of human experience.

E. argues that happiness is not a real possibility.

Popcorn is often associated with fun and festivities, both in and out of the home. It's eaten in theaters, usually after being salted and smothered in butter, and in homes, fresh from the microwave. But popcorn isn't just for fun—it's also a multimillion-dollar-a-year industry with a long and fascinating history.

While popcorn might seem like a modern invention, its history actually dates back thousands of years, making it one of the oldest snack foods enjoyed around the world. Popcorn is believed by food historians to be one of the earliest uses of cultivated corn. In 1948, Herbert Dick and Earle Smith discovered old popcorn dating back 4000 years in the New Mexico Bat Cave. For the Aztec Indians who called the caves home, popcorn (or *momochitl*) played an important role in society, both as a food staple and in ceremonies. The Aztecs cooked popcorn by heating sand in a fire; when it was heated, kernels were added and would pop when exposed to the heat of the sand.

The American love affair with popcorn began in 1912, when popcorn was first sold in theaters. The popcorn industry flourished during the Great Depression when it was advertised as a wholesome and economical food. Selling for five to ten cents a bag, it was a luxury that the downtrodden could afford. With the introduction of mobile popcorn machines at the World's Columbian Exposition, popcorn moved from the theater into fairs and parks. Popcorn continued to rule the snack food kingdom until the rise in popularity of home televisions during the 1950s.

The popcorn industry reacted to the decline in sales quickly by introducing pre-popped and unpopped popcorn for home consumption. However, it wasn't until microwave popcorn became commercially available in 1981 that at-home popcorn consumption began to grow exponentially. With the wide availability of microwaves in the United States, popcorn also began popping up in offices and hotel rooms. However, the home still remains the most popular popcorn eating spot: today, 70 percent of the 16 billion quarts of popcorn consumed annually in the United States are eaten at home.

21

The passage supports which of the following claims about popcorn?

A. People ate less popcorn in the 1950s than in previous decades because they went to the movies less.

B. Without mobile popcorn machines, people would not have been able to eat popcorn during the Great Depression.

C. People enjoyed popcorn during the Great Depression because it was a luxury food.

D. During the 1800s, people began abandoning theaters to go to fairs and festivals.

E. Today, popcorn is a popular snack food because of its wholesomeness and affordability.

22

As used in the passage, *staple* most nearly means

A. something produced only for special occasions.

B. something produced regularly in large quantities.

C. something produced by cooking.

D. something fastened together securely.

E. something of high nutritional value.

23

The primary purpose of the passage is to

A. explain how microwaves affected the popcorn industry.

B. show that popcorn is older than many people realize.

C. illustrate the history of popcorn from ancient cultures to modern times.

D. demonstrate the importance of popcorn in various cultures.

E. highlight the large increase in profits that the popcorn industry has seen in recent decades.

24

Which factor does the author of the passage credit for the growth of the popcorn industry in the United States?

A.   the use of popcorn in ancient Aztec ceremonies

B.   the growth of the home television industry

C.   the marketing of popcorn during the Great Depression

D.   the nutritional value of popcorn

E.   the introduction of pre-popped and unpopped popcorn to the market

25

What is the best summary of this passage?

A.   Popcorn is a popular snack food that dates back thousands of years. Its popularity in the United States has been tied to the growth of theaters and the availability of microwaves.

B.   Popcorn has been a popular snack food for thousands of years. Archaeologists have found evidence that many ancient cultures used popcorn as a food staple and in ceremonies.

C.   Popcorn was first introduced to America in 1912, and its popularity has grown exponentially since then. Today, over 16 billion quarts of popcorn are consumed in the United States annually.

D.   Popcorn is a versatile snack food that can be eaten with butter or other toppings. It can also be cooked in a number of different ways, including in microwaves.

E.   Popcorn is a versatile snack food that can be enjoyed in any number of locations such as theaters, festivals, at home, and even at work.

26

Which of the following is NOT a fact stated in the passage?

A.   Archaeologists have found popcorn dating back 4000 years.

B.   Popcorn was first sold in theaters in 1912.

C.   Consumption of popcorn dropped in 1981 with the growing popularity of home televisions.

D.   70 percent of the popcorn consumed in the United States is eaten in homes.

E.   The popcorn industry flourished during the Great Depression.

Go on →

27

Victoria won easily and had plenty of time to rest before her next scheduled match.

Based on the context, which of the following is the meaning of the word *match* in the sentence?

A.   a competitive event

B.   a suitable pair

C.   a slender piece of wood used to start a fire

D.   a prospective marriage partner

E.   another individual of equal skill or talent

Alexis de Tocqueville, a young Frenchman from an aristocratic family, visited the United States in the early 1800s. He observed: "Amongst the novel objects that attracted my attention during my stay in the United States, nothing struck me more forcibly than the general equality of conditions. [...] The more I advanced in the study of American society, the more I perceived that the equality of conditions is the fundamental fact from which all others seem to be derived, and the central point at which all my observations constantly terminated."

28

Which of the following best states the main idea of the passage?

A.   Alexis de Tocqueville has contributed substantially to the study of the nineteenth-century United States.

B.   Equality was the most important ideal in the nineteenth-century United States.

C.   In nineteenth-century American society, all people had rights.

D.   American society during the nineteenth century was more equal than French society.

E.   Alexis de Tocqueville observed America society closely in the hope of understanding how equality was achieved.

29

As used in the passage, *novel* most nearly means

A.   new.

B.   written.

C.   uncertain.

D.   confusing.

E.   interesting.

30

The author would most likely agree with which of the following statements about the United States in the nineteenth century?

A.   Right from the beginning at least three social classes emerged, with most people falling in the middle.

B.   American people were by nature competitive and individualistic.

C.   Since the birth of the United States, its citizens have been eager to achieve and prosper.

D.   In the early decades when America had just become an independent country with a new government, people lived in equality.

E.   American equality appeared more fragile the more closely it was observed.

I deny that Ireland has ever been really conquered; and even should the most sanguinary suggestions proposed in a nineteenth-century serial be carried out, I am certain she could not be. Ireland has never been permanently subdued by Dane or Norman, Dutchman or Saxon; nor has she ever been really united to England. A man is surely not united to a jailer because he is bound to him by an iron chain which his jailer has forged for his safe keeping. This is not union; and the term "United Kingdom" is in fact a most miserable misnomer. Unity requires something more than a mere material approximation.

31

The function of the second sentence of the passage is to

A.   elaborate on the idea that Ireland once engaged in a bloody war with northern countries.

B.   provide historical evidence that Ireland has never been entirely controlled by another country.

C.   describe the central problem of the Irish people.

D.   make an allusion to the many people who have settled in Ireland.

E.   provide an acknowledgement of the times Ireland has lost autonomy.

PASSAGE ONE

In the field of veterinary medicine, the inquiry into whether animals experience pain the same way humans do is especially important in the context of pain management. Although many advancements have been made in research sciences, and pain management is widely accepted as a necessary job of practitioners, a number of myths about animal pain still plague the field of veterinary medicine and prevent practitioners from making pain management a priority. According to veterinarian and writer Debbie Grant, three myths are especially detrimental to the cause.

The first of these is the myth that animals do not feel pain at all or that they feel it less intensely than humans; in fact, according to Grant, the biological mechanisms by which we experience pain are the very same mechanisms by which animals experience pain. Even the emotional reaction to a painful experience, like being afraid to return to the dentist after an unpleasant visit, is mirrored in animals.

The second myth that prevents the advancement of pain management practices is the myth that pain is a necessary part of an animal's recovery. While some veterinarians believe that pain may prevent a healing dog, for example, from playing too vigorously, Grant says this is simply not the case. In fact, restlessness and discomfort may even lead to unusually high levels of agitation and may consequently slow the recovery process even further.

Finally, contrary to the third myth, animals do not necessarily tolerate pain any better than humans do, though they may handle their pain differently. Grant emphasizes that veterinarians must be aware that a lack of obvious signs does not necessarily suggest that pain is not present: in fact, many animals are likely to conceal their pain out of an instinct to hide weaknesses that may make them easy targets for predators.

PASSAGE TWO

Unlike doctors, who typically have the benefit of discussing their patients' concerns, veterinarians cannot ask their patients whether and where they are experiencing discomfort. Additionally, veterinarians must be aware of the survival instinct of many animals to mask pain in response to stressful experiences or foreign environments. For these reasons, diagnostic tools and strategies are instrumental in the effective practice of veterinary medicine.

Veterinarians have a unique challenge when it comes to diagnosing their patients. In 2014, researchers of veterinary medicine at the University of Perugia in Italy completed a review of the diagnostic tools and strategies available to today's practitioners and found a number of them to be effective. Presumptive diagnosis, the first of these strategies, involves making a prediction about the animal's pain based on the observable damage to the body or body part. In addition to presumptive diagnosis, veterinarians can use close observation to assess changes in the animal's behavior.

The most common tool for performing diagnosis is the clinical exam, which can include both a physical exam and laboratory testing. As part of this process, a veterinarian might make use of an objective pain scale, by which he or she could assess the animal's condition according to a number of criteria. This tool is especially useful throughout the course of treatment, as it provides the practitioner with a quantitative measure for evaluating the effectiveness of various treatment options.

32

As it is used in Passage One, the term *detrimental* most nearly means

A.   mischievous.

B.   damaging.

C.   disturbing.

D.   advantageous.

E.   confusing.

33

The author of Passage 1 most likely includes the example of the unpleasant dentist visit in order to

A.   provide a relatable example of how pain can influence a person's emotions.

B.   challenge the reader to overcome his or her natural, emotional response to painful experiences.

C.   question a popular perception about the experience of going to the dentist.

D.   highlight a similarity in the way humans and animals respond to pain.

E.   remind the reader of how scary the dentist is for children.

34

As it is used in Passage 2, the term *foreign* most nearly means

A.   unfamiliar.

B.   inaccessible.

C.   distant.

D.   exotic.

E.   dangerous.

35

The author of Passage 1 indicates that despite advancements in veterinary sciences, many veterinarians

A.   do not see the value in pain management practices for their patients.

B.   still employ outdated methods of pain management.

C.   still believe that pain management is a responsibility of the pet owner.

D.   still have misguided beliefs and practices related to pain management in animals.

E.   do not have the technology to provide effective pain management options.

36

The author of Passage 2 indicates that veterinarians can improve their pain management practices by

A.   attempting to communicate with their patients about the pain they are experiencing.

B.   employing the best diagnostic practices in their field.

C.   encouraging pet owners to keep careful watch over their animals.

D.   inventing novel ways to assess and treat pain in animals.

E.   focusing on the causes of the pain rather than pain itself.

37

The author of Passage 2 indicates that objective pain measures are useful because

A.   they allow the veterinarian to compare an animal's pain level to the pain levels of other animals.

B.   they challenge the veterinarian to devise a treatment plan as quickly as possible.

C.   they discount the assumption that pain cannot be measured on an objective scale.

D.   they provide the veterinarian with a quantitative method for tracking pain levels over the course of an animal's treatment.

E.   they offer a new perspective on the management of pain in small animals.

38

The author of Passage 1 would most likely respond to the discussion of presumptive diagnosis in Passage 2 by

A.   asserting that substantial physical damage to an animal's form does not necessarily suggest the presence of pain.

B.   asserting that presumptive diagnosis is more effective for diagnosing humans and should not be used for diagnosing animals.

C.   asserting that similarities in methods of pain diagnosis for humans and animals are effective because of the biological similarities between them.

D.   asserting that veterinarians should not make use of presumptive diagnosis in evaluating and treating patients.

E.   asserting that the pain diagnosis is much more difficult in humans than in animals.

39

Which of the following best describes the relationship between the two passages?

A.   The first passage makes the claim that pain management should be a priority for veterinarians, while the second passage rejects this claim.

B.   The first passage emphasizes the veterinarian's responsibility to prioritize pain management in animals, while the second passage explores the tools by which veterinarians can execute this responsibility.

C.   The first passage seeks to dispel myths about pain management in animals, while the second passage denies that they are myths.

D.   The first passage sheds light on the shortcomings of veterinary sciences as they currently exist, while the second passage provides insight into how these shortcomings might be overcome.

E.   The first passage describes early approaches to pain management in animals, while the second passage highlights more modern approaches.

40

Both authors indicate that veterinarians

A. must be aware that a lack of obvious symptoms does not necessarily suggest an absence of pain.

B. should make pain management for their patients a priority.

C. ought to be familiar with the misguided assumptions that exist in their field.

D. need to conduct a thorough examination before releasing an animal back to its owner.

E. should prioritize oral health care in order to prevent the need for painful procedures.

41

The diagram represents the lock and key model of enzymes. According to the figure, the products are formed from which of the following?

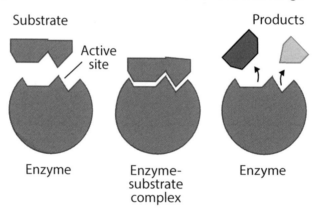

Substrate   Active site   Products

Enzyme   Enzyme-substrate complex   Enzyme

A. the enzyme

B. the enzyme-substrate complex

C. the substrate

D. the active site

E. none of these

Words are signs of natural facts. The use of natural history is to give us aid in supernatural history: the use of the outer creation, to give us language for the beings and changes of the inward creation. Every word which is used to express a moral or intellectual fact, if traced to its root, is found to be borrowed from some material appearance. Right means straight; wrong means twisted. Spirit primarily means wind; transgression, the crossing of a line; supercilious, the raising of the eyebrow. We say the heart to express emotion, the head to denote thought; and thought and emotion are words borrowed from sensible things, and now appropriated to spiritual nature. Most of the process by which this transformation is made, is hidden from us in the remote time when language was framed; but the same tendency may be daily observed in children.

42

Which of the following best describes the organization of the passage?

A.   cause and effect

B.   sequential

C.   chronological

D.   spatial details

E.   problem and solution

In *My Bondage and My Freedom*, Douglass emphasizes that having slaves is morally wrong, and people who have not been told otherwise know, intuitively, that it is wrong. However, these same people, after society has pressured them to conform to the practice of holding slaves, stop listening to their consciences. Such was the case with his mistress, as he explains, "Tommy, and I, and his mother, got on swimmingly together, for a time. I say for a time, because the fatal poison of irresponsible power, and the natural influence of slavery customs, were not long in making a suitable impression on the gentle and loving disposition of my excellent mistress. At first, Mrs. Auld evidently regarded me simply as a child, like any other child; she had not come to regard me as property. This latter thought was a thing of conventional growth. The first was natural and spontaneous. A noble nature, like hers, could not, instantly, be wholly perverted; and it took several years to change the natural sweetness of her temper into fretful bitterness." Specifically, when Douglass is brought to the home of Mrs. Auld in Baltimore, Mrs. Auld treats him as she treats her own child, Tommy. She begins teaching Douglass to read as she is teaching Tommy to read. When her husband realizes what his wife is doing, he corrects her and insists that she treat Douglass as property. Mrs. Auld stops educating Douglass and, over time, Mrs. Auld's temperament changes because she is violating what is natural and true.

43

Which of the following best states the main idea of the passage?

A.   People's consciences lead them to what is right; conformity to the majority may not.

B.   People are often pressured to follow social conventions.

C.   People who do not conform to society do not get along with others.

D.   Society sets up common practices so that people will know how to relate to each other.

E.   A person who breaks the rules of society causes problems.

44

As used in the passage, *conventional* most nearly means

A. current.

B. customary.

C. popular.

D. universal.

E. fashionable.

45

The author makes the unstated assumption that Mrs. Auld was told not educate Douglass because

A. he was a slave.

B. he had household chores to do.

C. Tommy would get less attention.

D. education would empower slaves.

E. educating slaves is a waste of time.

> I say moreover that you make a great, a very great mistake, if you think that psychology, being the science of the mind's laws, is something from which you can deduce definite programs and schemes and methods of instruction for immediate schoolroom use. Psychology is a science, and teaching is an art; and sciences never generate arts directly out of themselves. An intermediary inventive mind must make the application, by using its originality.

46

The passage is primarily concerned with

A. explaining that psychology is a science.

B. emphasizing that the science of psychology cannot determine educational programs and methods.

C. describing the artistic nature of educational practices, programming, and step-by-step planning.

D. comparing the values of art to those of science.

E. identifying specific laws of the human mind and expectations of day-to-day activities for teachers.

> Alan —
>
> I just wanted to drop you a quick note to let you know I'll be out of the office for the next two weeks. Elizabeth and I are finally taking that trip to France we've been talking about for years. It's a bit of a last-minute decision, but since we had the vacation time available, we figured it was now or never.

Anyway, my team's been briefed on the upcoming meeting, so they should be able to handle the presentation without any hiccups. If you have any questions or concerns, you can direct them to Joanie, who'll be handling my responsibilities while I'm out.

Let me know if you want any special treats. I don't know if you can take chocolate and cheese on the plane, but I'm going to try!

Best regards,

Michael

47

Which of the following most likely describes the relationship between the author and Alan?

A.   familial

B.   formal

C.   friendly

D.   strained

E.   intimate

48

The primary purpose of the author is to

A.   ask Alan if he wants any special treats from France.

B.   brag to Alan about his upcoming vacation.

C.   inform Alan that he will be out of the office.

D.   help Alan prepare for the upcoming meeting.

E.   introduce Alan to Joanie.

The bacteria, fungi, insects, plants, and animals that live together in a habitat have evolved to share a pool of limited resources. They've competed for water, minerals, nutrients, sunlight, and space—sometimes for thousands or even millions of years. As these communities have evolved, the species in them have developed complex, long-term interspecies interactions known as symbiotic relationships.

Ecologists characterize these interactions based on whether each party benefits. In mutualism, both individuals benefit, while in synnecrosis, both organisms are harmed. A relationship where one individual benefits and the other is harmed is known as parasitism. Examples of these relationships can easily be seen in any ecosystem. Pollination, for example, is mutualistic—pollinators get nutrients from the flower, and the plant is able to reproduce—while tapeworms, which steal nutrients from their host, are parasitic.

There's yet another class of symbiosis that is controversial among scientists. As it's long been defined, commensalism is a relationship where one species benefits and the other is unaffected. But is it possible for two species to interact and for one to remain completely unaffected? Often, relationships described as commensal include one species that feeds on another species' leftovers; remoras, for instance, will attach themselves to sharks and eat the food particles they leave behind. It might seem like the shark gets nothing from the relationship, but a closer look will show that sharks in fact benefit from remoras, which clean the sharks' skin and remove parasites. In fact, many scientists claim that relationships currently described as commensal are just mutualistic or parasitic in ways that haven't been discovered yet.

49

Which of the following is NOT a fact stated in the passage?

A.   Mutualism is an interspecies relationship where both species benefit.

B.   Synnecrosis is an interspecies relationship where both species are harmed.

C.   The relationship between plants and pollinators is mutualistic.

D.   The relationship between remoras and sharks is parasitic.

E.   Commensalism is a topic of controversy in the scientific community.

50

Epiphytes are plants that attach themselves to trees and derive nutrients from the air and surrounding debris. Sometimes, the weight of epiphytes can damage the trees on which they're growing. The relationship between epiphytes and their hosts would be described as

A.   mutualism.

B.   commensalism.

C.   parasitism.

D.   synnecrosis.

E.   atypical.

51

According to the passage, why is commensalism controversial among scientists?

A.   Many scientists believe that an interspecies interaction where one species is unaffected does not exist.

B.   Some scientists believe that relationships where one species feeds on the leftovers of another should be classified as parasitism.

C.   Because remoras and sharks have a mutualistic relationship, no interactions should be classified as commensalism.

D.   Only relationships among animal species should be classified as commensalism.

E.   Some scientists believe animals are incapable of interspecies interaction.

52

As used in the passage, *controversial* most nearly means

A. debatable.

B. objectionable.

C. confusing.

D. upsetting.

E. offensive.

53

The primary purpose of the passage is to

A. argue that commensalism isn't actually found in nature.

B. describe the many types of symbiotic relationships.

C. explain how competition for resources results in long-term interspecies relationships.

D. provide examples of the many different ways individual organisms interact.

E. explain the differences between commensalism and mutualism.

54

Which conclusion about symbiotic relationships is supported by the passage?

A. Scientists cannot decide how to classify symbiotic relationships among species.

B. The majority of interspecies interactions are parasitic because most species do not get along.

C. If two species are involved in a parasitic relationship, one of the species will eventually become extinct.

D. Symbiotic relationships evolve as the species that live in a community adapt to their environments and each other.

E. Mutualistic relationships are rare and difficult to maintain.

A fault of disproportionate height of ceilings must be avoided when renovating a house. During the renovation of an old house with high ceilings, walls are added to divide the original, but very large, rooms. In a modern house, if one room is large enough to require a lofty ceiling, the architect will manage to make his second floor upon different levels, so as not to inflict the necessary height of large rooms upon narrow halls and small rooms, which should have only a height proportioned to their size. A ten-foot room with a thirteen-foot ceiling makes the narrowness of the room doubly apparent; one feels shut up between two walls which threaten to come together and squeeze one between them, while, on the other hand, a ten-foot room with a nine-foot ceiling may have a really comfortable and cozy effect.

55

The passage suggests that with the rearrangement of walls in the renovation of an old house, which of the following may occur?

A.   The old house will end up with fewer rooms than it originally had.

B.   The lofty, high ceilings will make the new, smaller rooms seem large.

C.   The high ceiling of the new smaller room may make the room seem narrower than it is.

D.   Having smaller rooms will make the enormous house cozier.

E.   Instead of the spacious feeling of large rooms, the rooms will feel as though they are constricting.

The serfdom of the Irish tenant leads to misery. No one can understand the depth of Irish misery that has not lived in Ireland, and taken pains to become acquainted with the habits and manner of life of the lower orders. The tenant, who is kept at starvation point to pay his landlord's rent, has no means of providing for his family. He cannot encourage trade; his sons cannot get work to do, if they are taught trades. It is a cruel thing that a man who is willing to work should not be able to get it. I know an instance in which a girl belonging to a comparatively respectable family was taken into service, and it was discovered that for years her only food was dry bread. She and her family have gone to America.

56

Which of the following is the best statement of the central idea of the passage?

A.   Many Irish have been forced to leave their homes for America.

B.   The Irish people are not able to learn trades or to work, so they cannot feed their families.

C.   The Irish tenants have become slaves in their own country.

D.   The poor in Ireland are starving and lack important social programs to help families.

E.   The landlords promote the misery of Irish tenants by denying them work for their own benefit.

WRITING

USAGE

Each question consists of a sentence with underlined portions. Determine if any of the underlined parts contains inappropriate word use, poor or incorrect grammatical construction, or incorrect or omitted punctuation or capitalization that needs revision to produce a correct sentence. If there are no errors in the sentence as written, select "No error." No sentence has more than one error.

1

Ukrainians (A)<u>celebrate</u> a holiday called Malanka during which men (B)<u>dress in</u> costumes and masks and (C)<u>plays</u> tricks on (D)<u>their</u> neighbors. (E)<u>No error</u>

2

As juveniles (A), (B)<u>african</u> white-backed vultures are (C)<u>darkly</u> colored, developing their white feathers only as they (D)<u>grow into</u> adulthood. (E)<u>No error</u>

3

(A)<u>Because of</u> (B)<u>its</u> distance from the sun, the planet Neptune (C)<u>has seasons</u> that last the (D)<u>equivalent of</u> forty-one Earth years. (E)<u>No error</u>

4

Edward Jenner, (A)<u>considered</u> the father of immunology, invented the (B) <u>world's</u> first vaccine (C)<u>over infecting</u> a young boy with cowpox, successfully protecting him from the widespread (D)<u>,</u> and far more dangerous, smallpox virus. (E)<u>No error</u>

5

Everyday items like potatoes, (A)<u>bread,</u> onions, and even saliva (B)<u>is</u> the tools of art conservators, (C)<u>who</u> work to (D)<u>clean and restore</u> works of art. (E)<u>No error</u>

6

The Akhal-Teke horse breed, originally (A)<u>from</u> Turkmenistan, (B)<u>have</u> long enjoyed (C)<u>a reputation</u> for (D)<u>bravery and fortitude</u>. (E)<u>No error</u>

7

The employer (A)<u>decided</u> that he could not, (B)<u>due to</u> the high cost of health care, afford (C)<u>to offer</u> (D)<u>no other</u> benefits to his employees. (E)<u>No error</u>

8

Though Puerto Rico is known popularly for (A)<u>its</u> beaches, its landscape also (B)<u>includes</u> mountains, which (C)<u>are</u> home to many of the (D)<u>island's</u> rural villages. (E)<u>No error</u>

9

The photographer (A)<u>,</u> specializes in shooting portraits and taking still lifes, but she also (B)<u>likes</u> (C)<u>to accept</u> more challenging assignments, such as (D) <u>photographing</u> wildlife. (E)<u>No error</u>

10

In the fight (A)<u>against</u> obesity, (B)<u>countries'</u> around the world (C)<u>are</u> imposing taxes on sodas and other sugary drinks (D)<u>in hopes of</u> curbing unhealthy habits. (E)<u>No error</u>

11

The (A)<u>Black Death</u>, often thought of as a concern of times past, (B)<u>continued</u> to spread among rodent populations even today (C)<u>,</u> occasionally making (D)<u>its</u> way into a human host. (E)<u>No error</u>

12

Advances (A)<u>in</u> agricultural technology over the past five decades (B)<u>have led</u> to a steady increase in the global food (C)<u>supply, and</u> the (D)<u>population</u> of many countries around the world are benefiting. (E)<u>No error</u>

SENTENCE CORRECTION

In each of the following sentences, some part or all of the sentence is underlined. You are provided with five ways of writing the underlined part. The first choice is always the same as the original; the other four choices differ. Choose the answer that most effectively expresses the meaning of the sentence, while following the requirements of standard written English.

13

The famously high death toll at the end of the Civil War was not exclusively due to battle losses; <u>in addition,</u> large numbers of soldiers and civilians fell ill and died as a result of living conditions during the war.

A.   in addition,

B.   therefore,

C.   however,

D.   consequently,

E.   on the other hand,

14

The public defense attorney was able to maintain her optimism despite <u>her dearth of courtroom wins, lack of free time she had, and growing list of clients she was helping.</u>

A.   her dearth of courtroom wins, lack of free time she had, and growing list of clients she was helping.

B.   her dearth of courtroom wins, lack of free time, and how many clients she was helping.

C.   her dearth of courtroom wins, lack of free time, and growing list of clients.

D.   her dearth of courtroom wins, the free time she lacked, and the list of clients she was growing.

E.   the losses she had experienced, the free time she lacked, and her growing client list.

15

<u>Being invented in France in the early nineteenth century,</u> the stethoscope underwent a number of reiterations before the modern form of the instrument was introduced in the 1850s.

A.   Being invented in France in the early nineteenth century,

B.   Inventing in France in the early nineteenth century,

C.   It was invented in France in the early nineteenth century,

D.   Though it was invented in France in the nineteenth century,

E.   Invented in France in the early nineteenth century,

16

In 1983, almost twenty years after his death, T.S. Eliot won two Tony Awards for his contributions to the well-loved musical *Cats*, <u>it was based on a book of his poetry.</u>

A. it was based on a book of his poetry.

B. which was based on a book of his poetry.

C. because it was based on a book of his poetry.

D. being based on a book of his poetry.

E. having been based on a book of his poetry.

17

Because the distance between stars in the galaxy is far greater than the distance between planets, interstellar travel <u>is expected to be an even bigger challenge than</u> interplanetary exploration.

A. is expected to be an even bigger challenge than

B. will be expected to be an even bigger challenge than

C. is expected to be an even bigger challenge then

D. is expecting to be an even bigger challenge than

E. expects to be an even bigger challenge than

18

The <u>painters who are often confused for each other</u> Claude Monet and Édouard Manet actually did have a couple things in common: they were born only six years apart in Paris, France, and both contributed important early Impressionist works to the artistic canon.

A. painters who are often confused for each other

B. painters whose names are similar and who are sometimes confused as a result

C. common confused painters

D. painters who are confusing because of their similar names

E. commonly confused painters

19

The field of child development is concerned with <u>the emotional, the psychological, and biological developments</u> of infants and children.

A. the emotional, the psychological, and biological developments

B. the emotional, psychological, and biological developments

C. the emotional developments, the psychological, and the biological developments

D. emotional, psychological, and the biological developments

E. the emotional, psychological, and the biological developments

20

Though it is often thought of as an extreme sport, spelunking involves much more than adrenaline: enthusiasts dive into unexplored caves <u>to study structures of, take photographs, and create maps of</u> the untouched systems.

A.   to study structures of, take photographs, and create maps of

B.   to study structures of, to take photographs, and create maps of

C.   to study structures of, taking photographs of, and creating maps of

D.   to study structures, take photographs, and create maps of

E.   studying structures of, taking photographs, and creating maps of

21

In many European countries such as France, Spain, and Italy, <u>hot chocolate was made with real melted chocolate,</u> making for a beverage that is thick and rich.

A.   hot chocolate was made with real melted chocolate,

B.   hot chocolate had been made with real melted chocolate,

C.   hot chocolate has been made with real melted chocolate

D.   hot chocolate will be made with real melted chocolate,

E.   hot chocolate is made with real melted chocolate,

22

Parrots, among the most intelligent birds in the world, have been prized pets for many <u>centuries, in fact, the first recorded instance of parrot training was written in the thirteenth century.</u>

A.   centuries, in fact, the first recorded instance of parrot training was written in the thirteenth century.

B.   centuries, but the first recorded instance of parrot training was written in the thirteenth century.

C.   centuries, writing the first recorded instance of parrot training in the thirteenth century.

D.   centuries, so the first recorded instance of parrot training was written in the thirteenth century.

E.   centuries; in fact, the first recorded instance of parrot training was written in the thirteenth century.

23

Engineers <u>designed</u> seat belts to stop the inertia of traveling bodies by applying an opposing force on the driver and passengers during a collision.

A.   designed

B.   are designing

C.   design

D.   were designing

E.   will have designed

24

The artist Prince, whose death shocked America in April 2016, was one of the most successful musical artists ever, <u>ranking twenty-seventh</u> on *Rolling Stone*'s 2010 list of "100 Greatest Artists of All Time."

A.   ranking twenty-seventh

B.   ranked twenty-seventh

C.   he ranked twenty-seventh

D.   he was ranking twenty-seventh

E.   he was ranked twenty-seventh

REVISION IN CONTEXT

Passage One

The following passage is a draft of an essay that needs strengthening through editing and revision. Read the passage and choose the best answers for the questions that follow. Some questions will ask you to improve sentences or parts of sentences. Sometimes the portion in question may require no changes at all. Consider organization, development, tone, style, word choice, and the requirements of standard written English in answering the questions.

(1) For centuries, <u>artists and philosophers have long debated about the relationship between life and art.</u> (2) While some argue that art is an imitation of life, others believe that, just as often, life ends up imitating art. (3) In no other genre is the impact of art on our real lives more visible than in the realm of science fiction. (4) Great minds of science fiction such as Jules Verne, Gene Roddenberry, H. G. Wells, and Stanley Kubrick have introduced ideas that, though fantastical at the time of their inception, eventually became reality. (5) Many of these artists were dead before they ever saw their ideas come to life.

(6) Some of humanity's biggest accomplishments were achieved first in science fiction. (7) Jules Verne wrote about humanity traveling to the moon over a century before it happened. (8) Scientists Robert H. Goddard and Leo Szilard both credit his work—on liquid-fueled rockets and atomic power, respectively—to H. G. Wells and his futuristic novels. (9) Gene Roddenberry, the creator of *Star Trek*, dreamed up replicators long before 3-D printers were invented.

(10) Jules Verne's work, for example, was the inspiration for both the submarine and the modern-day helicopter. (11) H. G. Wells wrote about automatic doors long before they began to turn up in almost every grocery store in America. (12) Roddenberry's *Star Trek* is even credited as the inspiration for the creation of the mobile phone. (13) Kubrick's HAL from *2001: A Space Odyssey* represented voice control at its finest, long before virtual assistants were installed in all the new smartphone models.

25

In context, which revision to sentence 5 (reproduced below) is most needed?
Many of these artists were dead before they ever saw their ideas come to life.

A.   delete the sentence

B.   change *many* to *most*

C.   change *dead* to *deceased*

D.   change *saw* to *witnessed*

E.   change *their* to *they're*.

26

In context, which is the best version of the underlined portion of sentence 1 (reproduced below)?

artists and philosophers have long debated about the relationship between life and art.

A.   artists and philosophers have examined the facts and debated about the relationship between life and art.

B.   artists and philosophers have hemmed, hawed, and debated about the relationship between life and art.

C.   artists and philosophers have debated about the relationship between life and art.

D.   artists and philosophers have hemmed and hawed about the relationship between life and art.

E.   artists and philosophers have forever and always debated about the relationship between life and art.

27

Which of the following introductory phrases should be inserted at the beginning of sentence 6 (reproduced below)?

Some of humanity's biggest accomplishments were achieved first in science fiction.

A.   Therefore,

B.   In fact,

C.   However,

D.   In addition,

E.   Consequently,

28

In context, which revision to sentence 8 (reproduced below) is most needed?

Scientists Robert H. Goddard and Leo Szilard both credit his work—on liquid-fueled rockets and atomic power, respectively—to H. G. Wells and his futuristic novels.

A.   delete the sentence

B.   insert *always* after the word *both*

C.   change *his* to *their*

D.   delete the phrase inside the dashes

E.   change *futuristic* to *future*

29

In context, which of the following would provide the best introduction to the final paragraph?

A.   Transportation was of particular concern to science fiction writers, who dreamed up new ways for humanity to get around the world.

B.   These same authors had other interesting ideas as well.

C.   Sometimes science fiction is so much like life it is incredible.

D.   Many of the ideas life borrows from science fiction have infiltrated our everyday lives and our world to an even greater degree.

E.   Unfortunately, some of the dreams of these science fiction writers were more realistic than others.

30

In context, which of the following would provide the best conclusion to the essay?

A.   Science fiction will, no doubt, continue to influence our technology and our world for many years to come.

B.   These men are important figures in history for their ideas, and they should be respected as such.

C.   Many other times, the ideas that turn up in science fiction never make it to the design table.

D.   It is unfair that these creative individuals did not receive any money or rewards in exchange for their ideas.

E.   Science fiction is really an interesting topic, with many ideas and influential people to study and understand.

Passage Two

The following passage is a draft of an essay that needs strengthening through editing and revision. Read the passage and choose the best answers for the questions that follow. Some questions will ask you to improve sentences or parts of sentences. Sometimes the portion in question may require no changes at all. Consider organization, development, tone, style, word choice, and the requirements of standard written English in answering the questions.

(1) Since its birth, humanity has sought explanations for the unexplainable. (2) In ancient cultures, mythology explained the weather, the elements of nature, and even the creation of the universe. (3) More recently, as recently as the last two centuries, many cultures have turned to folklore and superstition to explain odd occurrences and behaviors. (4) In the folk traditions of European countries, <u>one creature in particular takes the blame when individuals, especially children, begin acting strangely, the changeling.</u>

(5) According to many folk traditions, <u>changelings were the children of fairies or elves, left in the places of human children who had been stolen from their families by the creatures.</u> (6) If an individual's family began to notice strange behaviors in the individual, they would assume he or she had been kidnapped and replaced with a changeling. (7) This provided, at least, some answers to families whose children suffered from unexplained ailments or disabilities.

(8) Many families believed there were specific actions that would encourage the changeling to leave and return the human child. (9) In Germany, Ireland, and Wales, for example, it was thought that brewing egg shells would surprise the changeling into admitting his or her true identity. (10) Unfortunately, however, the belief that changelings could be convinced to leave was not just <u>an innocuous superstition. (11) On some occasions,</u> harm came to the individual who was thought to be a changeling.

31

Which of the following is the best way to introduce sentence 3 (reproduced below)?

More recently, as recently as the last two centuries, many cultures have turned to folklore and superstition to explain odd occurrences and behaviors.

A.   More recently,

B.   These days,

C.   Therefore,

D.   On the other hand,

E.   In addition,

32

Which is the best revision for the underlined portion of sentence 4 (reproduced below)?

one creature in particular takes the blame when individuals, especially children, begin acting strangely, the changeling.

A.   as it is now

B.   one creature in particular takes the blame when individuals, especially children, begin acting strangely: the changeling.

C.   one creature in particular takes the blame when individuals—especially children, begin acting strangely—the changeling.

D.   one creature in particular takes the blame when individuals especially children begin acting strangely. The changeling.

E.   one creature in particular takes the blame, when individuals, especially children, begin acting strangely—the changeling.

33

Which of the following would NOT be an acceptable revision of the underlined portion of sentence 5 (reproduced below)?

changelings were the children of fairies or elves, left in the places of human children who had been stolen from their families by the creatures.

A. changelings were the children of fairies or elves, who were left in the places of human children who had been stolen from their families by the creatures.

B. changelings were the children of fairies or elves; they were left in the places of human children who had been stolen from their families by the creatures.

C. changelings were the children of fairies or elves, they were left in the places of human children who had been stolen from their families by the creatures.

D. changelings were the children of fairies or elves—left in the places of human children who had been stolen from their families by the creatures.

E. changelings were the children of fairies or elves. These creatures were left in the places of human children who had been stolen from their families by the creatures.

34

Which revision to sentence 7 (reproduced below) is most needed?

This provided, at least, some answers to families whose children suffered from unexplained ailments or disabilities.

A. delete the sentence

B. insert *explanation* after *this* and before *provided*

C. change *families* to *family's*

D. change *whose* to *who's*

E. change *ailments* to *illnesses*

35

What is the best placement for sentence 8 (reproduced below)?

Many families believed there were specific actions that would encourage the changeling to leave and return the human child.

A. where it is now

B. at the end of the second paragraph

C. after sentence 9

D. after sentence 10

E. after sentence 11

36

Which is the best way to revise and combine sentences 10 and 11 (reproduced below) at the underlined point?

Unfortunately, however, the belief that changelings could be convinced to leave was not just <u>an innocuous superstition. On some occasions,</u> harm came to the individual who was thought to be a changeling.

A.   an innocuous superstition, on some occasions,

B.   an innocuous superstition, so on some occasions,

C.   an innocuous superstition, but on some occasions,

D.   an innocuous superstition; however, on some occasions,

E.   an innocuous superstition: on some occasions,

RESEARCH SKILLS

The following questions test your familiarity with basic research skills. For each question, choose the best answer.

37

Which of the following style guides would be appropriate for a student who was writing a research paper about the effects of rewards on human behavior?

- A. APA Style
- B. MLA Style
- C. Chicago Style
- D. The student should choose his or her preferred style.
- E. No style guide is required for this type of project.

38

Which of the following is an example of a primary source document?

- A. an essay that reviews the findings of a handful of related studies, compiled by an expert in the field
- B. a condemning article about the government's response in the aftermath of a tragedy, written by a young journalist who conducted interviews and read eyewitness accounts
- C. a critical review of a recently released novel, written by a renowned literature critic
- D. a paper discussing the results of an original study, conducted by the author
- E. a summary of a famous speech, composed by a political science professor

39

Which of the following could be incorporated into a research paper as a secondary source?

- A. an interpretive essay about a famous piece of art, written by a well-respected art historian
- B. the court transcript of a high-profile murder trial, compiled by a court stenographer
- C. the journal entries of a student who witnessed a protest that turned riotous when police became involved
- D. a video recording of the aftermath of a natural disaster, shot by a resident of the featured neighborhood
- E. an audio recording of a politician admitting to wrongdoing, captured by a staff member

40

Harun is writing an essay about the migration patterns of birds. Which of the following facts would NOT be relevant to his research?

A. Within a species, the tendency to migrate might vary by the location of each population, as populations in areas that are warm year-round may not need to migrate in pursuit of food.

B. Only a small percentage of bird species actually migrate long distances, but some do complete shorter migratory journeys.

C. Of the species of bird that migrate, not all do so by flying: some bird species, such as the penguin, migrate in other ways, like by swimming.

D. Prior to the late eighteenth century, many people believed that birds hibernated during the winter; only later did they accept migration as an explanation for the absence of birds during winter.

E. Migration patterns may vary within a bird species based on age and gender.

ARGUMENTATIVE ESSAY

Discuss whether you agree or disagree with this opinion, and support your views with specific examples from your own observations, reading, or experience.

Prompt

It has been said that a "mob mentality" takes over when people gather in a crowd, and otherwise law-abiding people behave inappropriately or worse. History is full of such examples, including riots and wars. It is impossible for a large group of people to remain rational and thoughtful when confronted with an emotional situation.

SOURCE BASED ESSAY

You will have 30 minutes to read two short passages on a topic and then plan and write an informative essay on that topic based on the sources provided.

Passage One

Since the hugely successful launch of Paris's Velib public bicycle share program (PBSP) in 2007, PBSPs have become a worldwide movement. Over 100 programs operate in more than 150 cities around the world, including almost fifty US cities, providing alternative transportation to millions of people. However in cities like Seattle, Washington and Melbourne, Australia, mandatory helmet laws designed to reduce injuries among bikers are stunting the growth of the system. While bikes in London and New York are typically used three to six times a day, those in Melbourne are used once at most. In 2016, Seattle's city council had to intervene when its bike program reached an unsustainably low level of participation. Even though the programs in these cities attempt to facilitate helmet access through specialized vending machines and even the availability of free helmets, mandatory helmet usage is a hurdle that deters most casual riders: the target market of BPSPs. BPSPs are a vital component of modern cities: they decrease congestion, diversify transportation options, and provide a low-cost transportation alternative for both tourists and residents. These benefits greatly outweigh the potential risk of increased injury from lack of helmet use.

Passage Two

The negative impact of mandatory helmet laws on public bicycle share programs is indisputable. However, programs that operate without such regulations pose significant public health risks. Public bicycle share systems target the casual rider who is less likely to own or carry a helmet. In systems in which helmets are available but not required, helmet usage is extremely low. Concentrated in urban areas with heavy traffic patterns, these programs encourage relatively inexperienced riders to ride in challenging conditions with insufficient protection. A study conducted by the National Institute of Health found that in cities with public bicycle share systems, head injuries increased from 42.3 percent of bicycle-related injuries before implementation of the program to 50.1 percent after implementation, and that the proportion of bicycle-related head injuries that led to admission to a trauma center increased by 14 percent. Research since the first introduction of mandatory helmet laws in the 1990s shows a consistent decrease in bicycle-related traumatic brain injuries, ranging from a decrease of 45 to 75 percent. While fewer people may use the public bikes if a mandatory helmet law in place, it is a small price to pay to ensure the safety of those who do.

MATHEMATICS

The following questions test your familiarity with mathematics. For each question, choose the best answer.

1

Simplify: $10^2 - 7(3 - 4) - 25$

A.   −118

B.   −12

C.   2

D.   68

E.   82

2

What is the domain of the piece-wise function shown in the graph?

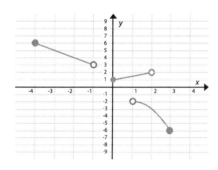

A. $D: (-4, -1) \cup (0, 3)$

B. $D: (-4, 3)$

C. $D: (-4, 1) \cup (0, 3)$

D. $D: (-4, -1) \cup (0, 1) \cup (1, 3)$

E. $D: (-4, -1) \cup (0, 2)$

3

If $\triangle ABD \sim \triangle DEF$ and the similarity ratio is 3:4, what is the measure of DE if $AB = 12$?

A.   6

B.   9

C.   12

D.   16

E.   96

4

The pie graph below shows how a state's government plans to spend its annual budget of $3 billion. How much more money does the state plan to spend on infrastructure than education?

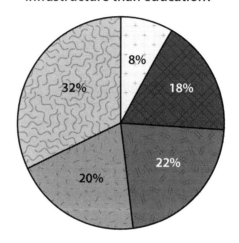

A. $60,000,000

B. $120,000,000

C. $300,000,000

D. $540,000,000

E. $600,000,000

5

40% of what number is equal to 17?

A.   2.35

B.   6.8

C.   42.5

D.   235

E.   680

6

Simplify: $\frac{7}{8} - \frac{1}{10} - \frac{2}{3}$

A. $\frac{1}{30}$

B. $\frac{4}{120}$

C. $\frac{13}{120}$

D. $\frac{4}{21}$

E. $\frac{4}{105}$

7

Which of the following is equivalent to $54z^4 + 18z^3 + 3z + 3$?

A. $18z^4 + 6z^3 + z + 1$

B. $3z(18z^3 + 6z^2 + 1)$

C. $3(18z^4 + 6z^3 + z + 1)$

D. $72z^7 + 3z$

E. $54(z^4 + 18z^3 + 3z + 3)$

8

If a student answers 42 out of 48 questions correctly on a quiz, what percentage of questions did she answer correctly?

A. 82.5%

B. 85%

C. 86%

D. 87.5%

E. 90%

9

If the surface area of a cylinder with radius of 4 feet is 48π square feet, what is its volume?

A. 1π ft.^{3}

B. 16π ft.^{3}

C. 32π ft.^{3}

D. 48π ft.^{3}

E. 64π ft.^{3}

10

Which of the following is a solution of the given equation?

$4(m + 4)^2 - 4m^2 + 20 = 276$

A. 3

B. 4

C. 6

D. 12

E. 24

11

Which of the following is the y-intercept of the given equation?

$7y - 42x + 7 = 0$

A. $(0, \frac{1}{6})$

B. $(6, 0)$

C. $(0, -1)$

D. $(-1, 0)$

E. $(0, 7)$

12

The line $f(x)$ is shown on the graph below. If $g(x) = f(x - 2) + 3$, which of the following points lies on $g(x)$?

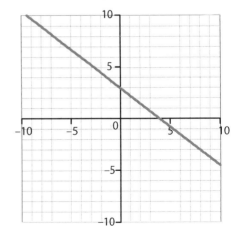

A. $(1, 2)$

B. $(2, 3)$

C. $(4, 0)$

D. $(6, 3)$

E. $(7, 2)$

13

If an employee who makes $37,500 per year receives a 5.5% raise, what is the employee's new salary?

A. $35,437.50

B. $35,625.00

C. $39,375.00

D. $39,562.50

E. $58,125.00

14

Which of the following is listed in order from least to greatest?

A. $-0.95, 0, \frac{2}{5}, 0.35, \frac{3}{4}$

B. $-1, -\frac{1}{10}, -0.11, \frac{5}{6}, 0.75$

C. $-\frac{3}{4}, -0.2, 0, \frac{2}{3}, 0.55$

D. $-1.1, -\frac{4}{5}, -0.13, 0.7, \frac{9}{11}$

E. $-0.0001, -\frac{1}{12}, 0, \frac{2}{3}, \frac{4}{5}$

15

Which inequality is represented by the following graph?

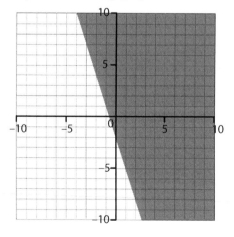

A. $y \geq -3x - 2$

B. $y \geq 3x - 2$

C. $y > -3x - 2$

D. $y \leq -3x - 2$

E. $y \geq -3x + 2$

16

Fifteen DVDs are to be arranged on a shelf. 4 of the DVDs are horror films, 6 are comedies, and 5 are science fiction. In how many ways can the DVDs be arranged if DVDs of the same genre must be placed together?

A. 1,800

B. 2,073,600

C. 6,220,800

D. 12,441,600

E. 131,216,200

17

50 shares of a financial stock and 10 shares of an auto stock are valued at $1,300. If 10 shares of the financial stock and 10 shares of the auto stock are valued at $500, what is the value of 50 shares of the auto stock?

A. $30

B. $20

C. $1,300

D. $1,500

E. $1,800

18

In a high school with 1,200 students, 200 students are in the band and 150 are in the math club. If 20 students are in both the band and the math club, how many students are in neither the band nor the math club?

A. 330 students

B. 350 students

C. 450 students

D. 870 students

E. 900 students

19

Points *B* and *C* are on a circle. Point *A* is located such that the line segments $\overline{AB}$ and $\overline{AC}$ are congruent. Which of the following could be true?

I.   *A* is the center of the circle.

II. *A* is on arc $\overset{\frown}{BC}$.

III. *A* is outside of the circle.

A.   I

B.   I and II

C.   I and III

D.   II and III

E.   I, II, and III

20

Michael is making cupcakes. He plans to give $\frac{1}{2}$ of the cupcakes to a friend and $\frac{1}{3}$ of the cupcakes to his coworkers. If he makes 48 cupcakes, how many will he have left over?

A.   8

B.   10

C.   12

D.   16

E.   24

21

Juan plans to spend 25% of his workday writing a report. If he is at work for 9 hours, how many hours will he spend writing the report?

A.   2.25

B.   2.50

C.   2.75

D.   3.25

E.   4.00

22

How many unique ways can the letters in the word *FOGGIER* be arranged?

A.   42

B.   210

C.   1050

D.   2520

E.   5040

23

Which of the following is a solution to the inequality $2x + y \leq -10$?

A. $(0, 0)$

B. $(10, 2)$

C. $(10, 10)$

D. $(-10, -10)$

E. $(0, 10)$

24

If the length of a rectangle is increased by 40% and its width is decreased by 40%, what is the effect on the rectangle's area?

A.   The area is the same.

B.   It increases by 16%.

C.   It increases by 20%.

D.   It decreases by 16%.

E.   It decreases by 20%.

25

Solve for *x*.

$x = 6(3^0)$

A.   0

B.   1

C.   6

D.   18

E.   180

26

An ice chest contains 24 sodas, some regular and some diet. The ratio of diet soda to regular soda is 1:3. How many regular sodas are there in the ice chest?

A.   1
B.   4
C.   6
D.   18
E.   24

27

The inequality $6 > x^2 - x$ is true for which of the following values of x?

I. $x < -2$
II. $-2 < x < -3$
III. $x > 3$

A.   I only
B.   II only
C.   III only
D.   I and III only
E.   I, II, and III

28

A cube is inscribed in a sphere such that each vertex on the cube touches the sphere. If the volume of the sphere is 972π cm³, what is the approximate volume of the cube in cubic centimeters?

A.   9
B.   104
C.   927
D.   1125
E.   1729

29

A bag contains 6 blue, 8 silver, and 4 green marbles. Two marbles are drawn from the bag. What is the probability that the second marble drawn will be green if replacement is not allowed?

A. $\frac{2}{51}$
B. $\frac{2}{9}$
C. $\frac{4}{17}$
D. $\frac{11}{17}$
E. $\frac{7}{9}$

30

An equilateral triangle is drawn next to a trapezoid as shown in the figure below. What is the approximate area of the new figure?

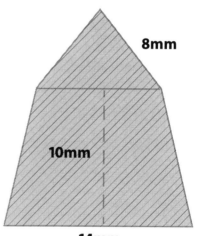

A.   128.0 mm²
B.   137.7 mm²
C.   140.5 mm²
D.   142.1 mm²
E.   149.0 mm²

31

What is $\frac{5}{8}$ as a percent?

A. 1.6%

B. 16%

C. 0.625%

D. 6.25%

E. 62.5%

32

In the fall, 425 students pass the math benchmark. In the spring, 680 students pass the same benchmark. What is the percentage increase in passing scores from fall to spring?

A. 37.5%

B. 55%

C. 60%

D. 62.5%

E. 80%

33

In the xy-plane, the line given by which of the following equations is parallel to the line $3x + 2y = 10$?

A. $y = -3x + 2$

B. $y = -\frac{3}{2}x - 10$

C. $y = \frac{1}{3}x + 5$

D. $y = \frac{2}{3}x - 10$

E. $y = 5x + 2$

34

Which number has the least value?

A. 0.305

B. 0.035

C. 0.35

D. 0.3

E. 3.5

35

Using the table, which equation demonstrates the linear relationship between x and y?

x	y
3	-18
7	-34
10	-46

A. $y = -6x - 6$

B. $y = -5x - 6$

C. $y = -4x - 6$

D. $y = -3x - 6$

E. $y = -2x - 6$

36

Robbie has a bag of treats that contains 5 pieces of gum, 7 pieces of taffy, and 8 pieces of chocolate. If Robbie reaches into the bag and randomly pulls out a treat, what is the probability that Robbie will get a piece of taffy?

A. $\frac{1}{13}$

B. $\frac{1}{7}$

C. $\frac{7}{20}$

D. $\frac{7}{13}$

E. $\frac{13}{20}$

37

In which quadrant is the point $(-3, -4)$ located?

A. I

B. II

C. III

D. IV

E. all of the above

38

Aprille has $50 to buy the items on her shopping list. Assuming there is no sales tax, about how much change will Aprille receive after buying all the items on her list?

Aprille's List	
Item	**Price**
Hammer	$13.24
Screwdriver	$11.99
Nails	$4.27
Wrench	$5.60

- A. $12
- B. $13
- C. $14
- D. $15
- E. $16

39

If angles *a* and *b* are congruent, what is the measurement of angle *c*?

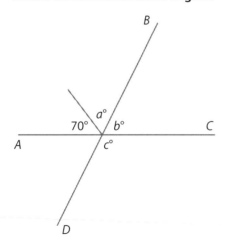

- A.   55°
- B.   70°
- C.   110°
- D.   120°
- E.   125°

40

Out of 1560 students at Ward Middle School, 15% want to take French. Which expression represents how many students want to take French?

- A.   1560 ÷ 15
- B.   1560 × 15
- C.   1560 × 0.15
- D.   1560 ÷ 0.15
- E.   1560 × 1.5

41

Justin has a summer lawn care business and earns $40 for each lawn he mows. He also pays $35 per week in business expenses. Which of the following expressions represents Justin's profit after *x* weeks if he mows *m* number of lawns?

- A. $40m - 35x$
- B. $40m + 35x$
- C. $35x(40 + m)$
- D. $35(40m + x)$
- E. $40x(35 + m)$

42

Lynn has 4 test scores in science class. Each test is worth 100 points, and Lynn has an 85% average. If Lynn scored 100% on each of the first 3 tests, what did she score on her 4th test?

- A.   40%
- B.   55%
- C.   60%
- D.   85%
- E.   100%

43

Erica is at work for $8\frac{1}{2}$ hours a day. If she takes one 30-minute lunch break and two 15-minute breaks during the day, how many hours does she work?

A.   6 hours, 30 minutes

B.   6 hours, 45 minutes

C.   7 hours, 15 minutes

D.   7 hours, 30 minutes

E.   7 hours, 45 minutes

44

Using the function table, what is the value of $f(20)$?

x	f(x)
5	12
10	22
15	32
20	
25	52

A.   20

B.   25

C.   40

D.   42

E.   50

45

If a car uses 8 gallons of gas to travel 650 miles, how many miles can it travel using 12 gallons of gas?

A.   870 miles

B.   895 miles

C.   915 miles

D.   975 miles

E.   1,025 miles

46

Two spheres are tangent to each other. One has a volume of 36π, and the other has a volume of 288π. What is the greatest distance between a point on one of the spheres and a point on the other sphere?

A.   6

B.   9

C.   18

D.   36

E.   63

47

A baby weighed 7.5 pounds at birth and gained weight at a rate of 6 ounces per month for the first six months. Which equation describes the baby's weight in ounces, y, after t months?

A. $y = 6t + 7.5$

B. $y = 6t + 120$

C. $y = 7.5t + 120$

D. $y = 6t + 7.5$

E. $y = 6t - 120$

48

A person earning a salary between $75,000 and $100,000 per year will pay $10,620 in taxes plus 20% of any amount over $75,000. What would a person earning $80,000 per year pay in taxes?

A. $10,620

B. $11,620

C. $12,120

D. $12,744

E. $15,620

49

New York had the fewest months with less than 3 inches of rain in every year except:

Number of Months with 3 or Fewer Than 3 Inches of Rain

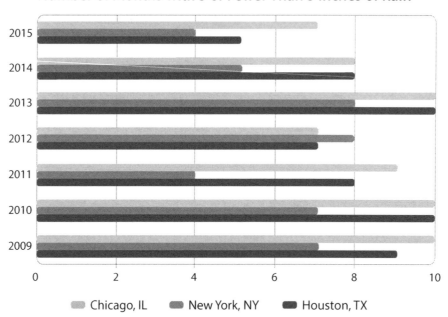

Chicago, IL   New York, NY   Houston, TX

A.   2011

B.   2012

C.   2013

D.   2014

E.   2015

50

Kim and Chris are writing a book together. Kim wrote twice as many pages as Chris, and together they wrote 240 pages. How many pages did Chris write?

A.   80

B.   100

C.   120

D.   160

E.   240

51

What is the probability of selecting either a king of spades or a king of clubs from a deck of 52 cards?

A. $\frac{1}{104}$

B. $\frac{1}{52}$

C. $\frac{1}{26}$

D. $\frac{3}{52}$

E. $\frac{1}{2}$

52

Which graph shows the solution to $y = 2x + 1$?

A.

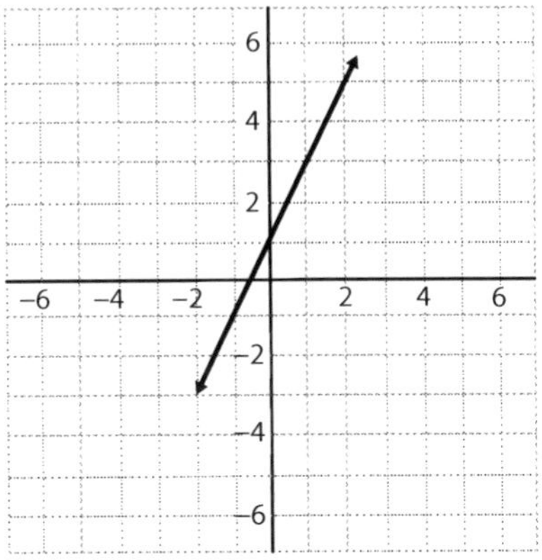

B.

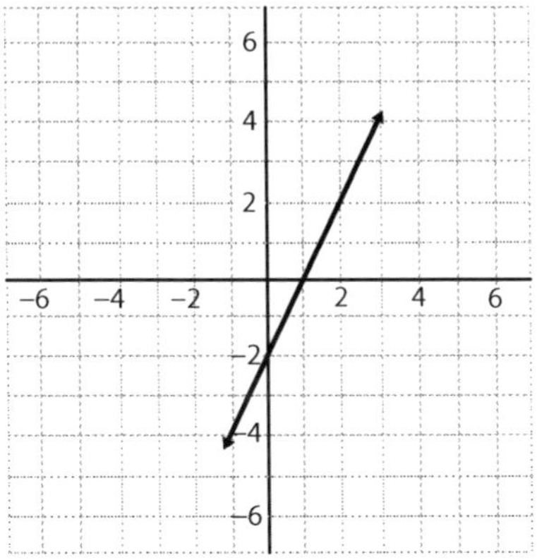

C.

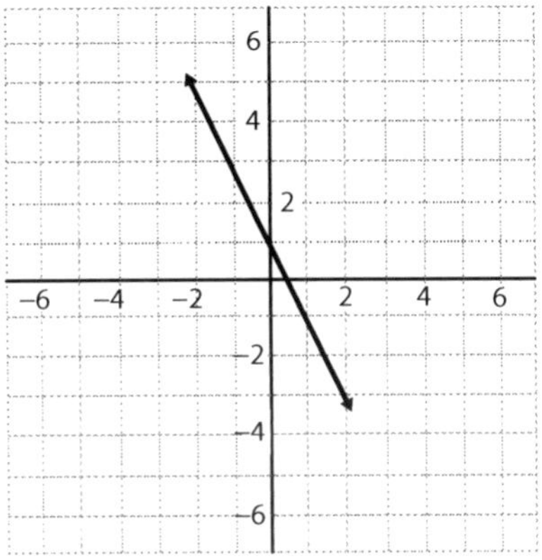

D.

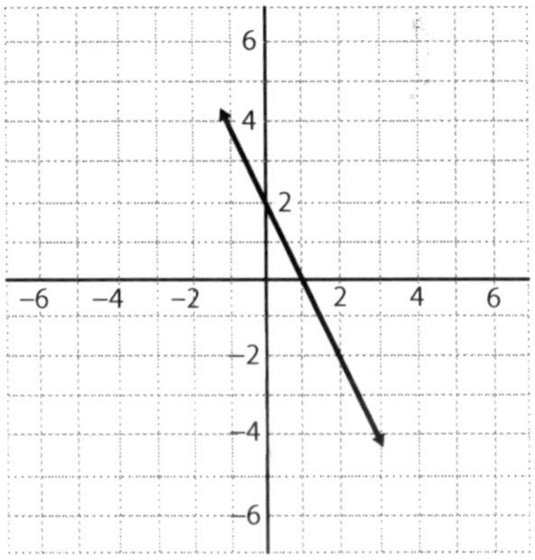

E.

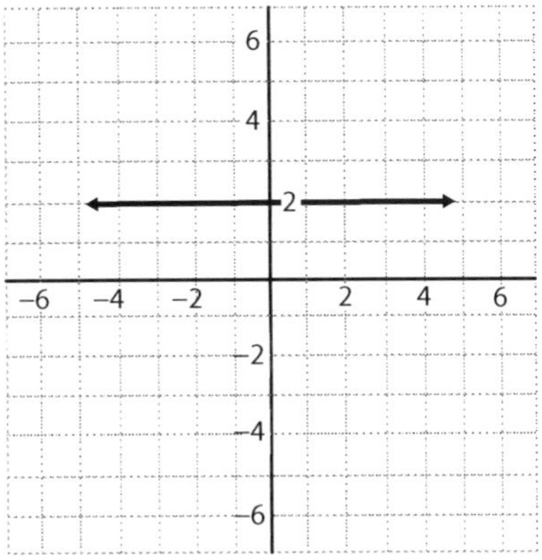

53

Which digit is in the hundredths place when 1.3208 is divided by 5.2?

A.   0

B.   4

C.   5

D.   8

E.   9

54

Solve for x: $5x - 4 = 3(8 + 3x)$

A. -7

B. $-\frac{3}{4}$

C. $\frac{3}{4}$

D.   7

E.   8

55

A grocery store sold 30% of its pears and had 455 pears remaining. How many pears did the grocery store start with?

A.   602

B.   650

C.   692

D.   700

E.   755

56

Solve the system of equations for y: $5x + 4y = 20$; $x = 2y + 1$

A. $y = \frac{2}{5}$

B. $y = \frac{4}{5}$

C. $y = \frac{15}{14}$

D. $y = \frac{5}{4}$

E. $y = 4$

Answer Key

READING

1)

A.   Incorrect. While the author points out that jazz is often associated with New Orleans, he does not indicate that this is a problem or that people should change how they think about jazz.

B.   Correct. The author writes that "[j]azz music was played by and for a more expressive and freed populace than the United States had previously seen." In addition to "the emergence of the flapper[,]" the 1920s saw "the explosion of African American art and culture now known as the Harlem Renaissance".

C.   Incorrect. Though this is mentioned in the passage, it is not the main idea.

D.   Incorrect. Though this is stated at the end of the passage, it is not the main idea.

E.   Incorrect. According to the passage, the first part of this statement is true, but the second part is not: in fact, the Jazz Age "saw major urban centers experiencing new economic, cultural, and artistic vitality" as well as suffrage for American women.

2)

A.   Correct. The author writes that "[j]azz music was played by and for a more expressive and freed populace than the United States had previously seen." In addition to "the emergence of the flapper[,]" the 1920s saw "the explosion of African American art and culture now known as the Harlem Renaissance."

B.   Incorrect. Though these artists are mentioned in the passage, the author does not indicate that they were the most important jazz musicians of the Harlem Renaissance, only that they were important.

C.   Incorrect. Though women's suffrage is mentioned in the passage, the author gives no indication that jazz music was the cause of this change.

D.   Incorrect. Though these artists are mentioned in the passage, the author does not indicate that they supported the movement for women's suffrage.

E.   Incorrect. Though the author says that the Roaring Twenties "saw major urban centers experiencing new economic, cultural, and artistic vitality[,]" he does not identify a causal relationship between jazz music and the country's economic prosperity.

3)

A.   Incorrect. The author writes, "Jazz music also provided the soundtrack for the explosion of African American art and culture now known as the Harlem Renaissance." However, this is not the primary purpose of the passage.

B.   Incorrect. Though the author names many of the important jazz musicians who were playing during the 1920s, this is not the primary purpose of the passage.

C.   Correct. The author opens the passage saying, "In recent decades, jazz has been associated with New Orleans and festivals like Mardi Gras, but in the 1920s, jazz was a booming trend whose influence reached into many aspects of American culture." He then goes on to elaborate on what these movements were.

D.   Incorrect. The author discusses the effects of jazz music on arts and culture in the 1920s but does not go into the history of the art.

E.   Incorrect. The author briefly mentions the modern association of jazz with festivals like Mardi Gras, but this is not the primary purpose of the passage.

4)

A.   Incorrect. In the first paragraph, the author writes, "In fact, the years between World War I and the Great Depression were known as the Jazz Age, a term coined by F. Scott Fitzgerald in his famous novel *The Great Gatsby*."

B.   Correct. At the end of the first paragraph, the author writes, "Ella Fitzgerald, for example, moved from Virginia to New York City to begin her much-lauded singing career, and jazz pioneer Louis Armstrong got his big break in Chicago."

C.   Incorrect. At the beginning of the second paragraph, the author writes, "Women gained the right to vote and were openly seen drinking and dancing to jazz music. This period marked the emergence of the flapper, a woman determined to make a statement about her new role in society."

D.   Incorrect. Toward the end of the second paragraph, the author writes, "Jazz music also provided the soundtrack for the explosion of African American art and culture now known as the Harlem Renaissance."

E.   Incorrect. In the first sentence, the author writes, "In recent decades, jazz has been associated with New Orleans and festivals like Mardi Gras, but in the 1920s, jazz was a booming trend whose influence reached into many aspects of American culture."

5)

A.   Incorrect. The author states that the term *Jazz Age* was "coined by F. Scott Fitzgerald in his famous novel *The Great Gatsby*" but does not elaborate on Fitzgerald's relationship to the artists of the age.

B.   Incorrect. The author does not discuss the current popularity of jazz, only that it is often associated with New Orleans.

C.   Correct. The author writes that "[j]azz music was played by and for a more expressive and freed populace than the United States had previously seen." In addition to "the emergence of the flapper[,]" the 1920s saw "the explosion of African American art and culture now known as the Harlem Renaissance."

D.   Incorrect. The passage does not indicate that flappers and African American musicians worked together, only that they both used jazz music as a way to express themselves.

E.   Incorrect. Though the author says that the Roaring Twenties "saw major urban centers experiencing new economic, cultural, and artistic vitality[,]" he does not identify a causal relationship between jazz music and the country's economic prosperity.

6)

A.   Incorrect. The passage implies that "the physical and biological consequences of nuclear war" have impacts that reach much further than the military.

B.   Incorrect. The second part of the second sentence suggests that the consequences of nuclear war—rather than the specific technology of nuclear weapons—are the focus of this student's paper.

C.   Incorrect. The author mentions the decision by world powers to cease testing nuclear weapons in the atmosphere; however, this is only one detail and is likely not the focus of the essay as a whole.

D.   Correct. The passage gives a short history of thermonuclear weapons and then introduces its main topic—the physical and biological consequences of nuclear war.

E.   Incorrect. Though the author mentions a testing ceasefire by world power, this is only one detail of the passage and is likely not the focus of the essay as a whole.

7)

A.   Incorrect. The author identifies the ideals associated with idealism but does not offer an opinion on or advocate for them.

B.   Correct. The purpose of the passage is to explain what an idealist believes in. The author does not offer any opinions or try to persuade readers about the importance of certain values.

C.   Incorrect. The author states that social and political discourse are "permeated with idealism" but does not suggest that this is destructive or wrong.

D.   Incorrect. The author provides the reader with information but does not seek to change the reader's opinions or behaviors.

E.   Incorrect. The author provides information about how idealists view the truth but does not necessarily intend for readers to question it.

8)

A.   Incorrect. According to the passage, gifts were assigned by Epimetheus and Prometheus, not purchased.

B.   Incorrect. The passage gives no indication that gifts were forgotten.

C.   Incorrect. The passage gives no indication that gifts were accepted by the animals, only that they were given by Epimetheus and Prometheus.

D.   Correct. The word *given* best describes the idea that the gifts have been handed out: "to the lion [Epimetheus] gave strength; to the bird, swiftness; to the fox, sagacity; and so on."

E.   Incorrect. The passage does not indicate that the gifts were lost.

9)

A.   Incorrect. The author does not suggest that the narrative of the Civil War as "a battle for individual identity" is a complicated one, only that it is untrue.

B.   Correct. The author writes, "All other explanations for the war are either a direct consequence of the South's desire for wealth at the expense of her fellow man or a fanciful invention to cover up this sad portion of our nation's history."

C.   Incorrect. The author does not discuss the extent to which the attempt to "cover up this sad portion of our nation's history" was successful or unsuccessful.

D.   Incorrect. Though the author may agree that the invention of the identity narrative is unfortunate, this is not the best answer choice to highlight her main assertion that it is untrue.

E.   Incorrect. This answer choice does not fit in the context of the passage.

10)

A.   Correct. The author writes, "But people who try to sell you this narrative are wrong. The Civil War was not a battle of cultural identities—it was a battle about slavery."

B.   Incorrect. Though the author describes the cultural differences between the North and South in the first half of the passage, her primary purpose is revealed when she states, "But people who try to sell you this narrative are wrong."

C.   Incorrect. The author makes no comment on the outcome of the Civil War.

D.   Incorrect. The author asserts that, despite the popular identity narrative, the cause of the Civil War was actually very clear: "The Civil War was not a battle of cultural identities—it was a battle about slavery."

E.   Incorrect. The author describes some of the factors that contributed to the Civil War but asserts that only one of those factors was actually the cause of the war: "The Civil War was not a battle of cultural identities—it was a battle about slavery."

11)

A.   Incorrect. The author asserts that, despite the popular narrative, cultural differences were not the cause of the Civil War.

B.   Correct. The author writes, "The Civil War was not a battle of cultural identities—it was a battle about slavery. All other explanations for the war are either a direct consequence of the South's desire for wealth at the expense of her fellow man or a fanciful invention to cover up this sad portion of our nation's history."

C.   Incorrect. The author does not discuss the strengths of the North or provide any reason for why it won the war.

D.   Incorrect. Though the author mentions these cultural beliefs, she does not suggest that these were the reasons the South was defeated.

E.   Incorrect. Though the author closes with this sentiment, it is not the main idea of the passage.

12)

A.   Incorrect. The author indicates that the house on Pine Street "had enough space inside[.]"

B.   Correct. The author says that the house on Pine Street "had enough space inside but didn't have a big enough yard for [their] three dogs."

C. Incorrect. The author does not mention the neighborhood of the Pine Street house.

D. Incorrect. The author does not mention the price of the Pine Street house.

E. Incorrect. The author indicates that the Pine Street house "had enough space inside" but does not mention the price of the house.

---

13)

A. Incorrect. Sam's Babysitting Service brought in a total of $200 during the month of April.

B. Correct. In February the service earned $1100, and in April it earned $200. The difference between the two months is $900.

C. Incorrect. Sam's Babysitting Service brought in a total of $1100 during the month of February.

D. Incorrect. Sam's Babysitting Service brought in a total of $1300 during February and April combined.

E. Incorrect. Sam's Babysitting Service did not bring in $1800 during February and April combined.

---

14)

A. Incorrect. The author's use of first person and exclamation marks signifies a more personal, less professional tone.

B. Correct. The author uses several markers of casual writing, including the first person, exclamation marks, and informal language.

C. Incorrect. The author writes that while recent months "have admittedly been a bit slow," she and her team are "hoping for a big summer once school gets out." While she recognizes that business has been slow, she does not seem concerned.

D. Incorrect. The author takes personal ownership over the business and expresses excitement about the busy Valentine's Day schedule and the upcoming summer.

E. Incorrect. Though the author mentions that recent months "have admittedly been a bit slow," she remains positive about the summer ahead.

---

15)

A. Correct. This detail is not stated in the passage.

B. Incorrect. The second paragraph states that "when a person can't breathe through his nose, he won't be able to keep his mouth closed long enough to get an accurate reading."

C. Incorrect. The final paragraph states that "no matter which method [of taking a temperature] is chosen, however, it's important to check the average temperature for each region, as it can vary by several degrees."

D. Incorrect. The second paragraph states that "the most common way people measure body temperature is orally."

E. Incorrect. The final paragraph states that "certain people, like agitated patients or fussy babies, won't be able to sit still long enough for an accurate reading."

---

16)

A. Incorrect. Thermometers that measure temperature in the ear and temporal artery are mentioned in the passage; however, they are a supporting detail for the author's primary purpose.

B. **Correct.** In the first paragraph, the author writes, "But what's the best way to get an accurate reading? The answer depends on the situation." She then goes on to describe various options and their applications.

C. Incorrect. Though this detail is mentioned, it is not the author's primary focus.

D. Incorrect. The author writes about how many people—not only nurses—use different types of thermometers in different situations.

E. Incorrect. The author does not go into detail about how to take a baby's temperature.

17)

A. Incorrect. The author indicates that "[t]aking a person's temperature is one of the most basic and common health care tasks" but does not suggest that everyone needs to know the various methods of completing this task.

B. **Correct.** The author indicates that "[t]he most common way people measure body temperature is orally" but that "[t]here are many situations [...] when measuring temperature orally isn't an option." She then goes on to describe these situations in the second and third paragraphs.

C. Incorrect. The author mentions this detail, but this choice does not provide an adequate summary of the passage as a whole.

D. Incorrect. The author indicates that there are many different ways to take temperature, but this does not provide an adequate summary of the author's main point.

E. Incorrect. The author mentions this detail, but this choice does not provide an adequate summary of the passage as a whole.

18)

A. **Correct.** The second paragraph of the passage states that "[u]sing the rectum also has the added benefit of providing a much more accurate reading than other locations can provide."

B. Incorrect. In the final paragraph, the author suggests that "certain people, like agitated patients or fussy babies" might have a difficult time sitting still but does not suggest that this is a problem for "many" people.

C. Incorrect. In the final paragraph, the author writes that "it's important to check the average temperature for each region, as it can vary by several degrees" but does not cite this as a reason to use a rectal thermometer.

D. Incorrect. The author does not mention access to thermometers as a consideration.

E. Incorrect. The author suggests that "agitated patients" and "fussy babies" who cannot sit still might require that their caretaker use ear or temporal artery thermometers.

19)

A. **Correct.** The final paragraph states that "agitated patients...won't be able to sit still long enough for an accurate reading[.]" The reader can infer that an agitated patient is a patient who is visibly upset, annoyed, or uncomfortable.

B. Incorrect. While some agitated patients may move quickly, this is not necessarily the meaning of the word in context.

C. Incorrect. The term *violently ill* does not necessarily explain why a patient would have a difficult time sitting still.

D.   Incorrect. The term *slightly dirty* does not explain why a patient would have a difficult time sitting still.

E.   Incorrect. A patient who was physically comfortable would not have a difficult time sitting still.

20)

A.   Incorrect. The passage states that, "Distances are not gauged, ellipses not measured, velocities not ascertained, times not known." However, it goes on to say, "Nevertheless, the recurrence is sure." In other words, people can be sure that things in life, including feeling happy or sad, recur at intervals.

B.   Incorrect. The passage indicates that suffering is periodic for people in general, not just some people.

C.   Correct. The passage concludes, "Happiness is not a matter of events; it depends upon the tides of the mind." The periodic fluctuations of a person's state of mind determine happiness.

D.   Incorrect. The passage is about mental experience having recurrent periods of happiness and unhappiness.

E.   Incorrect. This statement is inaccurate. Happiness is a real possibility, but it is a reflection of a person's state of mind.

21)

A.   Correct. The author states that "popcorn continued to rule the snack food kingdom until the rise in popularity of home televisions during the 1950s" when the industry saw a "decline in sales" as a result of the changing pastimes of the American people.

B.   Incorrect. The author indicates that "the introduction of the mobile popcorn machine" occurred "at the World's Columbian Exposition" after the Great Depression.

C.   Incorrect. The author indicates that the primary reason people consumed popcorn during the Great Depression was the it was advertised as a "wholesome and economical food[,]...a luxury the downtrodden could afford." This implies that the cost, not the luxuriousness, of popcorn was its primary appeal.

D.   Incorrect. The author indicates that "[t]he American love affair with popcorn began in 1912" and only after this did "popcorn move from the theater into fairs and parks."

E.   Incorrect. The author indicates that "[t]he popcorn industry flourished during the Great Depression when it was advertised as a wholesome and economical food" but does not suggest that these are the same reasons popcorn is popular today.

22)

A.   Incorrect. The author states that the Aztec people popped popcorn both for special occasions ("in ceremonies") and for regular consumption ("as a food staple").

B.   Correct. The author states, "For the Aztec Indians who called the caves home, popcorn (or *momochitl*) played an important role in society, both as a food staple and in ceremonies." This implies that the Aztec people popped popcorn both for special occasions ("in ceremonies") and for regular consumption ("as a food staple").

C.   Incorrect. Though the author does describe the process the Aztec peoples used to cook popcorn, this definition does not fit in the context of the sentence, when the author contrasts the phrase "as a food staple" with the phrase "in ceremonies."

D.   Incorrect. This definition does not fit in the context of the sentence.

E.   Incorrect. The author contrasts the phrase "as a food staple" with the phrase "in ceremonies" to show that popcorn was enjoyed for regular consumption, not to indicate the nutritional value of the snack.

23)

A.   Incorrect. Though the author does discuss the effect of the microwave on the popcorn industry ("it wasn't until microwave popcorn became commercially available in 1981 that at-home popcorn consumption began to grow exponentially"), this is not the primary purpose of the passage.

B.   Incorrect. Though this may be true, it is not the primary purpose of the passage; the author traces the history of popcorn from ancient to modern times.

C.   **Correct.** In the opening paragraph the author writes, "But popcorn isn't just for fun— it's also a multimillion-dollar-a-year industry with a long and fascinating history." The author then goes on to illustrate the history of popcorn from the ancient Aztecs, to early twentieth century America, to the present day.

D.   Incorrect. Though the author discusses the ancient Aztecs, the rest of the passage is focused on popcorn's history in American culture.

E.   Incorrect. Though the author mentions the rapid growth of the popcorn industry in recent decades ("it wasn't until microwave popcorn became commercially available in 1981 that at-home popcorn consumption began to grow exponentially"), this is not the primary focus of the passage.

24)

A.   Incorrect. The author mentions that popcorn was consumed "both as a food staple and in ceremonies" in Aztec culture but does not tie this to the popcorn industry in the United States.

B.   Incorrect. The author indicates that growth in popularity of home televisions actually hurt the popcorn industry: "Popcorn continued to rule the snack food kingdom until the rise in popularity of home televisions during the 1950s" when the industry saw "a decline in sales[.]"

C.   **Correct.** The author writes, "The popcorn industry flourished during the Great Depression when it was advertised as a wholesome and economical food."

D.   Incorrect. Though the nutritional value of popcorn is mentioned as a factor in its popularity during the Great Depression, the author does not indicate that this is the reason for its popularity in the United States.

E.   Incorrect. The author indicates that "the popcorn industry reacted to the decline in sales quickly by introducing pre-popped and unpopped popcorn for home consumption" but goes on to say that it was not until three decades later, with the rise in availability of the microwave, that the industry saw significant growth.

25)

A.   **Correct.** This statement summarizes the entire passage, including the brief history of popcorn in ancient cultures and the growth in the popularity of popcorn in America.

B.   Incorrect. Though the author does mention the history of popcorn in ancient cultures, this is not an adequate summary of the passage as a whole.

C.   Incorrect. Though the author discusses the history of popcorn in America, this is not an adequate summary of the passage as a whole.

D.   Incorrect. Though the author does mention the versatility and popularity of popcorn as a snack food, this is not an adequate summary of the passage as a whole.

E.   Incorrect. Though the author does mention the versatility and popularity of popcorn as a snack food, this is not an adequate summary of the passage as a whole.

26)

A.   Incorrect. The author writes, "In 1948, Herbert Dick and Earle Smith discovered old popcorn dating back 4000 years in the New Mexico Bat Cave."

B.   Incorrect. The author writes, "The American love affair with popcorn began in 1912, when popcorn was first sold in theaters."

C.   **Correct.** The author writes, "However, it wasn't until microwave popcorn became commercially available in 1981 that at-home popcorn consumption began to grow exponentially. With the wide availability of microwaves in the United States, popcorn also began popping up in offices and hotel rooms."

D.   Incorrect. The author writes, "However, the home still remains the most popular popcorn eating spot: today, 70 percent of the 16 billion quarts of popcorn consumed annually in the United States are eaten at home."

E.   Incorrect. The author writes, "The popcorn industry flourished during the Great Depression when it was advertised as a wholesome and economical food. Selling for five to ten cents a bag, it was a luxury that the downtrodden could afford."

27)

A.   **Correct.** Victoria's win implies that she played in a competitive event.

B.   Incorrect. The word *scheduled* makes this answer choice incorrect.

C.   Incorrect. This definition does not make sense in the context of the sentence.

D.   Incorrect. Victoria's win implies that the match refers to a game, not a personal relationship.

E.   Incorrect. Victoria's win indicates that this match refers to a game, not a person.

28)

A.   Incorrect. The author includes a quote from de Tocqueville's observations of life in the nineteenth century United States but does not indicate that his contributions to the field were substantial.

B.   **Correct.** The author notes de Tocqueville's observation: "The more I advanced in the study of American society, the more I perceived that the equality of conditions is the fundamental fact from which all others seem to be derived," implying that equality was the most important ideal in the United States.

C.   Incorrect. De Tocqueville makes note of a "general equality of conditions" but does not specify that this means all people had rights.

D.   Incorrect. De Tocqueville discusses conditions in America but makes no comment on nineteenth-century French society.

E.   Incorrect. De Tocqueville discovered the "general equality of conditions" as a result of his observations, but he does not indicate that he seeks to understand how this equality was achieved.

29)

A.   **Correct.** *New* best describes the idea that the writer is encountering things he has never seen before.

B.   Incorrect. De Tocqueville does not refer to any written objects but rather to the observable conditions of the American people.

C.   Incorrect. De Tocqueville gives the impression that he gets a strong sense about the equality of conditions in America, not that he is uncertain of them.

D.   Incorrect. De Tocqueville says he was "struck" by the "general equality of conditions" but does not indicate that was confused by them.

E.   Incorrect. Though de Tocqueville does seem to find the American way of life interesting, this interest seems to stem from the newness of the experience.

30)

A.   Incorrect. De Tocqueville references the "general equality of conditions" in the nineteenth century, suggesting that defined social classes have not yet emerged.

B.   Incorrect. De Tocqueville discusses the conditions of the American people as a whole but makes no comment about the natures of the people themselves.

C.   Incorrect. De Tocqueville makes no reference to achievement or prosperity, only to the "general equality of conditions" in the new country.

D.   **Correct.** "Equality of conditions" suggests that people's living conditions, in terms of economics and social status, were equal.

E.   Incorrect. In the final sentences of the quote, de Tocqueville indicates that the more he studied American equality, the more it appeared to be foundational to the American way of life.

31)

A.   Incorrect. The second sentence mentions several countries that at least partially conquered Ireland, but there is no mention of a war that led to that.

B.   **Correct.** The sentence identifies the countries that have conquered but not permanently subdued Ireland. It provides supporting information for the main point, the first sentence that states Ireland cannot be fully conquered.

C.   Incorrect. Although Ireland has experienced the attempts of other countries to conquer and subdue her, there is no mention of that being a central problem.

D.   Incorrect. Several countries are listed, but they are identified as conquerors, not settlers.

E.   Incorrect. The main point is that Ireland never has fully lost her independence.

32)

A.   Incorrect. This answer choice does not fit in the context of the sentence.

B.   **Correct.** The author writes that "a number of myths about animal pain still plague the field of veterinary medicine and prevent practitioners from making pain management a priority."

C.   Incorrect. The author does not imply that the myths are disturbing, only that they "prevent practitioners from making pain management a priority."

D.   Incorrect. The author indicates that the myths have a negative effect on the treatment of animals, not a positive one.

E.   Incorrect. The author does not imply that the myths are confusing, only that they "prevent practitioners from making pain management a priority."

33)

A.   Incorrect. The author does not seek to make the experience of animals relatable, only to indicate that it is similar to the way humans experience pain and that it should be considered during the course of treatment.

B.   Incorrect. The author does not seek to change the behavior of the reader.

C.   Incorrect. The author does not challenge popular perceptions about the experience of going to the dentist; she only suggests that the experience is similar to that of animals in pain at the veterinarian's office.

D.   **Correct.** The author writes that "[e]ven the emotional reaction to a painful experience (like being afraid to return to the dentist after an unpleasant visit) is mirrored in animals."

E.   Incorrect. The author does not address the fear that children have of going to the dentist.

34)

A.   **Correct.** The author writes that "veterinarians must be aware of the survival instinct of many animals to mask pain in response to stressful experiences or foreign environments."

B.   Incorrect. This answer choice does not fit in the context of the sentence.

C.   Incorrect. The author does not indicate that distance is a reason that animals might mask their pain.

D.   Incorrect. The author does not indicate that exoticism is a reason that animals might mask their pain.

E.   Incorrect. The author does not indicate that animals mask their pain only in dangerous environments.

35)

A.   Incorrect. The author writes that "pain management is widely accepted as a necessary job of practitioners."

B.   Incorrect. The author does not indicate that veterinarians employ outdated methods of pain management.

C.   Incorrect. The author writes that "pain management is widely accepted as a necessary job of practitioners."

D.   **Correct.** The author writes, "Though many advancements have been made in research sciences [...] a number of myths about animal pain still plague the field of veterinary medicine and prevent practitioners from making pain management a priority."

E.   Incorrect. The author does not indicate that veterinarians lack the technology for effective pain management.

36)

A.   Incorrect. The author does not suggest that veterinaries attempt to communicate with animals about their pain.

B.   Correct. The author writes that "veterinarians must be aware of the survival instinct of many animals to mask pain in response to stressful experiences or foreign environments. For these reasons, diagnostic tools and strategies are instrumental in the effective practice of veterinary medicine."

C.   Incorrect. The author suggests that veterinarians have a responsibility that extends beyond informing pet owners of the importance of close observation.

D.   Incorrect. The author indicates that veterinarians should rely on existing "diagnostic tools and strategies available to today's practitioners" that have been found "to be effective." She does not indicate that veterinarians should invent their own methods for assessing and treating pain.

E.   Incorrect. The author indicates that veterinarians should focus on treating pain in their animal patients.

37)

A.   Incorrect. The author does not indicate that objective pain scales are used to compare pain levels in different animals but that they are useful for "evaluating the effectiveness of various treatment options" in one animal.

B.   Incorrect. The author does not indicate that this is an application of the objective pain scale.

C.   Incorrect. The author does not indicate that objective pain scales are useful for this reason.

D.   Correct. The author writes that to diagnose pain in animals, "a veterinarian might make use of an objective pain scale, by which he or she could assess the animal's condition according to a number of criteria. This tool is especially useful throughout the course of treatment, as it provides the practitioner with a quantitative measure for evaluating the effectiveness of various treatment options."

E.   Incorrect. The author does not indicate that objective pain scales are useful for this reason.

38)

A.   Incorrect. The author of Passage 1 gives no indication that physical damage and pain are unrelated.

B.   Incorrect. The author of Passage 1 does not indicate that presumptive diagnosis is ineffective when used with animals.

C.   Correct. The author of Passage 1 indicates that "according to Grant, the biological mechanisms by which we experience pain are the very same mechanisms by which animals experience pain." This indicates that the author believes that pain, and the process of pain management, is somewhat similar in animals and humans.

D.   Incorrect. The author of Passage 1 does not indicate that presumptive diagnosis is ineffective when used with animals.

E.   Incorrect. The author of Passage 1 does not indicate that pain diagnosis is more difficult in animals.

39)

A. Incorrect. The second passage does not reject the claim that pain management should be a priority of veterinarians.

B. Correct. The author of the first passage writes that "a number of myths about animal pain still plague the field of veterinary medicine and present practitioners from making pain management a priority." This implies that the author believes pain management should be a priority of veterinarians. The second author writes that "diagnostic tools and strategies are instrumental in the effective practice of veterinary medicine" and then goes on to describe some of these tools.

C. Incorrect. The author of the second passage does not contradict that the myths in the first passage are untrue.

D. Incorrect. The authors do not discuss shortcomings of veterinary medicine in broad terms; they only address the issue of pain management.

E. Incorrect. The first author does not discuss early approaches to pain management in animals.

40)

A. Correct. The first author writes, "Grant emphasizes that veterinarians must be aware that a lack of obvious signs does not necessarily suggest that pain is not present: in fact, many animals, especially those that are prey animals in the wild, are likely to conceal their pain out of an instinct to hide weaknesses that may make them easy targets for predators." The second author agrees, saying that "veterinarians must be aware of the survival instinct of many animals to mask pain in response to stressful experiences or foreign environments."

B. Incorrect. While the first author indicates that pain management should be priority for veterinarians, the second author does not discuss the prioritization of pain management in relation to other responsibilities.

C. Incorrect. The first author seeks to dispel myths that exist in the world of veterinary medicine; the second author does not.

D. Incorrect. The second author indicates that thorough examinations must be conducted; the first author does not.

E. Incorrect. Neither author emphasizes the importance of oral health in animals.

41)

A. Incorrect. The diagram indicates that products require an interaction between the enzyme and the substrate, and that they are formed from the substrate.

B. Incorrect. The diagram indicates that products require an interaction between the enzyme and the substrate, and that they are formed from the substrate.

C. Correct. The diagram indicates that products are formed when the substrate is broken apart.

D. Incorrect. The diagram indicates that the active site is an area on the enzyme.

E. Incorrect. The diagram indicates that products are formed when the substrate is broken apart.

42)

A.   **Correct.** He tells us that natural facts cause or give us words; then, the words are the effects that signify the spiritual ideas understood or signified by natural facts, like *Right* means straight; *wrong* means twisted.

B.   Incorrect. He does not explain the sequence of steps or actions that led to "the process by which this transformation is made," only that it "is hidden from us."

C.   Incorrect. He does not explain how language was formed over time, only that connections between words and natural facts happened in the remote past.

D.   Incorrect. Spatial details are used to describe a place or object; in this passage, the author is explaining an idea.

E.   Incorrect. The text is not about a problem, although the reader may have problems understanding the philosophical idea expressed.

43)

A.   Incorrect. Slavery was current practice, but the present time does not make sense in the context of Mrs. Auld's growth.

B.   **Correct.** Mrs. Auld had to accept and grow into the customs of her social group.

C.   Incorrect. The word "growth" implies the development of her thinking, which is unrelated to popularity.

D.   Incorrect. The growth is Mrs. Auld's growth, not universal or general growth.

E.   Incorrect. "Fashionable" is the same as "popular" in this context. While slavery was widely accepted, the context implies Mrs. Auld's growth of thinking, not simply subscribing to popular belief.

44)

A.   **Correct.** Mrs. Auld treats Douglass well and educates him when she is following her natural response to a child. By following her husband's instruction to not educate a slave, she goes against her conscience.

B.   Incorrect. This is true; Mrs. Auld was pressured by her husband. However, it is not the central idea.

C.   Incorrect. If Mrs. Auld had continued to teach Douglass to read, she would most likely have experienced marital discord. However, this is not the central idea.

D.   Incorrect. The common practice of slavery was to deny enslaved persons education and to treat them as property. This is not the central idea.

E.   Incorrect. Mrs. Auld broke the rules, which upset her husband. When she obeyed her husband and stopped teaching Douglass to read, her disposition became bitter. However, this is not the central idea.

45)

A.   Incorrect. This is a fact stated in the passage.

B.   Incorrect. He probably did, but that's not the implicit reason.

C.   Incorrect. This is not true because she was teaching them together.

D.   **Correct.** To give slaves any power is antithetical to keeping people in slavery.

E.   Incorrect. It is true that a slave could not use his education to advance, but being educated has value in other ways, making the statement false.

46)

A.   Incorrect. Although the passage states that psychology is a science, it does not explain the science. The primary concern is distinguishing the science of psychology from the art of teaching.

B.   Correct. The text states that educational programs and plans cannot be deduced from the laws of the mind.

C.   Incorrect. Although the text indicates that teaching is an art, the practices and plans of educational programs are not described.

D.   Incorrect. The focus of the art of teaching and of the science of psychology is identified, but their values are not mentioned.

E.   Incorrect. The specific activities and laws are not included, but the passage does convey the idea that the art of teaching involves programs and plans.

47)

A.   Incorrect. Though the author mentions some details of his personal life, most of his letter is concerned with work-related matters.

B.   Incorrect. Though the author's letter is primarily concerned with work-related matters, he includes personal details and friendly language.

C.   Correct. The author and Alan have a friendly relationship, as evidenced by the author's casual tone and his offer to bring Alan a gift from his vacation.

D.   Incorrect. The author's tone is casual, and he includes details that suggest he is not concerned or stressed about how things will go in his absence.

E.   Incorrect. Though the author shares some personal details in his letter, he does not share very many, and he is more focused on communicating about work-related matters.

48)

A.   Incorrect. Though the author does ask Alan if he wants any special treats, this is not his main purpose, as evidenced by the fact that he mentions it only in the final sentences of the letter.

B.   Incorrect. The author's tone is not boastful; he spends more time on professional matters and offers to bring Alan a gift, showing consideration.

C.   Correct. The author is writing to tell Alan that he will be out of the office. The details about his trip and the meeting support this idea.

D.   Incorrect. Though the author mentions the upcoming meeting, he does not intend to help Alan prepare for the meeting, only to inform him of the team's plans.

E.   Incorrect. The author mentions Joanie but does not suggest that he is introducing them for the first time.

49)

A.   Incorrect. The author writes, "In mutualism, both individuals benefit, while in synnecrosis, both organisms are harmed."

B.   Incorrect. The author writes, "In mutualism, both individuals benefit, while in synnecrosis, both organisms are harmed."

C.   Incorrect. The author writes, "Pollination, for example, is mutualistic[:]pollinators get nutrients from the flower, and the plant is able to reproduce[.]"

D.   **Correct.** The author writes, "Often, relationships described as commensal include one species that feeds on another species' leftovers; remoras, for instance, will attach themselves to sharks and eat the food particles they leave behind. It might seem like the shark gets nothing from the relationship, but a closer look will show that sharks in fact benefit from remoras, which clean the sharks' skin and remove parasites."

E.   Incorrect. The author writes, "There's yet another class of symbiosis that is controversial among scientists. As it's long been defined, commensalism is a relationship where one species benefits and the other is unaffected. But is it possible for two species to interact and for one to remain completely unaffected?"

50)

A.   Incorrect. The author writes, "In mutualism, both individuals benefit[.]"

B.   Incorrect. The author writes, "As it's long been defined, commensalism is a relationship where one species benefits and the other is unaffected."

C.   **Correct.** The author writes, "A relationship where one individual benefits and the other is harmed is known as parasitism."

D.   Incorrect. The author writes, "In mutualism, both individuals benefit, while in synnecrosis, both organisms are harmed."

E.   Incorrect. The relationship described is an example of a typical parasitic relationship; it is not atypical.

51)

A.   **Correct.** The author writes, "But is it possible for two species to interact and for one to remain completely unaffected?... In fact, many scientists claim that relationships currently described as commensal are just mutualistic or parasitic in ways that haven't been discovered yet."

B.   Incorrect. The author does not indicate that scientists disagree about the classification of relationships, only that they recognize that they do not fully understand all relationships yet and may, therefore, be classifying some of them based on incomplete information.

C.   Incorrect. The author does not indicate that the example of remoras and sharks is the reason for the controversy about commensalism, only that it illustrates this controversy well.

D.   Incorrect. The author does indicate that the controversy around commensalism is limited to discussions of animal species only.

E.   Incorrect. The author writes that commensalism is controversial because scientists are not sure if it is "possible for two species to interact and for one to remain completely unaffected"; however, this does not imply that scientists think animals are altogether incapable of interspecies interaction.

52)

A.   **Correct.** The author writes that "[t]here's another class of symbiosis that is controversial among scientists" and goes on to say that "many scientists claim the relationships currently described as commensal are just mutualistic or parasitic in ways that haven't been discovered yet." This implies that scientists debate about the topic of commensalism.

B. Incorrect. The author does not imply that scientists disapprove of or protest commensalism, only that they disagree about whether it truly exists.

C. Incorrect. The author does not imply that scientists are confused about commensalism, only that they disagree about whether it truly exists.

D. Incorrect. The author does not imply that scientists are upset about commensalism, only that they disagree about whether it truly exists.

E. Incorrect. The author does not imply that scientists are offended about commensalism, only that they disagree about whether it truly exists.

53)

A. Incorrect. Though the author explores this idea in the final paragraph, it is not the main focus of the passage as a whole.

B. Correct. The author writes that "[a]s these communities have evolved, the species in them have developed complex, long-term interspecies interactions known as symbiotic relationships." She then goes on to describe the different types of symbiotic relationships that exist.

C. Incorrect. Though the author introduces the passage with this idea, it is not the main focus of the passage as a whole.

D. Incorrect. Though the author does provide examples of interspecies interaction, this is not the primary purpose of the passage; rather, the examples provide further detail about the main topic—symbiotic relationships.

E. Incorrect. Though the author does explain the various types of symbiotic relationships, she does not focus on comparing commensalism and mutualism.

54)

A. Incorrect. The author does not indicate that scientists disagree about the classification of relationships, only that they recognize that they do not fully understand all relationships yet and may, therefore, be classifying some of them based on incomplete information.

B. Incorrect. The author provides no support for this in the passage.

C. Incorrect. The author provides no support for this in the passage.

D. Correct. The author writes, "The bacteria, fungi, insects, plants, and animals that live together in a habitat have evolved to share a pool of limited resources...As these communities have evolved, the species in them have developed complex, long-term interspecies interactions known as symbiotic relationships."

E. Incorrect. The author provides no support for this in the passage.

55)

A. Incorrect. In the renovation of a large old house, if new walls are added to divide large rooms, there will be more rooms.

B. Incorrect. The opposite is true; the height of the ceiling needs to be proportionate to the width of the room.

C. Correct. The text points out, "A ten-foot room with a thirteen-foot ceiling makes the narrowness of the room doubly apparent."

D. Incorrect. Small rooms can feel cozy if the height of the ceiling is "proportioned to their size."

E.   Incorrect. This is only true of the rooms with high ceilings that have been divided into two small rooms.

56)

A.   Incorrect. At the end of the passage, there is mention of one family that went to America. The other inaccurate part of the statement is about the Irish leaving their homes; the Irish tenants do not own their homes and are forced to pay their landlords high prices in order to have a place to live.

B.   Incorrect. The text says, "He cannot encourage trade; his sons cannot get work to do, if they are taught trades. It is a cruel thing that a man who is willing to work should not be able to get it." The Irish people are taught trades, but still cannot get jobs.

C.   Incorrect. The text says, "The serfdom of the Irish tenant leads to misery." Serfdom is a condition of servitude, which is close to, but not exactly, slavery. The Irish tenants must work like servants for their landlords, but are technically not slaves.

D.   Incorrect. The Irish tenants are close to starvation. There is no mention of social programs.

E.   **Correct.** The text indicates that "The tenant, who is kept at starvation point to pay his landlord's rent, has no means of providing for his family."

WRITING

USAGE

1)

A. Incorrect. *Celebrate* provides a plural verb for the plural subject *Ukrainians*.

B. Incorrect. *Dress* is a singular, present-tense verb that agrees with its subject (*men*) and the rest of the sentence (*celebrate*); *in* is the appropriate preposition to complete the idiom *dress in*, meaning "wear."

C. **Correct.** *Plays* is a singular verb and does not correctly pair with the plural subject *men*; *men dress* and *play*.

D. Incorrect. *Their* is a possessive pronoun describing whose neighbors are being referred to in the sentence (*the men's*).

E. Incorrect. A subject-verb agreement error exists in this sentence (C).

2)

A. Incorrect. The comma is used correctly here to set off an introductory phrase (*as juveniles*).

B. **Correct.** *African* is derived from the name of a place (Africa) and is therefore a proper noun and needs to be capitalized.

C. Incorrect. *Darkly* is an adverb describing the adjective *colored*.

D. Incorrect. *Grow into* is an idiomatic phrase that describes a transition.

E. Incorrect. A capitalization error exists in this sentence (B).

3)

A. Incorrect. *Because of* is an introductory phrase that accurately describes the relationship between a cause (Neptune's distance from the sun) and its effect (length of seasons).

B. Incorrect. *Its* is a possessive pronoun describing whose distance (Neptune's) from the sun.

C. Incorrect. *Has* is a singular verb, referring to a singular noun (Neptune); *seasons* is the direct object of the verb *has*.

D. Incorrect. As a noun, *equivalent* is typically followed by *of* (the equivalent of something); as an adjective, *equivalent* is usually followed by *to* (something is equivalent to something else).

E. **Correct.** No errors are present in this sentence.

4)

A. Incorrect. *Considered* begins an adjectival phrase that describes the subject of the sentence (Jenner).

B. Incorrect. *World's* must be possessive, as it refers to the first vaccine *of* the world.

C. **Correct.** The preposition *over* does not accurately illustrate the relationship between the vaccine and the young boy's infection; more appropriate would be the preposition *by*.

D. Incorrect. The comma after *widespread* is needed to set off the appositive phrase *and far more dangerous*.

E. Incorrect. A preposition error exists in this sentence (C).

5)

A. Incorrect. *Bread* is correctly punctuated in this sentence; it is followed by a comma to offset it from the next item in the list, *onions*.

B. Correct. The verb in this sentence (*is*) must be edited in order to create agreement between the subject (*items like potatoes, bread, onions, and even saliva*) and the verb (which should be *are*).

C. Incorrect. *Who* is the subjective form of the pronoun, used here to describe the noun *art conservators*.

D. Incorrect. *Clean and restore* is a compound verb phrase; both verbs are correctly formatted as plural.

E. Incorrect. A subject-verb agreement error exists in this sentence (B).

6)

A. Incorrect. *From* is an appropriate preposition in this context, as it describes the origin (*originally from*) of the horse breed.

B. Correct. The subject of this sentence is the singular *breed*; though it is separated from the subject by an adjectival phrase, the verb must also be singular (*has*).

C. Incorrect. *A reputation* is a singular noun, acting as the direct object; it should remain singular to show that one reputation is held by the breed as a whole.

D. Incorrect. *Bravery* and *fortitude* are grammatically similar nouns, both being used to name the qualities for which the breed is known.

E. Incorrect. A subject-verb agreement error exists in this sentence (B).

7)

A. Incorrect. *Decided* is a past-tense verb, which matches the tense of the phrase *could not*.

B. Incorrect. *Due to* accurately describes the relationship between cause (*high cost of health care*) and effect (*could not...afford*).

C. Incorrect. *To offer* is an infinitive phrase, acting as the direct object of the complete verb phrase *could not afford*.

D. Correct. Because it is a negative, *no other* inaccurately discounts the first negative (*not*) and creates a double negative (*could not afford no other*); it should be changed to *any other*.

E. Incorrect. A misleading double negative exists in this sentence (D).

8)

A. Incorrect. *Its* is a singular possessive pronoun, used here to refer to the *beaches* of the singular subject *Puerto Rico*.

B. Incorrect. *Includes* is a singular verb describing the state of the singular noun *landscape*.

C. Incorrect. *Are* is a plural verb for the plural subject *mountains*.

D. Incorrect. *Island's* is the singular possessive form of *island*, used here to refer to the *rural villages* of the singular *island* of Puerto Rico.

E. Correct. No error exists in this sentence.

9)

A. **Correct.** A comma should not be included in this location, as it separates the subject (*photographer*) and the verb (*specializes*).

B. Incorrect. *Likes* is a singular verb describing the behavior of the singular subject *she*.

C. Incorrect. *To accept* is an infinitive phrase, acting as the direct object of *likes*.

D. Incorrect. *Photographing* matches in format the other (parallel) ideas in the sentence; the photographer likes *shooting* (*portraits*), *taking* (*still lifes*), and *photographing* (*wildlife*).

E. Incorrect. A comma error exists in this sentence (A).

10)

A. Incorrect. *Against* is the appropriate preposition in this context, as its object is something the subject is fighting to end, not something the subject is supporting.

B. **Correct.** *Countries'* is a plural possessive but should be acting as a plural subject; the correct format of the word is *countries* (*around the world*).

C. Incorrect. *Are* is a plural helping verb describing the actions of to the plural subject *countries*.

D. Incorrect. *In hopes of* is a prepositional idiom describing the goals (*curbing unhealthy habits*) of the action (*are imposing taxes*).

E. Incorrect. A punctuation error exists in this sentence (B).

11)

A. Incorrect. *Black Death* is a colloquial name of a particular disease; it is a proper noun and is, therefore, correctly capitalized.

B. **Correct.** *Continued* is a past-tense verb; however, it should be present tense (*continues*) in order to align with the time mentioned later in the sentence (*even today*).

C. Incorrect. This comma correctly offsets the final participial phrase (*occasionally making its way into a human host*).

D. Incorrect. *Its* is a possessive pronoun renaming the disease.

E. Incorrect. A verb tense error exists in this sentence (B).

12)

A. Incorrect. *In* is the appropriate preposition to complete the prepositional idiom *advances in* meaning "advances that have occurred in."

B. Incorrect. *Have led* is a plural verb phrase; its subject, *advances*, is also plural.

C. Incorrect. A comma and conjunction pair is being used correctly to join two independent clauses.

D. **Correct.** Because the people *of many countries* are benefiting, multiple populations are benefiting: *the population[s] of many countries*.

E. Incorrect. An agreement error exists in this sentence (D).

SENTENCE CORRECTION

13)

A. **Correct.** *In addition* is the appropriate introductory phrase to signify the additive relationship between the two clauses.

B. Incorrect. *Therefore* incorrectly suggests a cause-and-effect relationship between the two clauses.

C. Incorrect. *However* incorrectly suggests a contradictory relationship between the two clauses.

D. Incorrect. *Consequently* incorrectly suggests a cause-and-effect relationship between the two clauses.

E. Incorrect. *On the other hand* incorrectly suggests a contradictory relationship between the two clauses.

14)

A. Incorrect. Though all three items begin with noun phrases (*dearth of, lack of,* and *list of*), the second and third are followed by unnecessary verb phrases (*she had* and *she was helping*).

B. Incorrect. The first two are noun phrases (*dearth of* and *lack of*), while the third is not.

C. **Correct.** In this iteration, all items in the list are nouns (*dearth, lack,* and *list*), followed by prepositions (*of*) and objects of the prepositions (*wins, time,* and *clients*).

D. Incorrect. While the first item in the list is a noun phrase (*dearth of courtroom wins*), the second two include unnecessary verb phrases (*she lacked* and *she was growing*).

E. Incorrect. While the first two items in the list include verb phrases (*she had experienced* and *she lacked*), the third does not.

15)

A. Incorrect. *Being invented* is wordy; the same idea can be communicated by beginning the sentence with *invented.*

B. Incorrect. *Inventing* suggests that the subject of the sentence is doing the action of inventing rather than being invented.

C. Incorrect. Joining these two independent clauses with a comma would make this sentence a comma splice.

D. Incorrect. *Though* suggests a contradiction between the clauses; no such contradiction exists between these two clauses.

E. **Correct.** *Invented*, the past participle of *invent*, appropriately introduces this participial phrase that provides more information about the subject of the sentence (*stethoscope*).

16)

A. Incorrect. As written, these two independent clauses, joined by a comma, form a comma splice.

B. **Correct.** *Which* is used correctly here to introduce an additional, nonrestrictive clause about an element of the sentence (the musical).

C.   Incorrect. Although *because* works in the context of the sentence, it does not work grammatically; the information following *because* is grammatically essential to the sentence and therefore should not be separated with a comma.

D.   Incorrect. *Being based on* leaves some ambiguity as to who or what this additional clause is describing.

E.   Incorrect. *Having been based on* is a perfect participle, a form that is rarely used because of its wordiness.

17)

A.   **Correct.** *Is* is a present-tense verb, used correctly to refer to current mindsets; *than* is used correctly to show comparison.

B.   Incorrect. *Will be expected* is future tense, suggesting that the mindset on interstellar travel does not yet exist; *than* is used correctly to show comparison.

C.   Incorrect. *Is* is a present-tense verb, used correctly to refer to current mindsets; *then* is used incorrectly to show comparison when it should refer to time.

D.   Incorrect. *Is expecting to be* suggests that interstellar travel itself has expectations about the future.

E.   Incorrect. *Expects* suggests that interstellar travel itself has expectations about the future.

18)

A.   Incorrect. This phrasing is unnecessarily wordy.

B.   Incorrect. This phrasing is unnecessarily wordy.

C.   Incorrect. *Common* and *confused* are both adjectives that, in this case, are both referring to the painters.

D.   Incorrect. This phrasing is unnecessarily wordy.

E.   **Correct.** *Commonly* is an adverb describing *confused*, which is an adjective describing *painters*.

19)

A.   Incorrect. The first two phrases share a structure (article + adjective) while the third does not (adjective + noun).

B.   **Correct.** The three phrases share a structure; they are parallel adjectives.

C.   Incorrect. The first and third phrases share a structure (article + adjective + noun), while the second one does not (article + adjective).

D.   Incorrect. The first two phrases share a structure (adjective only), while the third does not (article + adjective + noun).

E.   Incorrect. None of the phrases share a structure (article + adjective; adjective only; article + adjective + noun).

20)

A.   Incorrect. The first and third phrases in the list end with a preposition (*of*), while the second one does not.

B. Incorrect. None of the phrases share a structure; while the first and second begin with infinitives, the third does not; the first and third end with a preposition (*of*), while the second does not.

C. Incorrect. The third phrase includes a participle (*creating*), while the first and second do not.

D. Correct. The three phrases have a similar (parallel) structure (verb + direct object).

E. Incorrect. Though all three begin with a participle, the first and third end with a preposition (*of*), while the second does not.

21)

A. Incorrect. Because the sentence states a general fact (*a beverage that is*), it should not be in past tense.

B. Incorrect. Because the sentence states a general fact (*a beverage that is*), it should not be in past perfect tense.

C. Incorrect. Because the sentence states a general fact (*a beverage that is*), it should not be in present perfect tense.

D. Incorrect. Because the sentence states a general fact (*a beverage that is*), it should not be in present perfect tense.

E. Correct. Because the sentence states a general fact, it should be written in present tense (*hot chocolate is made*).

22)

A. Incorrect. As written, this sentence is a comma splice with two independent clauses (*parrots have been...* and *the first recorded instance...*).

B. Incorrect. Though a comma plus conjunction can be used to join clauses, this conjunction (*but*) does not fit with the meaning of the sentence, as the clauses are not contradictory.

C. Incorrect. *Writing* begins a participial phrase that, in this case, is modifying nothing.

D. Incorrect. Though a comma plus conjunction can be used to join clauses, this conjunction (*so*) does not fit with the meaning of the sentence, as the clauses are not related by cause and effect.

E. Correct. The semicolon is used appropriately here to join two independent, related clauses; *in fact* signifies an interesting detail to follow.

23)

A. Incorrect. Because the sentence states a general fact (how seat belts work), it should not be written in past tense.

B. Incorrect. Because the sentence states a general fact (how seat belts work), it should not be written in present progressive tense.

C. Correct. Because the sentence states a general fact (how seat belts work), it should be written in present tense.

D. Incorrect. Because the sentence states a general fact (how seat belts work), it should not be written in past progressive tense.

E. Incorrect. Because the sentence states a general fact (how seat belts work), it should not be written in future perfect tense.

24)

A. **Correct.** *Ranking* sets off a participial phrase that provides additional information about the subject of the sentence (*Prince*).

B. Incorrect. *Ranked* incorrectly sets off the participial phrase with the past participle (*ranked*) rather than the present participle (*ranking*).

C. Incorrect. This independent clause, if inserted into the sentence, would create a comma splice of two independent clauses.

D. Incorrect. This independent clause, if inserted into the sentence, would create a comma splice of two independent clauses.

E. Incorrect. This independent clause, if inserted into the sentence, would create a comma splice of two independent clauses.

REVISION IN CONTEXT

25)

A. **Correct.** This information is unnecessary and detracts from the point of the passage.

B. Incorrect. *Many* and *most* have similar meanings and are both grammatically correct in this case.

C. Incorrect. *Deceased* is a more formal word for *dead*, but neither is incorrect.

D. Incorrect. *Witnessed* is a more formal word for *saw*, but neither is incorrect.

E. Incorrect. *Their* is the correct word, as it is being used to show possession (*their ideas*).

26)

A. Incorrect. This choice is unnecessarily wordy, as *examined the facts* is implied in *debated*.

B. Incorrect. This choice is ambiguous, as *hemmed* and *hawed* are colloquial, which does not match the rest of the passage, whereas *debate* implies a more serious tone. Furthermore, this choice is wordy.

C. **Correct.** This is the clearest, most concise choice for communicating this idea.

D. Incorrect. *Hemmed and hawed* is a colloquial saying, which does not match the tone of the rest of the passage.

E. Incorrect. *Forever and always* is unnecessary to our understanding of the sentence, as it opens with *for centuries*.

27)

A. Incorrect. *Therefore* does not fit in the context of this sentence, as no cause-and-effect relationship exists.

B. **Correct.** *In fact* can be used correctly in this instance to draw attention to interesting information that builds on the previous sentence.

C. Incorrect. *However* does not fit in the context of this sentence, as no contradictory relationship exists.

D. Incorrect. *In addition* does not fit in the context of this sentence, as this sentence builds on the previous one and does not introduce a new idea.

E. Incorrect. *Consequently* does not fit in the context of this sentence, as no cause-and-effect relationship exists.

28)

A.   Incorrect. The sentence provides important information about two scientists who point to science fiction as the inspiration for their work.

B.   Incorrect. *Always* is unnecessary to the reader's understanding of the sentence.

C.   Correct. *His* should become *their* because the work belongs to two people (Goddard and Szilard).

D.   Incorrect. The phrase inside the dashes is not grammatically necessary, but it is helpful to the reader's understanding of the sentence.

E.   Incorrect. *Futuristic* is an adjective, used correctly here to modify *novels*.

29)

A.   Incorrect. This choice is too specific, as only one sentence of the final paragraph relates to transportation.

B.   Incorrect. This sentence adds very little to the meaning of the paragraph.

C.   Incorrect. The tone of this sentence is conversational, and it does not fit with the rest of the passage.

D.   Correct. This choice provides a brief but interesting overview of the information to come.

E.   Incorrect. This sentence is not relevant, as all of the inventions being discussed were, in the end, realistic.

30)

A.   Correct. This sentence relates directly to the overall idea of the passage—that science fiction has a natural influence on real life.

B.   Incorrect. This sentence does not relate to the overall topic of the passage—the relationship between science fiction and reality.

C.   Incorrect. Though this may be true, the sentence does not provide any useful information and detracts from the main idea of the passage.

D.   Incorrect. This sentence is inappropriately argumentative when compared with the rest of the passage, and it detracts from the main idea of the passage.

E.   Incorrect. This sentence is too general and provides no additional insight to the reader.

31)

A.   Correct. As it is written, *more recently* provides the reader with information about the time period being referred to as well as its relationship to the time period that was discussed in the previous sentence.

B.   Incorrect. *These days* in a colloquial expression used to refer to the present day; it does not agree with the meaning the author hopes to convey.

C.   Incorrect. *Therefore* incorrectly suggests a cause-and-effect relationship between this sentence and the preceding sentence.

D.   Incorrect. *On the other hand* incorrectly suggests a contradictory relationship between this sentence and the preceding sentence.

E.   Incorrect. *In addition* incorrectly suggests an additive relationship between this sentence and the preceding sentence.

32)

A. Incorrect. The final phrase *the changeling* is incorrectly set off from its descriptor with only a comma.

B. Correct. The final phrase *the changeling* is appropriately set off from the rest of the sentence—its descriptor—with a colon.

C. Incorrect. The dashes in this sentence incorrectly set off information that is essential to the meaning.

D. Incorrect. This choice creates a fragment by placing *the changeling* in its own sentence.

E. Incorrect. This choice includes an unnecessary comma after blame, which separates the essential adverbial phrase (*when individuals begin...*) from the rest of the sentence.

33)

A. Incorrect. This choice correctly turns the second clause into a subordinate clause by adding *who* and joins it to an independent clause with a comma.

B. Incorrect. This choice correctly joins two related independent clauses with a comma.

C. Correct. This choice incorrectly joins two independent clauses with a comma (*changelings were...* and *they were left...*).

D. Incorrect. The dash correctly joins the subordinate clause (*left in the places...*) to the main sentence.

E. Incorrect. This choice correctly forms two complete sentences by separating two independent clauses with a period and starting each with a capital letter.

34)

A. Incorrect. This choice provides a meaningful conclusion to the paragraph by explaining why people may have been invested in the changeling legend.

B. Correct. *Explanation* adds an important detail about what the demonstrative pronoun *this* refers to.

C. Incorrect. *Families* is used correctly in the sentence to signify multiple families and does not need to be changed.

D. Incorrect. *Whose* is used correctly in the sentence to signify possession (the children *of* the families) and does not need to be changed.

E. Incorrect. *Ailments* and *illnesses* are synonyms, so no change is necessary.

35)

A. Correct. As written, the sentence acts appropriately as an introductory sentence, providing a summary of the topic that will be discussed; additionally, it gives meaning to the phrase *for example* in sentence 9.

B. Incorrect. The content of the sentence is better aligned with the content of the third paragraph, as encouraging the changelings to leave was not an idea that was discussed in paragraph 2.

C. Incorrect. In this placement, the sentence above is notably vague compared to the sentences around it; as such, it works best as an introductory statement that summarizes the similarities between the various examples.

D. Incorrect. In this placement, the sentence above is notably vague compared to the sentences around it; as such, it works best as an introductory statement that summarizes the similarities between the various examples.

E. Incorrect. In this placement, the sentence above is notably vague compared to the sentences around it; as such, it works best as an introductory statement that summarizes the similarities between the various examples.

36)

A. Incorrect. This choice creates a comma splice by combining two independent clauses with a comma.

B. Incorrect. This choice combines the independent clauses correctly with a comma and a conjunction; however, the meaning of the conjunction *so* suggests a cause-and-effect relationship, which does not exist here.

C. Incorrect. This choice combines the independent clauses correctly with a comma and a conjunction; however, the meaning of the conjunction *but* suggests a contradictory relationship, which does not exist here.

D. Incorrect. This choice combines the independent clauses correctly with a semicolon and an introductory word; however, the meaning of *however* suggests a contradictory relationship, which does not exist here.

E. Correct. The choice correctly joins the independent clauses with a colon, signifying that the information in the second clause somehow builds or expands on the first.

RESEARCH SKILLS

37)

A. Correct. APA Style is derived from guidelines published by the American Psychological Association; it should be used when writing in a field of the social sciences.

B. Incorrect. MLA Style is derived from guidelines published by the Modern Language Association; it should be used when writing in the fields of liberal arts or humanities.

C. Incorrect. Though Chicago Style can be used for many types of papers, it is most commonly seen in the fields of history and anthropology and is not common for psychology research.

D. Incorrect. Students should receive explicit instruction in the various style guides and should be instructed on the appropriate use of each.

E. Incorrect. Style guides should be used in order to provide information on how students should cite their research.

38)

A. Incorrect. A paper that reviews other studies is not introducing unique or novel information and is considered a secondary source.

B. Incorrect. Because the journalist is interpreting the events and interviews to draw conclusions about the government's efforts, the article would be considered a secondary source.

C. Incorrect. Because the review critiques another author's work, it would be considered a secondary source.

D.   **Correct.** Because the results of the study are original and are being published by the author of the study, this paper would be considered a primary source.

E.   Incorrect. A summary of another's work is considered a secondary source.

39)

A.   **Correct.** Because the art historian must filter the information (the art) through his or her own perspective, this interpretive essay would be considered a secondary source.

B.   Incorrect. Because court transcripts come directly from the proceedings in the courtroom (without interpretation), they would be considered primary source documents.

C.   Incorrect. Because the journal entries reflect the student's personal experience of the event, they would be considered primary sources.

D.   Incorrect. Because the video provides a firsthand account of the aftermath, it would be considered a primary source.

E.   Incorrect. Because the audio recording provides a firsthand account of the politician's admission (without interpretation), it would be considered a primary source.

40)

A.   Incorrect. Population variance is relevant to the topic of bird migration.

B.   Incorrect. A discussion of different types of migration is relevant to the reader's understanding of bird migration.

C.   Incorrect. Methods of movement are relevant to the topic of bird migration.

D.   **Correct.** Though it is interesting, the history of humanity's understanding of bird migration is not necessarily relevant to an essay about bird migration.

E.   Incorrect. Variations in migration patterns are relevant to an essay about bird migration.

ARGUMENTATIVE ESSAY

History provides countless examples of crowds that have become unruly, dangerous, even deadly. However, a commanding leader can make a difference. When a charismatic leader harnesses the emotions of the crowd, he or she can stir it up or calm it down with thoughtful and evocative words and actions. During the Great Depression, US President Franklin D. Roosevelt's speeches and "Fireside Chats" calmed Americans fearful of losing their savings and quelled financial panic. However, powerful speakers have the power to trigger violence. In the 1930s, Adolf Hitler's nationalist speeches in Germany inspired anti-Semitism, racism, and violent acts like Kristallnacht. A large crowd can remain calm in an emotional situation, but only with the right leadership.

Consumer panic makes an economic crisis into a catastrophe when people withdraw their funds from banks all at once, and social unrest can soon follow. FDR's public speeches and radio addresses, known as "Fireside Chats," were intended to calm the public while allowing bank reform and economic recovery to occur. Famously, in describing emergency measures to close the banks, he explained economic policy in plain language, reassuring Americans that their money would still be available when banks reopened. He also stayed positive and optimistic, using euphemisms like "bank holiday" and "inconvenience." His word choice and demeanor encouraged people to stay calm and cooperate with financial reforms. In fact, in his inaugural address, he proclaimed that there was "nothing to fear but fear itself," inspiring faith rather than panic in a time of national crisis when social unrest was feared.

On the other hand, Adolf Hitler rose to power in Germany on a platform of nationalism and discrimination. At the time, much like the United States, Germany was suffering from an economic depression and struggling to rebuild following the First World War. Unlike FDR, Hitler used negative language and scapegoated minority groups, especially Jewish people. He encouraged violence among his followers such as book burnings, property damage, and deadly acts against Jewish people and other minority groups. As the Nazis became more powerful, Jewish people were subject to discriminatory laws and oppressive treatment. Jewish businesses were attacked and looted on Kristallnacht. Hitler's harsh rhetoric had contributed to a social and political environment where this abuse was acceptable, and it led to the Holocaust.

Overall, crowds are driven by emotion, and even people who remain rational within them cannot take control. Some people helped the Jews and other persecuted people in Nazi Germany, but they did so in secret, no match for the power of Hitler and Nazi ideology over the nation. Yet, as shown by FDR's leadership during the Great Depression, it is possible for a huge group—an entire nation—to stave off irrational, panicky behavior even with something as important as money. A crowd, despite its essential emotional nature, can be rendered rational and calm by the right leader.

SOURCE BASED ESSAY

As public bicycle share programs (PBSPs) increase in popularity, significant debate has emerged over helmet requirements in cities that implement these systems. Both sides of the debate agree that helmets improve safety for bicycle riders. Historically, mandatory bicycle laws have greatly increased helmet usage and had a significant impact on reducing traumatic brain injuries. Both sides of the debate also agree that PBSPs provide both transportation and environmental benefits to cities. They can decrease congestion and provide low-cost and flexible transportation options for commuters and tourists. Finally, both perspectives agree that mandatory helmet laws hamper the development of bicycle-based urban public transportation, by discouraging riders from partaking in the system. The conflict between the two camps centers on how cities should balance their responsibility to individual safety and public policy goals.

Cities with mandatory helmet laws have struggled to get their programs off the ground, experiencing significantly decreased participation rates. For example, according to Passage 1, Melbourne, which has a mandatory helmet law, has a participation rate anywhere from 67 to 83 percent lower than London, which has no such law. Without extensive participation, the societal benefits of PBSPs are greatly diminished. While Melbourne's system still offers a transportation alternative, it is clearly not viewed as a viable one by most of the population, and so provides little benefit in that way. Also, with such markedly low participation rates, impact on congestion and pollution would be negligible.

On the other hand, PBSP riders typically do not have extensive experience riding in urban environments whose increased traffic can pose greater risk of an accident.

According to Passage 2, a recent study shows that PBSPs that do not mandate helmets increase the chance of a rider suffering a traumatic brain injury during a biking accident. This increase could potentially create new policy problems as it impacts one of the city government's primary goals: ensuring the safety of its people.

Some cities have attempted to make helmets more accessible by installing helmet vending machines near bike stations or even leaving free helmets out for riders, according to Passage 1. However, according to Passage 2, few people take advantage of these options. This indicates that people would rather opt out than use a helmet; perhaps issues beyond accessibility factor into the equation. For example, while people are willing to share bicycles, they may not be willing to share headgear, which could be perceived as unsanitary. Or riders could be concerned with fitting, as helmets come in a variety of sizes. The nature of PBSPs can also be a factor. The majority of PBSP users are casual riders according to Passage 1, who are attracted by the flexibility and ease of use the programs. This includes tourists or commuters who perhaps did not even intend to ride a bike when they set out. Even if it does not actually require any increased effort, such users may simply feel that helmet laws detract from the open nature of PBSPs.

Because both sides of the debate agree that helmet usage is preferable and that PBSPs are beneficial, several questions on this topic are open to further research. For example, researchers should examine the overall number of injuries in cities with PBSPs compared to those without, and how the volume of users impacts both rider and vehicle safety on the road. They could also look at how the modification of roads to accommodate bikers by installing protected bike lanes, for example, impacts safety numbers. Finally, researchers could explore alternative ways to encourage helmet use beyond legislation.

MATHEMATICS

1)

E.   Simplify using PEMDAS.

$10^2 - 7(3 - 4) - 25$

$= 10^2 - 7(-1) - 25$

$= 100 + 7 - 25$

$= 107 - 25 = \mathbf{82}$

2)

A.   The domain is the possible values of x from left to right. Here, the domain starts at -4, inclusive, and stops at -1, exclusive. It starts again at 0, inclusive, and goes to 3, inclusive. The two line segments from 0 to 3 cross over each other, so the domain includes this whole interval. Note that closed circles represent inclusion (square bracket), and open circles represent exclusions (round bracket).

3)

D.   Set up a proportion and solve.

$\frac{AB}{DE} = \frac{3}{4}$

$\frac{12}{DE} = \frac{3}{4}$

$3(DE) = 48$

$\boldsymbol{DE = 16}$

4)

A.   Find the amount the state will spend on infrastructure and education, and then find the difference.

$infrastructure = 0.2(3,000,000,000) = 600,000,000$

$education = 0.18(3,000,000,000) = 540,000,000$

$600,000,000 - 540,000,000 = \mathbf{\$60,000,000}$

5)

C.   Use the equation for percentages.

$whole = \frac{part}{percentage} = \frac{17}{0.4} = \mathbf{42.5}$

6)

C.   Convert each fraction to the LCD and subtract the numerators.

$\frac{7}{8} - \frac{1}{10} - \frac{2}{3}$

$= \frac{7}{8}\left(\frac{15}{15}\right) - \frac{1}{10}\left(\frac{12}{12}\right) - \frac{2}{3}\left(\frac{40}{40}\right)$

$= \frac{105}{120} - \frac{12}{120} - \frac{80}{120} = \mathbf{\frac{13}{120}}$

7)

C.   Factor the expression using the greatest common factor of 3.

$54z^4 + 18z^3 + 3z + 3 =$

$\mathbf{3(18z^4 + 6z^3 + z + 1)}$

8)

D.   Use the formula for percentages.

$percent = \frac{part}{whole}$

$= \frac{42}{48}$

$= 0.875 = \mathbf{87.5\%}$

9)

C.   Find the height of the cylinder using the equation for surface area.

$SA = 2\pi rh + 2\pi r^2$

$48\pi = 2\pi(4)h + 2\pi(4)^2$

$h = 2$

Find the volume using the volume equation.

$V = \pi r^2 h$

$V = \pi(4)^2(2) = \mathbf{32\pi \ ft.^3}$

10)

C.   Plug each value into the equation.

$4(3 + 4)^2 - 4(3)^2 + 20 = 180 \neq 276$

$4(4 + 4)^2 - 4(3)^2 + 20 = 240 \neq 276$

$4(6 + 4)^2 - 4(6)^2 + 20 = \mathbf{276}$

$4(12 + 4)^2 - 4(12)^2 + 20 = 468 \neq 276$

$4(24 + 4)^2 - 4(24)^2 + 20 = 852 \neq 276$

11)

C. Plug 0 in for x and solve for y.

$7y - 42x + 7 = 0$

$7y - 42(0) + 7 = 0$

$y = -1$

The y-intercept is at **(0, −1)**.

12)

C. The function $g(x) = f(x - 2) + 3$ is a translation of $\langle 2, 3 \rangle$ from $f(x)$. Test each possible point by undoing the transformation and checking if the point lies on $f(x)$.

$(1, 2) \to (-1, -1)$: This point is not on $f(x)$.

$(2, 3) \to (0, 0)$: This point is not on $f(x)$.

$(4, 0) \to (2, -3)$: This point is not on $f(x)$.

$(6, 3) \to (4, 0)$: **This point is on $f(x)$.**

$(7, 2) \to (5, -1)$: This point is not on $f(x)$.

13)

D. Find the amount of change and add to the original amount.

amount of change = original amount × percent change

$= 37{,}500 \times 0.055 = 2{,}062.50$

$37{,}500 + 2{,}062.50 = $ **\$39,562.50**

14)

D. Write each value in decimal form and compare.

$-0.95 < 0 < 0.4 < 0.35 < 0.75$
FALSE

$-1 < -0.1 < -0.11 < 0.8\overline{3} < 0.75$
FALSE

$-0.75 < -0.2 < 0 < 0.\overline{66} < 0.55$
FALSE

$-1.1 < -0.8 < -0.13 < 0.7 < 0.\overline{81}$
TRUE

$-0.0001 < -0.\overline{83} < 0 < 0.\overline{66} < 0.8$
FALSE

15)

Eliminate answer choices that don't match the graph.

A. Correct.

B. The graph has a negative slope while this inequality has a positive slope.

C. The line on the graph is solid, so the inequality should include the "or equal to" symbol.

D. The shading is above the line, meaning the inequality should be "y is greater than."

E. The y-intercept is −2, not 2.

16)

D. Use the fundamental counting principle to determine how many ways the DVDs can be arranged within each category and how many ways the 3 categories can be arranged.

ways to arrange horror = 4! = 24

ways to arrange comedies = 6! = 720

ways to arrange science fiction = 5! = 120

ways to arrange categories = 3! = 6

$(24)(720)(120)(6) = $ **12,441,600**

17)

D. Set up a system of equations and solve using elimination.

$f = $ the cost of a financial stock

$a = $ the cost of an auto stock

$50f + 10a = 1300$

$10f + 10a = 500$

$\begin{aligned} 50f + 10a &= 1300 \\ + \; -50f - 50a &= -2500 \\ \hline -40a &= -1{,}200 \\ a &= 30 \end{aligned}$

$50(30) = $ **1,500**

18)

D. Let B equal the set of students in the band and C equal the set of students in the math club. Use set theory to find the number of students in either the band or the math club, then subtract this number from the total number of students in the school.

$B \cup C = B + C - B \cap C = 200 + 150 - 20$
$= 330$

$1,200 - 330 = $ **870**

19)

E. As shown in the figure, A can be placed inside, on, or outside the circle.

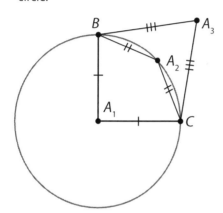

20)

A. Add the number of cupcakes he will give to his friend and to his coworkers, then subtract that value from 48.

# of cupcakes for his friend:
$\frac{1}{2} \times 48 = 24$

# of cupcakes for his coworkers:
$\frac{1}{3} \times 48 = 16$

$48 - (24 + 16) = $ **8**

21)

A. Use the equation for percentages.

part = whole × percentage =
$9 \times 0.25 = $ **2.25**

22)

D. Use the fundamental counting principle to find the number of ways the letters can be arranged. Because

the two Gs are indistinguishable, divide by the number of ways those 2 letters can be arranged.

$\frac{7!}{2!} = (7)(6)(5)(4)(3) = $ **2520**

23)

D. Plug in each set of values and determine if the inequality is true.

$2(0) + 0 \leq -10$ FALSE

$2(10) + 2 \leq -10$ FALSE

$2(10) + 10 \leq -10$ FALSE

$2(-10) + (-10) \leq -10$ TRUE

$2(0) + 10 \leq -10$ FALSE

24)

D. Use the formula for the area of a rectangle to find the increase in its size.

$A = lw$

$A = (1.4l)(0.6w)$

$A = 0.84lw$

The new area will be 84% of the original area, a decrease of **16%**.

25)

C. $6(3^0) = 6(1) = $ **6**

26)

C. One way to find the answer is to draw a picture.

Put 24 cans into groups of 4. One out of every 4 cans is diet (light gray) so there is 1 light gray can for every 3 dark gray cans. That leaves 18 dark gray cans (regular soda).

Alternatively, solve the problem using ratios.

$\frac{Regular}{Total} = \frac{3}{4} = \frac{x}{24}$

$4x = 72$

$x = 18$

27)

B. Move the terms to the same side and factor. Use the zeros to find the intervals where the inequality is true.

$6 > x^2 - x$

$0 > x^2 - x - 6$

$0 > (x + 2)(x - 3)$

For $x < -2$:

$0 \not> (x + 2)(x - 3)$

For $-2 < x < -3$:

$0 > (x + 2)(x - 3)$

For $x > 3$:

$\mathbf{0 \not> (x + 2)(x - 3)}$

28)

D. Use the formula for the volume of a sphere to find its radius.

$V = \frac{4}{3}\pi r^3$

$972\pi = \frac{4}{3}\pi r^3$

$r = 9$

Use the super Pythagorean theorem to find the side of the cube.

$d^2 = a^2 + b^2 + c^2$

$18^2 = 3s^2$

$s \approx 10.4$

Use the length of the side to find the volume of the cube.

$V = s^3$

$V \approx (10.4)^3$

$\mathbf{V \approx 1125}$

29)

B. Find the probability that the second marble will be green if the first marble is blue, silver, or green, and then add these probabilities together.

$P(\text{first blue and second green}) =$
$P(\text{blue}) \times P(\text{green}|\text{first blue}) = \frac{6}{18}$
$\times \frac{4}{17} = \frac{4}{51}$

$P(\text{first silver and second green}) =$
$P(\text{silver}) \times P(\text{green}|\text{first silver}) = \frac{8}{18}$
$\times \frac{4}{17} = \frac{16}{153}$

$P(\text{first green and second green}) =$
$P(\text{green}) \times P(\text{green}|\text{first green}) = \frac{4}{18}$
$\times \frac{3}{17} = \frac{2}{51}$

$P(\text{second green}) = \frac{4}{51} + \frac{16}{153} + \frac{2}{51}$
$= \frac{2}{9}$

30)

B. Add the area of the trapezoid and the area of the triangle.

trapezoid: $A = \frac{h(b_1 + b_2)}{2} = \frac{10(14 + 8)}{2} =$ 110 mm^2

triangle: $A = \frac{1}{2}bh = \frac{1}{2}(8)(4\sqrt{3}) =$ $16\sqrt{3}$ mm^2

$110 + 16\sqrt{3} \approx \mathbf{137.7}$ **mm^2**

31)

E. $5 \div 8 = 0.625$

$0.625 \times 100 = 62.5\%$

32)

C. Use the formula for percent change.

$percent\ change = \frac{amount\ of\ change}{original\ amount}$

$= (680 - 425) / 425$

$= 255/425 = 0.60 = \mathbf{60\%}$

33)

B. Find the slope of the given line. Any parallel lines will have the same slope.

$3x + 2y = 10$

$2y = -3x + 10$

$\mathbf{y = -\frac{3}{2}x + 5}$

34)

B. Write each decimal as a fraction and compare the numerators.

A. $0.305 = \frac{305}{1000}$

B. $0.035 = \frac{\mathbf{35}}{\mathbf{1000}}$

C. $0.35 = \frac{350}{1000}$

D. $0.3 = \frac{300}{1000}$

E. $3.5 = \frac{3500}{1000}$

35)

C. Substitute one (x, y) pair into each answer choice to find the correct equation.

A. $y = -6x - 6; (3, -18)$

$y = -6(3) - 6$

$y = -18 - 6$

$y = -24 \neq -18$

B. $y = -5x - 6; (3, -18)$

$y = -5(3) - 6$

$y = -15 - 6$

$y = -24 \neq -18$

C. $y = -4x - 6; (3, -18)$

$y = -4(3) - 6$

$y = -12 - 6$

$\mathbf{y = -18}$

D. $y = -3x - 6; (3, -18)$

$y = -3(3) - 6$

$y = -9 - 6$

$y = -15 \neq -18$

E. $y = -2x - 6; (3, -18)$

$y = -2(3) - 6$

$y = -6 - 6$

$y = -12 \neq -18$

36)

C. Use the equation for probability.

$probability = \frac{possible\ favorable\ outcomes}{all\ possible\ outcomes}$

$= \frac{7}{(5 + 7 + 8)} = 20$

$= \frac{7}{20}$

37)

C. **Correct.**

A. Points in quadrant I have a positive x and a positive y coordinate.

B. Points in quadrant II have a negative x and a positive y coordinate.

C. Points in quadrant III have a negative x and a negative y coordinate.

D. Points in quadrant IV have a positive x and a negative y coordinate.

E. See above.

38)

D. To estimate the amount of the change, round the price of each item to the nearest dollar amount and subtract from the total.

$\$50 - (\$13 + \$12 + \$4 + \$6)$

$= \$50 - \$35 = \mathbf{\$15}$

39)

E. Use the two sets of linear angles to find b and then c.

$a = b$

$a + b + 70 = 180$

$2a + 70 = 180$

$a = b = 55°$

$b + c = 180°$

$55 + c = 180$

$c = \mathbf{125°}$

40)

C. Use the formula for finding percentages. Express the percentage as a decimal.

$part = whole \times percentage = \mathbf{1560 \times 0.15}$

41)

A. His profit will be his income minus his expensions. He will earn $40 for each lawn, or $40m$. He pays $35 is expenses each week, or $35x$.

$\mathbf{profit = 40m - 35x}$

42)

A. To calculate the average, add all of the scores and divide by the total number of scores. Use the variable x in place of the missing score.

$$\frac{(100 + 100 + 100 + x)}{4} = 85$$

$$\frac{(300 + x)}{4} = 85$$

$$(300 + x) = 340$$

$x = 40\%$

43)

D. Find the time that Erica spends on break and subtract this from her total time at work.

$30 + 2(15) = 1$ hour

$8\frac{1}{2} - 1 = 7\frac{1}{2} =$ **7 hours, 30 minutes**

44)

D. $f(x) = 2x + 2$

$f(20) = 2(20) + 2 =$ **42**

45)

D. Set up a proportion and solve.

$$\frac{8}{650} = \frac{12}{x}$$

$12(650) = 8x$

$x = 975$ miles

46)

C. The greatest distance will be between two points at opposite ends of each sphere's diameters. Find the diameter of each sphere and add them.

$36\pi = \frac{4}{3}\pi r_1^3$

$r_1 = 3$

$d_1 = 2(3) = 6$

$288\pi = \frac{4}{3}\pi r_2^3$

$r_2 = 6$

$d_2 = 2(6) = 12$

$d_1 + d_1 = 6 + 12 =$ **18**

47)

B. There are 16 ounces in a pound, so the baby's starting weight is 120

ounces. He gained 6 ounces per month, or $6t$. So, the baby's weight will be his initial weight plus the amount gained for each month: **$y = 6t + 120$**.

48)

B. Add the base amount and the tax on the extra percentage of the person's income.

$10,620 + 0.2(80,000 - 75,000) =$ **$11,620**

49)

B. In 2012, New York had more months with less than 3 inches of rain than either Chicago or Houston.

50)

A. $p =$ number of pages written by Chris

$2p =$ number of pages written by Kim

$p + 2p = 240$

$p = 80$

51)

C. Use the formula for probability.

$$probability = \frac{desired\ outcomes}{possible\ outcomes} =$$

$$\frac{2\ cards}{52\ cards} = \frac{1}{26}$$

52)

A. The line $y = 2x + 1$ will have a slope of 2 and y-intercept of 1. The lines shown in graphs C and D have negative slopes. The line in graph B has a y-intercept of -2.

Alternatively, use a table to find some coordinates, and identify the graph that contains those coordinates.

x	y
0	1
1	3
2	5

53)

C. Divide 1.3208 by 5.2.

$$\begin{array}{r} .254 \\ 52\overline{)13.208} \\ \underline{104} \\ 280 \\ \underline{260} \\ 208 \\ \underline{208} \\ 0 \end{array}$$

There is a **5** in the hundredths place.

54)

A. Isolate the variable x on one side of the equation.

$5x - 4 = 3(8 + 3x)$

$5x - 4 = 24 + 9x$

$-4 - 24 = 9x - 5x$

$-28 = 4x$

$\frac{-28}{4} = \frac{4x}{4}$

$x = -7$

55)

B. Set up an equation. If p is the original number of pears, the store has sold $0.30p$ pears. The original number minus the number sold will equal 455.

$p - 0.30p = 455$

$p = \frac{455}{0.7} =$ **650 pears**

56)

C. Solve the system of equations using substitution:

$5x + 4y = 20; x = 2y + 1$

$5(2y + 1) + 4y = 20$

$y = \frac{15}{14}$

Go to **http://www.cirrustestprep.com/praxis-core-academic-skills-for-educators-online-resources** to access your second Praxis Core Academic Skills practice test and other online study resources.

Sources

Anthony, Susan B., "On Women's Right to Vote," 1873.

Bailliet, Thomas M. "Preface." *In Gulliver's Travels* by Jonathan Swift, 1900.

Curtis, William. *Curtis's Botanical Magazine*, 1790.

Cusack, Mary Frances. *An Illustrated History of Ireland from AD 400 to 1800*, 1868.

Dalton Frank Eugen. "Swimming Scientifically Taught," 1912.

Emerson, Ralph Waldo. *Nature*, 1836.

James, William. *Talks to Teachers on Psychology*, 1899.

Meynell, Alice. *The Rhythm of Life*, 1905.

Paine, Thomas. *Common Sense*, 1776.

Shelley, Mary Wollstonecraft. *Frankenstein*, 1818.

de Tocqueville, Alexis. *Democracy in America*, 1835.

Truman, Harry. Statement to Congress (Truman Doctrine), March 12, 1947.

Twain, Mark. "The Oldest Inhabitant—The Weather of New England," 1876.

United States Arms Control and Disarmament Agency. *Worldwide Effects of Nuclear War: Some Perspectives*, 1996.

Vest, George Graham. "Tribute to the Dog," c. 1855.

Washington, George. Farewell Address to Congress, December 19, 1796.

Wheeler, Candace. *Principles of Home Decoration, With Practical Examples*, 1903.

Wilson, Woodrow. *On Being Human*, 1897.

Made in the USA
Columbia, SC
12 July 2017